THE WORLD BANK GROUP

RESEARCH AND INFORMATION
GUIDES IN BUSINESS, INDUSTRY, AND
ECONOMIC INSTITUTIONS
(VOL. 4)

GARLAND REFERENCE LIBRARY
OF SOCIAL SCIENCE
(VOL. 572)

Research and Information Guides in Business, Industry, and Economic Institutions

General Editor: Wahib Nasrallah

THE WORLD BANK GROUP
A Guide to
Information Sources

Carol R. Wilson

GARLAND PUBLISHING, INC. • NEW YORK & LONDON
1991

Library of Congress Cataloging-in-Publication Data

Wilson, Carol R., 1955–
    The World Bank Group ; a guide to information sources / Carol R.
Wilson.
        p. cm. — (Research and information guides in business,
industry, and economic institutions ; vol. 4) (Garland reference
library of social sciences ; vol. 572)
    Includes index.
    ISBN 0-8240-4429-0
    1. World Bank Group—Bibliography. 2. Banks and banking,
International—Bibliography. I. Title. II. Series: Research and
information guides in business, industry, and economic institutions ;
4. III. Series: Garland reference library of social sciences ; v.
572.
HG3881.5.W57W55   1991
016.3321'532—dc20   91–17364
                                                       CIP

Printed on acid-free, 250-year-life paper
Manufactured in the United States of America

CONTENTS

SERIES FOREWORD

The new information society has exceeded everyone's expectations in providing new and exciting media for the collection and dissemination of data. Such proliferation has been matched by a similar increase in the number of providers of business literature. Furthermore, many emerging technologies, financial fields, and management processes have amassed an amazing body of knowledge in a short period of time. Indicators are that packaging of information will continue its trend of diversification, confounding even the experienced researcher. How then will information seekers identify and assess the adequacy and relevancy of various packages to their research needs?

It is my hope that Garland's *Research and Information Guides in Business, Industry, and Economic Institutions* series will bridge the gap between classical forms of literature and new alternative formats. Each guide will be devoted to an industry, a profession, a managerial process, an economic institution, or a field of study. Organization of the guides will emphasize subject access to formats such as bibliographic and numeric databases on-line, distributed databases, CD-ROM products, loose-leaf services, government publications and books, and periodical articles. Although most of the guides will serve as locators and bridges to bodies of knowledge, some may be reference books with self-contained information.

Since compiling such guides requires substantial knowledge in the organization of information or the field of study, authors are selected on the basis of their expertise as information professionals or subject specialists. Inquiries about the series and its content should be addressed to the Series Editor.

Wahib Nasrallah
Langsam Library
University of Cincinnati

PREFACE

The purpose of this guide is to pull together
various information sources about the World Bank Group.
The World Bank Group refers primarily to the
International Bank for Reconstruction and Development
(IBRD), International Development Association (IDA),
and International Finance Corporation (IFC). Sources
about the International Centre for the Settlement of
Investment Disputes (ICSID), Multilateral Investment
Guarantee Agency (MIGA), and Consultative Group on
International Agricultural Research (CGIAR) are also
included where available.

This guide's scope is to gather works about the
World Bank Group that were published or translated into
English from 1944 to 1988; although some works from
1989 and 1990 are also included. Books, periodical
articles, government publications, pamphlets, and
reference works are cited. Although the focus is on
U.S. publications, other English works are also
included where found. This scope reflects the intended
audience; it is a specialized bibliography aimed at
academic/research libraries, business/economic
libraries, corporate libraries, and others interested
in international organizations.

Within the bibliography, entries are arranged by
the affiliate or division within the Bank Group. In
addition to the members of World Bank Group, Bretton
Woods is used as a heading for works related to the
1944 UN Conference at which the World Bank was founded.
Major divisions within IBRD are also used as headings,
for example: Economic Development Institute (a
training unit). Works not related to a specific
heading are found under the heading: International Bank
for Reconstruction and Development. Entries are
arranged alphabetically, and then chronologically under
each heading. Each entry is assigned an identification
number which is used in cross-references and the index.
The full entry is listed only once, under the heading
reflecting the primary focus. For a work covering
several affiliates, the full entry is found under the
more general heading with additional references in the
index. For example, a work covering the policies of
the World Bank has the full entry under IBRD, with
cross-references under IFC, IDA, and ICSID in the

ix

index. The index provides access by title, subject (broad topical and geographical), and personal name (authors, editors, and chiefs of World Bank missions), as well as references to other affiliates or divisions.

In addition to the identification number, entries include basic bibliographic elements (author, title, and imprint), as well as pagination, ISBN, and LCCN where available. The latter two elements are included to aid in the actual retrieval of the items at the user's own libraries, since retrieval using the numbers is often faster. Brief annotations or descriptive statements are provided wherever possible; however, many items were not available when this research was conducted. Items not seen are indicated by (*) at the end of the entry. Some of these "unseen" items will have descriptive statements based on information originally found in the source consulted (see Appendix D). The appendices also contain significant dates in the World Bank's history, their information products, related works, an organizational chart, and information about the availability of citations about the World Bank in electronic format.

I would like to acknowledge the support of my family and friends, and the helpful comments of Margaret Taylor, Catherine Warner, Wahib Nasrallah, and Marie Ellen Larcada throughout this endeavor.

Carol R. Wilson

INTRODUCTION

The International Bank for Reconstruction and Development (IBRD), or the World Bank as it is more commonly called, was founded as a result of the 1944 UN Monetary and Financial Conference at Bretton Woods, New Hampshire. The International Monetary Fund (IMF) was also founded at this conference. Because of their common roots, these two institutions are often called the Bretton Woods twins. Like other siblings, there are differences and similarities between them. Each has a distinct purpose: IMF focuses on currency stabilization through short-term financing or trade deficits, while IBRD focuses on longer term financing of development projects within a country. A discussion of one Bretton Woods institution cannot avoid references to the other; nevertheless, these comparisons will be kept to a minimum.

The World Bank, an intergovernmental institution, is owned by its 150 member countries. It was designed to lend or to guarantee loans for rebuilding nations after the destruction following World War II. Later World Bank assistance was focused more on developing countries and their economic growth. Throughout its history, several sectors have been recognized as critical to IBRD-supported development projects: food, agriculture, transportation, and education.

In the 16 years following the Bretton Woods conference, Economic Development Institute (EDI), International Development Association (IDA), and International Finance Corporation (IFC) were established. Each was designed to complement IBRD's original purpose. EDI is the internal college or training institute for government officials from developing countries. IFC is designed to work with private enterprise in developing countries, while IDA is designed to make loans for projects similar to those financed by the Bank but with longer terms. (IBRD loans are generally 15 years while IDA loans are 50 years; in fact, IDA loans are called "credits" rather than loans.) Of the two, IDA maintains closer links with IBRD, sharing the same president, management, and staff. When one speaks of the World Bank, it is assumed that IDA is also included. IFC, on the other hand, is a separate entity, sharing only the president

xi

of the World Bank while maintaining its own staff and
management. IBRD membership is a prerequisite for IFC
membership. IDA and IBRD activities are covered in the
World Bank's annual report, while IFC's activities are
covered in a separate report. The Board of Governors,
which meets once a year to approve the annual reports,
are the same for all three units.

EDI's goal has been to improve the quality of
economic management in developing countries by training
their senior government officials. Founded in 1955,
EDI utilizes both World Bank and IFC staff members, as
well as specialists from other international
organizations to act as lecturers. A six-month general
development course covering the problems and policies
of development, forms the nucleus of the curricula.
Two by-products of the EDI are the supplementary
libraries program and publications program (seminar
papers, teaching materials, and case studies). In
EDI's library program, small collections were assembled
during the early 1960s to provide basic reference
materials on development.

The World Bank Group consists of these three
complementary institutions (IBRD, IDA, and IFC), and
several affiliates; although they are separate
entities, their missions are related. International
Center for the Settlement of Investment Disputes
(ICSID) was established under World Bank auspices to
assist the flow of private capital between developed
and developing countries by serving as a resource for
arbitration of investment disputes. Consultative Group
on International Agricultural Research (CGIAR) is
headed by the World Bank, and cosponsored by FAO and
UNDP. CGIAR is designed to finance international
agricultural research centers aimed at increasing food
production in developing countries. The research and
training programs of CGIAR-supported centers seek to
equip developing countries with superior varieties of
crops and improved farming systems for the production
of animals and food plants. Research results from
these centers are disseminated through publications,
conferences, and training scientists from both
developed and developing nations.

Multilateral Investment Guarantee Agency (MIGA),
the newest affiliate, was designed to provide technical
assistance on ways to encourage foreign investors. It

promotes the flow of international investments to developing countries by issuing guarantees against noncommercial risks, as well as providing a range of advisory services.

The Joint Ministerial Committee of the Board of Governors of the World Bank and the International Monetary Fund on the Transfer of Real Resources to Developing Countries (Development Committee) was formed to advise the Board of Governors on problems of developing nations that are most affected by balance of payment difficulties. It is not a decision making body but a forum to provide guidance and advice to the executive boards of IMF and IBRD. Heads of other international economic organizations are invited to participate in its meetings as observers. Committee members are high-ranking leaders in finance from both developed and developing nations.

In addition to financial support, the World Bank has provided technical assistance to developing countries (i.e., various advisory services). World Bank teams of experts analyze the economy, conduct feasibility studies, and make recommendations on long range development programs. Calling upon these experts to provide information on the profitability of projects, impacts on the local economy, and other considerations enables the World Bank to analyze loan requests. General survey missions were sent to select countries to study development prospects, while permanent regional missions were also established in countries where development problems were more complex. These missions generated a number of reports intended primarily for internal World Bank use. Later these mission reports were replaced by a country economic reports program.

An outgrowth of EDI's library program is the World Bank Depository Library Plan in which several hundred institutions in member countries participate. This plan provides free access to most World Bank publications; one depository library per country is permitted, although some developing countries may have more than one. In the United States, the Joint Library of the IBRD and IMF serves as the official U.S. depository. World Bank publications are available through interlibrary loan from the Joint IBRD-IMF Library. These publications are also registered with the National Technical Information Service (NTIS), allowing access to out-of-print as well as current titles.

The Joint IBRD-IMF Library serves the World Bank Group and the International Monetary Fund. In addition to collecting materials from both, the Joint Library collects the major official publications from all its member countries, as well as those from other international organizations like FAO, OECD, and UN. The Joint Library has an extensive collection of serials, monographs, and research paper series, as well as a Bretton Woods collection (materials in chronological order about the history and activities of the World Bank and IMF). A number of bibliographies have been produced by the Joint IBRD-IMF Library. Although normally restricted to Bank and Fund staff members, the library is open to scholars who apply for permission to use their research materials.

As a result of its expanded financial and technical assistance over the past decade, the World Bank has become more international in focus, and its activities have attracted more attention. Bank policies and activities are explained in various media to foster the exchange of knowledge and experience with others interested in development. Their role in the international community encompasses a range of activities from intellectual to operational through relationships with the academic community, the UN and its specialized agencies, and others.

Because of its research, the World Bank produces documents and publications of great interest to those in the field of international development, as well as policy makers, universities, and libraries. A wide range of materials are offered for sale from various distributors throughout the world (see Appendix B). Documents tend to be restricted in their distribution, while publications are more widely distributed. Some of these publications are published by the Bank itself while others are copublished by commercial publishers (primarily Johns Hopkins University Press). Similar to government organizations, IGOs (intergovernmental organizations) like the World Bank Group produce a variety of materials: monographs, periodicals, directories, summaries of meetings, manuals, research reports, working papers, and so on. Some are announced through a publications unit, while others are announced through indexes produced by their library, like the Joint Library's LIST OF RECENT PERIODICAL ARTICLES.

My research indicates that a bibliography on the World Bank has not been written, and therefore this guide will not duplicate another work. It would be similar to bibliographies for other international organizations, should they exist. Some of these international agencies include: IMF, UN, EEC, League of Nations, and OECD. A number of bibliographies exist for the official and sales publications for the United Nations, while only a few works exist for some of the other agencies mentioned (see Appendix D).

There are very few bibliographies about the individual international agencies. For instance, Baer's INTERNATIONAL ORGANIZATIONS does not include coverage of the World Bank or IMF (both were founded in 1944 and his work covers 1918-1945). INTERNATIONAL ECONOMIC INSTITUTIONS by Meerhaeghe includes a brief bibliography, but it contains only a few citations to works about these agencies. Works by Collester and Palmer appear to be the only guides written about individual agencies, while the IMF article is written by and about the IMF. Even Hajnal's recent work INTERNATIONAL INFORMATION tends to focus on the nature of intergovernmental organizations and uses the UN as an example. The World Bank is mentioned, as are a number of other international agencies. His emphasis, however, is not on the individual agencies but on the selection, collection, and arrangement of materials from international organizations. This guide, then, fills a gap by providing a bibliography of materials specifically about the World Bank Group.

ABBREVIATIONS

AID	Agency for International Development (US)
BIS	Bank for International Settlements
CGIAR	Consultative Group on International Agricultural Research
EEC	European Economic Community
EDI	Economic Development Institute
EMGF	Emerging Markets Growth Fund
FAO	Food and Agriculture Organization of the United Nations
GATT	General Agreement on Tariffs and Trade
GDP	Gross Domestic Product
GPO	Government Printing Office (US)
GRIP	Guaranteed Recovery of Investment Principal
HMSO	Her Majesty's Stationery Office (UK)
IADB	Inter-American Development Bank
IBRD	International Bank for Reconstruction and Development (World Bank)
ICSID	International Centre for Settlement of Investment Disputes
IDA	International Development Association
IDS	Institute for Development Studies
IFAD	International Fund for Agricultural Development
IFC	International Finance Corporation
IGO	Intergovernmental Organization
ILO	International Labour Organisation
ITO	International Trade Organization
IMF	International Monetary Fund
ITU	International Telecommunications Union
LDC	Less Developed Country
MIGA	Multilateral International Guarantee Agency
MITI	Ministry of International Trade and Industry (Japan)
NAC	National Advisory Council for Monetary and Financial Problems
NBER	National Bureau for Economic Research
NGO	Nongovernmental Organization
OAS	Organization of American States
OAU	Organization for African Unity
ODA	Overseas Development Administration (UK)
ODI	Overseas Development Institute
OECD	Organization for Economic Cooperation and Development
OPEC	Organization of Petroleum Exporting Countries
PLO	Palestine Liberation Organization

UK	United Kingdom
UN	United Nations
UNCTAD	United Nations Conference on Trade and Development
UNDP	United Nations Development Program
UNIDO	United Nations Industrial Development Organization
US	United States
WHO	World Health Organization

The World Bank Group

DIVISION/AFFILIATE BIBLIOGRAPHY

BRETTON WOODS

1.   ABC OF BRETTON WOODS. New York: Crowell-
          Collier, 1945. *

2.   Acheson, A.L.K., J.F. Chant, and M.F.J.
          Pradnowny (eds.). BRETTON WOODS
          REVISITED: EVALUATIONS OF THE
          INTERNATIONAL MONETARY FUND AND THE
          INTERNATIONAL BANK FOR RECONSTRUCTION
          AND DEVELOPMENT. Toronto, Canada:
          University of Toronto Press, 1972.
          xxiv,138 p. ISBN 0-8020-1847-5
          LCCN 72-185697

              Papers delivered at a conference
          held in honor of the 25th anniversary of
          the Bretton Woods Agreements. Reviews
          the historical background of Bretton
          Woods, and its accomplishments. Presents
          forecasts by international finance
          scholars.

3.   American Bankers Association. PRACTICAL
          INTERNATIONAL FINANCIAL ORGANIZATION,
          THROUGH AMENDMENTS TO THE BRETTON WOODS
          PROPOSALS. New York: 1945. *

4.   Arndt, H.W. "Bretton Woods: Progress to
          Date in the Establishment of the
          International Monetary Fund and
          International Bank." PUBLIC
          ADMINISTRATION (Australia), vol. 6 (June
          1947): 321-328. *

5.   Baer, George (ed.). INTERNATIONAL
          ORGANIZATIONS 1918-1945: A GUIDE TO
          RESEARCH AND RESEARCH MATERIALS.
          Wilmington, DE: Scholarly Resources,
          1981. ISBN 0-8420-2179-5

Cites a few references to Bretton Woods institutions, but mostly to League of Nations.

6.   "Bank and the Fund: the Story Continued." MIDLAND BANK REVIEW (February 1951): 1-9.

Reviews achievements during 1948-1950. Claims IMF made larger contribution to monetary order, while the World Bank made larger contribution to economic development. Improvements are needed to increase their usefulness.

7.   Bareau, Paul. "Bretton Woods Institutions." INSTITUTE OF BANKERS IN IRELAND JOURNAL, vol. 51 (January 1949): 30-43. *

Address before the Institute, in Dublin Centre (Ireland) in October 1948.

8.   Bareau, Paul. "Bretton Woods Institutions and Britain's External Economic Policy." INSTITUTE OF BANKERS IN SCOTLAND, LECTURES TO LOCAL CENTRES (1947/1948): 71-88. *

Address in Glasgow and Dundee Centres (Scotland) in January 1948.

9.   Bareau, Paul. "Is It Good-bye to Bretton Woods?" THREE BANKS REVIEW, vol. 13 (March 1952): 3-18.

States IMF and IBRD were largely initiated by the US. Discusses problems of international economic relations and balance of payments under US leadership.

10.   Bratter, Herbert. "Four Years After Bretton Woods." BANKING, vol. 84 (September 1948): 50-53. *

11.   Bratter, H.M. "Fund and Bank: The First
       Full Year." BANKER, vol. 83 (September
       1947): 147-152. *

12.   "Bretton Woods Agreements." CANTERBURY
       CHAMBER OF COMMERCE BULLETIN (New
       Zealand) (December 1946): 1-2. *

13.   "Bretton Woods Twins." THE ECONOMIST,
       vol. 155, no. 5482 (September 25, 1948):
       506-507.

           Argues decision to establish
       Washington, D.C. as permanent
       headquarters, has placed these
       institutions too much under the
       influence of the US government. Claims
       operations of both have decreased, while
       operating expenses have increased.

14.   "Bretton Woods Twins." HYDERABAD GOVERNMENT
       BULLETIN ON ECONOMIC AFFAIRS (India),
       vol. 1, no. 9 (December 1948): 940-943.

           Same text as Entry 13. Argues
       staff size is inflated, not proportional
       to output. Calls for reduction in
       excess staffing.

15.   Bokil, S.V. MECHANICS OF INTERNATIONAL
       MONEY: A STUDY OF THE BRETTON WOODS
       SYSTEM. Madras, India: Macmillan, 1971.
       vii,184 p.

           Studies international monetary
       systems during post-war period, and
       calls for international monetary
       unification. Claims Special Drawing
       Rights are a move in this direction.
       Examines Bretton Woods system, and calls
       for new international monetary system -
       one in which the dollar is not used

the reserve currency. Argues in favor
of flexible exchange rate system.

16. Cassius (pseud.). BRETTON WOODS PLAN (FOR
WORLD DOMINATION BY THE U.S.A.):
BLUEPRINTS FOR A THIRD WORLD WAR (WITH)
THE HAVANA TRADE CHARTER (THE ORIGINAL
BRETTON WOODS PLAN). Wellington, New
Zealand: Democracy Publications, 1948.
15 p. *

17. Citizens Conference in International Economic
Union. BRETTON WOODS AGREEMENTS -- AND
WHY IT IS NECESSARY. New York: 1944.
50 p. *

Abstracts the Bretton Woods
Agreements and the public meeting
speeches (edited by H. Alfred).

18. "Establishment of Bretton Woods
Institutions." FEDERAL RESERVE
BULLETIN, vol. 32 (April 1946): 361-372.

Describes how IMF and IBRD held
their first meeting in March, and are
expected to commence operations by late
1946. Provides background on their
establishment, distribution of voting,
and prospects. Concludes that World
Bank and IMF are essential in fostering
national development.

19. "Fund and the Bank: A Great International
Experiment." MIDLAND BANK REVIEW (May
1948): 1-7.

Four years after Bretton Woods
conference, reviews events leading up to
the creation of the World Bank and IMF,
as well as their separate but
complementary functions, and cooperative
relationships with other international

organizations. Concludes the Bretton
Woods institutions do not have
sufficient resources, on their own, to
bring about international financial and
economic stability.

20. Haberler, Gottfried. "Reflections on the
Future of the Bretton Woods System."
AMERICAN ECONOMIC REVIEW, vol. 43, no. 2
(May 1953), Papers & Proceedings:
81-103.

Focuses on both IMF and IBRD
(although more on IMF) as international
multilateral organizations. Discusses
balance of payments, US, UK, Germany,
and Netherlands exports in relation to
both the World Bank and IMF.

21. Hackett, William T.G. BRETTON WOODS.
Toronto: Canadian Institute of
International Affairs, 1945. *

22. Halasi, Augustus. BRETTON WOODS AND FULL
EMPLOYMENT. New York: American Labor
Conference on International Affairs,
1945. *

23. Halm, George Nikolaus. INTERNATIONAL
MONETARY COOPERATION. Chapel Hill, NC:
University of North Carolina Press,
1945. vii,355 p.

Contrasts Bretton Woods Agreements
with earlier proposals (especially the
Keynes Plan and the White Plan).
Presents text of the Articles of
Agreement for both IMF and World Bank.
Summarizes the controversy surrounding
the establishment of IMF.

24.   Hawtrey, Ralph G. BRETTON WOODS, FOR BETTER
           OR WORSE. London, UK: Longmans, 1946.
           vii,142 p. *

25.   Heilperin, Michael A. INTERNATIONAL MONETARY
           RECONSTRUCTION: THE BRETTON WOODS
           AGREEMENTS. New York: American
           Enterprise Association, 1945. 112 p.   *

26.   Institute of International Finance. BRETTON
           WOODS MONETARY AND FINANCIAL CONFERENCE.
           New York: 1944. *

27.   "International Bank." THE ECONOMIST,
           vol. 147 (September 9, 1944): 355-356.

           Discusses the Bretton Woods
           Agreements, focussing on the World Bank.
           States if the Bank is not established,
           the international capital market will be
           severely hampered in the years following
           World War II. Proposes the creation of
           the World Bank as a return to the
           principles of world order (economic
           stability and mutual assistance).

28.   International Bank for Reconstruction and
           Development. BRETTON WOODS AT FORTY
           1944-84: A SERIES OF ARTICLES
           COMMEMORATING THE FORTIETH ANNIVERSARY
           OF THE UNITED NATIONS MONETARY AND
           FINANCIAL CONFERENCE HELD AT BRETTON
           WOODS, NEW HAMPSHIRE, JULY 1-22, 1944.
           Washington, D.C: 1984. 20 p.

           Reprints from FINANCE AND
           DEVELOPMENT (March to December 1984).
           Focuses on individuals who were involved
           with Bretton Woods itself, or either the
           IMF or World Bank during the early days.

29.   Kindleberger, Charles P. "Bretton Woods
      Reappraised." INTERNATIONAL
      ORGANIZATION, vol. 5 , no. 1 (February
      1951): 32-47.

          Reviews first 4 years of
      operations. Calls IMF and IBRD as
      inadequate to meet the economic problems
      after World War II. Contrasts World
      Bank activity with IMF passivity.

30.   Knorr, Klaus. "Bretton Woods Institutions in
      Transition." INTERNATIONAL
      ORGANIZATION, vol. 2, no. 1 (February
      1948): 19-38.

          Compares IMF and IBRD similarities
      (i.e., policy making, structure), as
      well as examines the policies and
      purpose of each. Reviews current
      problems in light of dollar crisis.

31.   Meade, J.E. "Bretton Woods, Havana, and the
      United Kingdom Balance of Payments."
      LLOYDS BANK REVIEW, series 2, no. 7
      (January 1948): 1-18.

          Discusses whether UK decision to
      support IMF and World Bank was right.
      Examines the Bretton Woods Agreements
      and the ITO charter (the latter was
      presented at World Conference on Trade
      and Employment in Havana).

32.   Metzger, Laure. "Bretton Woods -- Three
      Years After." AMERICAN PERSPECTIVE,
      vol. 2 (December 1948): 378-381.

          Comments on IMF and World Bank
      annual reports and their inability to
      accomplish as much as possible (due to
      current world economic conditions).
      Points out administrative expenditures

are out of proportion to other
activities. Argues that instead of
attempting to be profitable in the short
run, they should be more risk-taking on
programs that are economically sound in
the long run.

33.   Morgan, Carlyle. BRETTON WOODS: CLUES TO A
        MONETARY MYSTERY. Boston: World Peace
        Foundation, 1945.

        Summarizes Articles of Agreement
        and major issues involved in Bretton
        Woods. Provides understanding of
        problems of economic security after
        World War II for general audience.

34.   Newcomer, M. MONETARY PLANS FOR THE UNITED
        NATIONS. Washington, D.C.: American
        Association of University Women, 1944.*

35.   Oliver, R.W. ORIGINS OF THE INTERNATIONAL
        BANK FOR RECONSTRUCTION AND DEVELOPMENT.
        Ann Arbor, MI: University Microfilm
        International, 1959. Collation of
        original as determined by the film:
        4,x,792 p. *

36.   Oliver, Robert W. INTERNATIONAL ECONOMIC
        COOPERATION AND THE WORLD BANK. London,
        UK: Macmillan, 1975. xxii,421 p.
        ISBN 0-333-18402-5 LCCN 75-328642

        Presents proposals for
        international economic cooperation
        following the collapse of Europe after
        World War I. Discusses reasons why US
        planned for international economic
        cooperation in 1930s and 1940s, how the
        US proposal led to the draft plan, and
        how the Articles were negotiated.
        Describes main features of White Plan
        and its evolution.

37.   Oliver, Robert W.   EARLY PLANS FOR A WORLD
      BANK (Princeton Studies in International
      Finance, 29).   Princeton, NJ: 1971.
      57 p.   LCCN 70-171848

          Discusses early proposals which led
      to the establishment of the World Bank.
      Emphasizes the work of Harry Dexter
      White and the US Department of Treasury,
      comparing the White and Keynes Plans.

38.   Peddie, John T.   CRITICISM OF THE BRETTON
      WOODS PROPOSALS.   London: Economic
      Equity, 1944.   *

39.   Petersmann, H.G.   "Operations of the World
      Bank and the Evolution of its
      Institutional Functions Since Bretton
      Woods (1944-1984)."   GERMAN YEARBOOK
      OF INTERNATIONAL LAW, vol. 26 (1983):
      7-53.   *

40.   Piest, Oskar.   TOWARD STABILITY OF WORLD
      ECONOMY: DEFENSE AND CRITICISM OF THE
      BRETTON WOODS AGREEMENTS.   New York: J.
      Messner, 1945.   61 p.

          Explains the world economy and
      economic aspects of peace to the general
      audience.   Published while Congress was
      debating the Bretton Woods Agreements,
      summarizes the Bretton Woods Agreements.

41.   "Quartets Old and New."   THE ECONOMIST,
      vol. 297 (October 5, 1985): 6+.   *

42.   "Retreat from Bretton Woods."   BANKER,
      vol. 106, no. 369 (October 1956):
      605-610.   *

43. Shields, Murray (ed.). INTERNATIONAL
     FINANCIAL STABILIZATION: A SYMPOSIUM.
     New York, NY: Irving Trust, 1944.
     xvii,186 p.

          Reviews the Bretton Woods
     Agreements (by E.A. Goldenweiser and A.
     Bourneuf). Presents the views of six
     American monetary economists (J. Bogen,
     A. Hansen, E. Kemmerer, J. Viner, R.
     Westerfield, and J. Williams). Reviews
     proposals for stability in post-war
     international financial relationships.

44. Tether, C.G. "Bretton Woods and the
     Crisis." BANKER, vol. 84 (October
     1947): 32-35. *

          Discusses the World Bank's role in
     the dollar crisis.

45. Tyrer, A.J., and N.G. Crowley. WILL
     BRETTON WOODS WORK? AN ECONOMIC
     ANALYSIS. Melbourne, Australia: F.J.
     Hilton, 1946. 63 p. *

46. UN Monetary and Financial Conference,
     (Bretton Woods, NH, 1944). "Bretton
     Woods Agreements: International Monetary
     Fund and International Bank for
     Reconstruction and Development."
     INTERNATIONAL CONCILIATION, vol. 413,
     Section 2 (September 1945): 561-639.

          Presents the full text (without
     comments) of the Articles of Agreements.

47. US Board of Governors of the Federal
     Reserve System. BRETTON WOODS
     AGREEMENTS: A BIBLIOGRAPHY, APRIL
     1943-DECEMBER 1945. Washington, D.C.:
     Federal Reserve System Library, 1946. *

48.   US Department of State. INTERNATIONAL BANK
      FOR RECONSTRUCTION AND DEVELOPMENT:
      ARTICLES OF AGREEMENT BETWEEN THE UNITED
      STATES OF AMERICA AND OTHER POWERS;
      signed at Washington, D.C., December 27,
      1945, effective December 17, 1945
      (Treaties and Other Internal Acts
      Series, 1502; Publication 2511).
      Washington, D.C.: GPO, 1946. 33 p.   *

49.   US Department of State. PROCEEDINGS AND
      DOCUMENTS OF THE U.N. MONETARY AND
      FINANCIAL CONFERENCE, BRETTON WOODS, NEW
      HAMPSHIRE, JULY 1-22, 1944, vol. 1 & 2
      (International Organizations and
      Conferences, series 1, 3; Publication
      2866). Washington, D.C.: GPO, 1948.
      1808 p.

          Presents working papers issued at
      the UN conference, as well as pre-
      conference documents, press releases,
      and other related papers.

50.   Van Dormael, Armand. BRETTON WOODS: BIRTH OF
      A MONETARY SYSTEM. London: Macmillan,
      1978. xi,322 p. ISBN 0-333-23369-7

          Tells history of Bretton Woods from
      its birth in 1944. Covers what
      happened, how, and why, as well as the
      background during the few years (1939-
      1944) prior to UN conference. Includes
      quotes from documents and speeches.

51.   "World's Money Needs Unsolved: International
      Agencies Face Biggest Tests." U.S. NEWS
      AND WORLD REPORT, vol. 27, no. 5 (July
      29, 1949): 50-51.

          Claims World Bank is unable to
      finance development, and IMF is unable
      solve currency problem. Both were meant

to straighten out the currency problem
and provide capital to repair war
damage, but neither has done these
functions. Yet both have the resources
to do so, giving rise to criticism.
Argues Bretton Woods institutions were
designed for 1939 problems, and both
charters may need to change to deal with
1940s problems.

52.   Young, John Parke. "Developing Plans for an
        International Monetary Fund and a World
        Bank." U.S. DEPARTMENT OF STATE
        BULLETIN, vol. 23, no. 593 (November 13,
        1950): 778-790.

        Discusses how US proposals for
        worldwide stabilization fund was
        prepared, and how it eventually led to
        the UN conference. Compares the US
        proposal (Harry D. White) and UK
        proposal (John M. Keynes), how the two
        were reconciled, resulting in a joint
        statement in early 1944. Summarized the
        IMF and IBRD Articles of Agreement.

CONSULTATIVE GROUP ON INTERNATIONAL
AGRICULTURAL RESEARCH

53.   Baum, Warren C. PARTNERS AGAINST HUNGER: THE
        CONSULTATIVE GROUP ON INTERNATIONAL
        AGRICULTURAL RESEARCH. Washington,
        D.C.: Published for CGIAR by IBRD, 1986.
        xiii,337 p.

        Describes CGIAR's history, 13
        international agricultural research
        institutions, and activities. Written
        in honor of its 15th anniversary by its
        chair (Baum) for 10 years.

54.   Consultative Group on International
        Agricultural Research. CONSULTATIVE
        GROUP ON INTERNATIONAL AGRICULTURAL
        RESEARCH. Washington, D.C.: 1980.
        vii,50 p.

            Presents an overview of CGIAR's
        corporate effort and describes
        CGIAR-supported centers.

ECONOMIC DEVELOPMENT INSTITUTE

55.   Adler, Hans A. ECONOMIC APPRAISAL OF
        TRANSPORT PROJECTS: A MANUAL WITH CASE
        STUDIES. Bloomington, IN: Indiana
        University Press, 1971. xi,205 p.
        ISBN 0-0253-31900-5; 0-0253-31901-3
        (paper) LCCN 73-12604

            Discusses the costs and benefits of
        transport projects using case studies.

56.   Adler, Hans A. ECONOMIC APPRAISAL OF
        TRANSPORT PROJECTS: A MANUAL WITH CASE
        STUDIES, rev. edition. Baltimore, MD:
        Published for the World Bank by Johns
        Hopkins University Press, 1987. *

            Updates Entry 55.

57.   Adler, John H. "Economic Development
        Institute of the World Bank: Training
        Programs for Developers." INTERNATIONAL
        DEVELOPMENT REVIEW, vol. 5 (March 1963):
        7-13.

            Since 1956, EDI has provided
        training in economic development.
        Describes selection of participants,
        curriculum, instruction methodology, and
        staffing.

58.   Austin, James E. AGROINDUSTRIAL PROJECT
       ANALYSIS (EDI Series in Economic
       Development). Baltimore, MD: Published
       for EDI by Johns Hopkins University
       Press, 1981. x,213 p.
       ISBN 0-8018-2412-5; 0-8018-2413-3
       (paper) LCCN 80-550

            Advises systems approach, and
       financial and economic analysis in
       evaluating agroindustrial projects.
       Urges consideration of nutritional
       consequences in project design.

59.   Bhatt, V.V. ASPECTS OF DEVELOPMENT BANKING
       POLICY (EDI Seminar Paper, 12).
       Washington, D.C.: EDI, 1975. *

60.   Bhatt, V.V. SOME ASPECTS OF FINANCIAL
       POLICIES AND CENTRAL BANKING IN
       DEVELOPING COUNTRIES (EDI Seminar
       Paper, 11). Washington, D.C.: EDI,
       1974. *

61.   Bhatt, V.V. STERILITY OF EQUILIBRIUM
       ECONOMICS: AN ASPECT OF SOCIOLOGY OF
       SCIENCE (EDI Seminar Paper, 9).
       Washington, D.C.: EDI, 1974. *

62.   Bhatt, V.V. "World Bank's Economic
       Development Institute." FINANCE AND
       DEVELOPMENT, vol. 19 (December 1982):
       18-19.

            Discusses basic function, topics of
       courses, and geographical distribution
       of participants in EDI.

63.   Cairncross, A.K. SHORT TERM AND THE LONG IN
       ECONOMIC PLANNING. Washington, D.C.:
       EDI, 1966. ii,30 p.

In honor of its 10th anniversary, EDI's first director (Cairncross) lectures on the role of long term and short term planning in economic development.

64. Deutsch, Richard. "World Bank's EDI: Laying the Groundwork to Attract Foreign Investment." DEVELOPMENT BUSINESS: THE BUSINESS ED. OF DEVELOPMENT FORUM (March 16, 1988): 66. *

65. Diamond, William. DEVELOPMENT BANKS. Baltimore, MD: Published for EDI by Johns Hopkins Press, 1957. xi,128 p. LCCN 57-13429

Uses Turkey, India, and Mexico as examples for discussion in EDI seminars. Describes principles of investment and general problems of operating a development bank. See also Entry 174.

66. Economic Development Institute. CURRICULA OF COURSES HELD AT EDI FROM SEPTEMBER 1974-AUGUST 1975. Washington, D.C.: 1976. 207 p.

Reading lists and assignments used in EDI courses. See also Entry 70.

67. Economic Development Institute. DIRECTORY OF FELLOWS. Washington, D.C.: 1974-

List of EDI participants.

68. Economic Development Institute. EDI COURSE PROGRAM 1976-1977. Washington, D.C.: 1976. *

69.   Economic Development Institute. SELECTED
        READINGS AND SOURCE MATERIALS ON
        ECONOMIC DEVELOPMENT: A LIST OF BOOKS,
        ARTICLES AND REPORTS INCLUDED IN A SMALL
        LIBRARY ASSEMBLED BY THE ECONOMIC
        DEVELOPMENT INSTITUTE. Washington,
        D.C.: 1962. vi, 66 p.

        Bibliography of English language
        publications donated to 55 member
        countries in 1960-1961. The small
        library program was created to initiate
        collections on economic development in
        the Third World.

70.   Economic Development Institute. SELECTED
        READINGS AND SOURCE MATERIALS ON
        ECONOMIC DEVELOPMENT: FOR GENERAL
        DEVELOPMENT COURSE OF THE ECONOMIC
        DEVELOPMENT INSTITUTE. Washington,
        D.C.: 1962-   40 p.

        Reading lists and assignments of
        EDI classes. See also Entry 66.

71.   Economic Development Institute. TRAINING FOR
        DEVELOPMENT -- A REPORT OF THE WORLD
        BANK'S ECONOMIC DEVELOPMENT INSTITUTE.
        Washington, D.C.: 1974.   40 p.

        Describes role of EDI in the World
        Bank Group and in member countries.

72.   Espadas, Orlando T. SELECTED BIBLIOGRAPHY ON
        AGRICULTURAL PROJECT EVALUATION (EDI
        Seminar Paper, 1). Washington, D.C.:
        EDI, 1972. *

73.   Gittinger, J. Price (ed.). AGRICULTURAL
        PROJECTS CASE STUDIES AND WORK EXERCISES
        (EDI Seminar Paper, 4). Washington,
        D.C.: EDI, 1973. *

74.   Gittinger, J. Price (ed.). COMPOUNDING AND
       DISCOUNTING TABLES FOR PROJECT
       EVALUATION (EDI Teaching Materials, 1).
       Washington, D.C.: EDI, 1973. 143 p.

           Presents compounding, discounting,
       summary present worth, and narrow
       interval compounding tables, as well as
       the formulas used in teaching project
       analysis.

75.   Gittinger, J. Price. ECONOMIC ANALYSIS OF
       AGRICULTURAL PROJECTS. Baltimore, MD:
       Published for EDI by Johns Hopkins
       Press, 1972. vii,221 p.
       ISBN 0-8018-1386-7; 0-8018-1403-0
       (paper) LCCN 75-186503

           Applies probable outcome
       discounting techniques. Compares
       investment and production costs with
       benefits produced. See Entry 76.

76.   Gittinger, J. Price. ECONOMIC ANALYSIS OF
       AGRICULTURAL PROJECTS, 2nd ed. (EDI
       Series in Economic Development).
       Baltimore, MD: Published for EDI by
       Johns Hopkins University Press, 1982.
       xxi,505 p. ISBN 0-8018-2912-7;
       0-8018-2913-5 (paper) LCCN 82-15262

           Revised edition describes the
       project concept, as well as financial
       and economic aspects of project
       analysis. See Entry 75.

77.   International Bank for Reconstruction and
       Development. ECONOMIC DEVELOPMENT
       INSTITUTE. Washington, D.C.: 1956-

           Discusses the work of the EDI (a
       staff college for senior government
       officials from underdeveloped

countries). Describes the curriculum
and facilities.

78.   Kamarck, Andrew M. CLIMATE AND ECONOMIC
       DEVELOPMENT (EDI Seminar Paper, 2).
       Washington, D.C.: EDI, 1972. *

79.   King, John A., Jr. ECONOMIC DEVELOPMENT
       PROJECTS AND THEIR APPRAISAL: CASES AND
       PRINCIPLES FROM THE EXPERIENCE OF THE
       WORLD BANK. Baltimore, MD: Published
       for EDI by Johns Hopkins Press, 1967.
       xii,530 p. LCCN 67-22895

           Describes electric power,
       transportation, and industrial projects
       to illustrate project appraisal process.

80.   Lamson-Scribner, Frank H. (ed.). INDUSTRY
       CASE STUDIES AND WORK EXERCISES (EDI
       Seminar Paper, 3). Washington, D.C.:
       EDI, 1973. *

81.   Lamson-Scribner, Frank H., and Nicholas R.
       Burnett (eds.). WATER SUPPLY CASE
       STUDIES AND WORK EXERCISES (EDI Seminar
       Paper, 8). Washington, D.C.: 1973.   *

82.   Mulvaney, John. ANALYSIS BAR CHARTING.
       Washington, D.C.: EDI, 1975. *

83.   Schuster, Helmut. AGRICULTURAL ROADS (EDI
       Seminar Paper, 7). Washington, D.C.:
       EDI, 1973. *

84.   Tinbergen, Jan. DESIGN OF DEVELOPMENT.
       Baltimore, MD: Published for EDI, World
       Bank by Johns Hopkins Press, 1958.
       viii,99 p. LCCN 58-9458

           Discusses development policies,
       project appraisals, and problems with
       programming.

85. Vasiliades, Kanella C., and Cecille Shannon.
     BIBLIOGRAPHY FOR PROGRAMMING IN
     AGRICULTURE (EDI Seminar Paper, 6).
     Washington, D.C.: EDI, 1973. *

86. Waterston, Albert. DEVELOPMENT PLANNING:
     LESSONS OF EXPERIENCE. Baltimore, MD:
     Published for EDI by John Hopkins Press,
     1965. 706 p. LCCN 65-26180

          Compares planning in Morocco,
     Pakistan, and Yugoslavia. Draws
     "lessons" based on Waterson's
     experience. See Entries 87, 88 and 89.
     See also Entry 429.

87. Waterson, Albert. PLANNING IN MOROCCO:
     ORGANIZATION AND IMPLEMENTATION.
     Baltimore, MD: Published for EDI by
     Johns Hopkins Press, 1962. 72 p.

          Draws on author's experience in
     Morocco (1961). Used in teaching EDI
     courses. See also Entry 86.

88. Waterson, Albert. PLANNING IN PAKISTAN:
     ORGANIZATION AND IMPLEMENTATION.
     Baltimore, MD: Published for EDI by
     Johns Hopkins Press, 1963.

          Draws on author's experience in
     Pakistan, and used in EDI courses.
     Shows that if development planning is to
     be carried out, government support is
     needed. See also Entry 86.

89. Waterson, Albert. PLANNING IN YUGOSLAVIA:
     ORGANIZATION AND IMPLEMENTATION.
     Baltimore, MD: Published for EDI by
     Johns Hopkins Press, 1962.

Draws on experience in Yugoslavia.
Studied in EDI courses on development
planning. See also Entry 86.

90.   Waterson, Albert. PREPARING A PROGRAM FOR
Washington, D.C.: EDI, 1973. *

INTERNATIONAL BANK FOR RECONSTRUCTION AND DEVELOPMENT

91.   Adelman, Irma, and Cynthia Taft Morris.
SOCIETY, POLITICS, AND ECONOMIC
DEVELOPMENT: A QUANTITATIVE APPROACH.
Baltimore, MD: Johns Hopkins Press,
1967. LCCN 67-21582

Studies the relationship between
economic, social, and political factors
in economic development by applying
factor analysis. Using 41 indicators
in 74 countries, argues that large-scale
projects have little or no effect on
development.

92.   Adelman, Irma, and Sherman Robinson. INCOME
DISTRIBUTION POLICY IN DEVELOPING
COUNTRIES: A CASE STUDY OF KOREA.
Stanford, CA: Published for the World
Bank by Stanford University Press, 1978.
346 p.   ISBN 0-8047-0925-4
LCCN 76-14269

Examines Korean economy using
general equilibrium model as instrument
for planning income distribution.
Concludes policy interventions in short
to medium term are ineffective, while
significant improvements are possible
with a large-scale policy change.

93. Alexandrowicz, Charles Henry. WORLD ECONOMIC
    AGENCIES: LAW AND PRACTICE. New York:
    Praeger, 1962. xiv,310 p.
    LCCN 62-17301

        Institutional analysis of GATT,
    IMF, WHO, ILO, FAO, World Bank and other
    contributors to world economic
    development. Examines their role in law
    making, and discusses law against the
    background of international economic
    relations.

94. "All Quiet on the Potomac." ECONOMIST
    FINANCIAL REPORT, vol. 12 (October 1,
    1987): 1-2. *

95. Allen, Gary. "Stop the Bank Gang." AMERICAN
    OPINION, vol. 22, no. 2 (February 1979):
    11-18,101-110.

        Argues that the creation of IMF and
    IBRD was part of a plan for a single
    world government, Harry White was a
    Soviet spy, the World Bank supports
    communism, and the Bank actually
    promotes poverty through its loan
    conditions. Calls for cessation of
    World Bank funding, which in return will
    cease inflation.

96. Allen, William R. "Domestic Investment, the
    Foreign Trade Balance and the World
    Bank." KYKLOS, vol. 15, no. 2 (1962):
    353-373.

        Examines relationship between
    domestic investment and balance of
    payments. Suggest implications for
    World Bank lending policy based on this
    relationship.

97.   Almeida, Pauline. "World Bank Report: Irony
        of a Pledge." MALAYSIAN BUSINESS
        (November 1, 1988): 53-55. *

98.   Amerasinghe, Chittharanjan. CASE LAW OF THE
        WORLD BANK ADMINISTRATIVE TRIBUNAL.
        Washington, D.C.: World Bank, 1984.
        LCCN 84-179662 *

99.   Amerasinghe, Chittharanjan Felix. INDEX TO
        DECISIONS OF THE WORLD BANK
        ADMINISTRATIVE TRIBUNAL. Washington,
        D.C.: World Bank, 1983. iii,20 p.
        LCCN 84-179873 *

100.   Amerasinghe, Chittharanjan Felix. MAIN
        POINTS IN DECISIONS OF THE WORLD BANK
        ADMINISTRATIVE TRIBUNAL. Washington,
        D.C.: World Bank, 1985.
        LCCN 86-176071 *

101.   Anderson, Robert S., and Walter Huber. HOUR
        OF THE FOX: TROPICAL FORESTS, THE WORLD
        BANK, AND INDIGENOUS PEOPLE IN CENTRAL
        INDIA. University of Washington Press,
        1988. 202 p. *

102.   Annis, Sheldon. "Shifting Grounds of Poverty
        Lending at the World Bank." BETWEEN TWO
        WORLDS: THE WORLD BANK'S NEXT DECADE, by
        R. Feinberg, et al. New Brunswick, NJ:
        Transaction Books, 1986. p. 87-110.

            Argues that in their poverty
        orientation to development, the Bank
        should not neglect to correct the
        mistakes of its past poverty alleviation
        research. See also Entry 283.

103.   Annis, Sheldon. "Next World Bank? Financing
        Development from the Bottom Up."
        GRASSROOTS DEVELOPMENT, Vol. 11, No. 1
        (1987): 24-29. *

104.   Annis, Sheldon. "World Bank Needs New Ideas
        to Stay Relevant." DEUTSCHE BUNDESBANK,
        AUSZUGE AUS PRESSEARTIKLEN, no. 59
        (August 17, 1987): 12. *

105.   Applegate, Charles, and Susan Fennell.
        "Cooperating for Growth and Adjustment."
        FINANCE AND DEVELOPMENT, vol. 22
        (December 1985): 50-53.

        Comments on the October 1985
        meeting of the Board of Governors in
        Seoul, which focused on sustained growth
        and development as its main themes.

106.   "Arab Financier in Model Debt/Equity Swap."
        MIDDLE EAST ECONOMIC DIGEST, vol. 31,
        no. 42 (October 17-23, 1987): 9,11.

        Describes first World Bank-assisted
        debt/equity swap in Africa. Involves
        the restructuring of banking systems in
        Mauritania, and would allow local banks
        to reopen credit lines, providing a more
        effective channel for future Bank loans.

107.   Ardalan, Cyrus, and Alex Fleming. "Changing
        Thrust of the World Bank's Funding: the
        World Bank Has Been Developing New
        Financing Techniques and Tapping New
        Markets to Keep Pace with the Growth of
        its Lending." BANKER, vol. 135 (June
        1985): 50-53+. *

        Describes the World Bank's
        initiatives during 1983-1985.

108.   "Argentina, China, Tanzania Gas Projects
        Backed." OIL & GAS JOURNAL, vol. 83
        (July 8, 1985): 30-1. *

109.   Asher, Robert E. "Reflections on Reaching
        the Age of Thirty." INTERNATIONAL
        DEVELOPMENT REVIEW, vol. 18, no. 2
        (1976): 36-37.

            Written in diary format, presents
        World Bank's reflections on celebrating
        its 30th anniversary. Acknowledges how
        the World Bank has become a major source
        of technical assistance, and source of
        data on LDCs. Comments on how the Bank
        needs reorganizing, how rigid it had
        been in earlier years, how less pompous
        it is now, and how rates of return had
        determined investments.

110.   Ascher, William. "New Development Approaches
        and the Adaptability of International
        Agencies: the Case of the World Bank."
        INTERNATIONAL ORGANIZATION, vol. 37,
        no. 3 (Summer 1983): 415-439.

            Examines World Bank and its
        response to change, especially staff
        resistance to reorientation. Tries to
        help determine whether reorientation
        efforts should be directed at staff, or
        member countries that control the staff.
        Examines recent proposals for change
        (priorities, economic growth strategies,
        and North-South balance).

111.   Assetto, Valerie J. SOVIET BLOC IN THE IMF
        AND THE IBRD. Boulder, CO: Westview
        Press, 1987. 216 p. ISBN 0-8133-7236-4
        LCCN 86-7800

            Examines political impact in IBRD
        and IMF lending operations for East
        European countries (Romania, Hungary,
        Poland, and Yugoslavia). Investigates
        IBRD-IMF relations, and traces Soviet
        Union's role since Bretton Woods.

112. Awanohara, Susumo. "How Japan Saw Hori's Speech." FAR EASTERN ECONOMIC REVIEW, vol. 94 (1976): 46,49.

Reports the responses of Japan's Foreign Ministry, MITI, Economic Planning Agency, and Finance Ministry, in light of World Bank Executive Director Taro Hori's farewell remarks.

113. Awanohara, Susomo. "Japan Steps up Eurodollar Race." FAR EASTERN ECONOMIC REVIEW, vol. 97 (September 9, 1977): 56,59.

Discusses how Japanese banks are seeking to give loans after a low profile during 1974-1977.

114. Aufderheide, Pat. "Missing Link in Global Links." COLUMBIA JOURNALISM REVIEW, vol. 27 (May/June 1988): 41-42.

Criticizes Washington, D.C. public TV station WETA and World Bank jointly produced documentary GLOBAL LINKS. Claims that the question is not whether the World Bank should exist, but how the World Bank defines development and who benefits from World Bank-financed projects.

115. Avramovic, Dragoslav, and Ravi Gulhati. DEBT SERVICING PROBLEMS OF LOW-INCOME COUNTRIES, 1956-1958. Baltimore, MD: Johns Hopkins Press, 1960. 74 p. LCCN 60-14700

Examines changes in economic conditions in LDCs by the end of the 1950s, and emphasizes the continuing need for economic development.

116.   Avramovic, Dragoslav, et al. ECONOMIC GROWTH
        AND EXTERNAL DEBT. Baltimore, MD: Johns
        Hopkins Press, 1964. 207 p.
        LCCN 64-25065

            Discusses factors influencing debt
        serving capacity for a nation. Attempts
        to provide a framework to analyze data
        and forecast "external indebtedness."

117.   Ayres, Robert L. BANKING ON THE POOR: THE
        WORLD BANK AND WORLD POVERTY.
        Cambridge, MA: MIT Press, 1983.
        xiv,282 p. ISBN 0-262-01070-4
        LCCN 82-17961

            Comprehensive analysis of World
        Bank's transformation under McNamara,
        especially in terms of poverty
        alleviation. Presents Ayres'
        projections for the future under
        Clausen.

118.   Ayres, Robert L. "Breaking the Bank."
        FOREIGN POLICY, vol. 43 (Summer 1981):
        104-120.

            Analyzes Reagan administration's
        reevaluation of foreign aid and its
        negative impact on IDA and IBRD.
        Describes legacy left by McNamara for
        incoming World Bank President Clausen.
        Discusses the conflict between being a
        "bank" versus a "development agency."

119.   Ayub, Mahmood Ali. MADE IN JAMAICA: THE
        DEVELOPMENT OF THE MANUFACTURING SECTOR
        (World Bank Occasional Paper, 31).
        Baltimore, MD: Published for the World
        Bank by Johns Hopkins University Press,
        1981. xii,128 p. ISBN 0-8018-2568-7
        (paper) LCCN 80-27765

Based on Ayub's experience in Jamaica during 1977-1979. Assesses the importance of factors used in determining the structure of the manufacturing sector. Examines prospects, and makes policy recommendations.

120.   Babington, E.A. "Installing a Computerized Planning System in Ghana." LONG RANGE PLANNING, vol. 20 (August 1987): 110-117.

Part of the World Bank program to improve the exports industry in Ghana. Uses corporate planning methods and management information reporting. Presents techniques of planning, budgeting, and management information using microcomputers.

121.   Baer, Werner. "World Bank Group and the Process of Socio-economic Development in the Third World." WORLD DEVELOPMENT, vol. 2, no. 6 (June 1974): 1-10.

Draws on works by Mason and Asher (Entry 603), Lewis and Kapur (Entry 588), Reid (Entry 684), and McNamara (Entry 598) to comment on the World Bank's past performance and to make recommendations for its future role. Examines the potential and limitations of multilateral institutions assisting LDCs with socioeconomic development.

122.   Balassa, Bela A., et al. STRUCTURE OF PROTECTION IN DEVELOPING COUNTRIES. Baltimore, MD: Published for the World Bank, and IADB by Johns Hopkins Press, 1971. 375 p. ISBN 0-8018-1257-7 LCCN 77-147366

Reports results of research
sponsored by the World Bank and IADB in
Brazil, Chile, Mexico, Malaysia,
Pakistan, and the Philippines. Compares
the evaluation of country studies, and
examines the effects on expenditures,
economic growth, and resource
allocation. Concludes with the
guidelines for the "perfect" protection
policy.

123.   Baldwin, David A. "International Bank in
        Political Perspective." WORLD POLITICS,
        vol. 18, no. 1 (October 1965): 68-81.

        Looks at political aspects of Bank
        loans, allocation of funds, and impacts
        on developing countries' governments.
        Examines how World Bank takes political
        considerations into account when
        determining credit-worthiness, even
        though they are not supposed to be
        affected by them.

124.   Baldwin, George B. "Economics and Economists
        at the World Bank." ECONOMISTS IN
        INTERNATIONAL AGENCIES: AN EXPLORATORY
        STUDY, ed. by A.W. Coats. New York:
        Praeger, 1986. xi,197 p.
        ISBN 0-275-92010-0 LCCN 85-16750.

        Based on 1983 conference at
        Institute for International Economics.
        See also Entry 220.

125.   "Baker's Plan." BANKER, vol. 135 (November
        1985): 3. *

126.   "Baker Plan Bears Some Fruit." FORTUNE,
        vol. 113 (April 28, 1986): 9.

        US Secretary of Treasury James
        Baker calls for new approach to Third

World loans. The Baker Plan advocates increased lending to Brazil, Argentina and Sub-Saharan Africa. Discusses the need for more cooperation between IMF and the World Bank on various programs.

127. "Bank President Stresses Need to Combat Poverty." IMF SURVEY, vol. 16 (October 19, 1987): 299-300.

Describes World Bank President Barber Conable's opening remarks at the September 1987 Board of Governors Annual Meeting, focusing on the promotion of economic growth and fighting poverty.

128. "Bank's Budget: Interview with Barber Conable." BANK'S WORLD, vol.7 (August 1988): 2-3. *

129. "Bank's Gift Horse." ECONOMIST FINANCIAL REPORT, vol. 12 (May 12, 1988): 3. *

130. "Bank's Mission in a Changing World." FINANCE AND DEVELOPMENT, vol. 23 (December 1986): 2-5.

Presents Barber Conable's general impressions. Discusses the adequacy of the World Bank, and its long-term development issues and resources.

131. Barber, Lionel. "World Bank Agrees Capital Base Boost." FINANCIAL TIMES (February 17, 1988): 1. *

132. "Barber Conable Outlines World Bank Agenda." BANK'S WORLD, vol. 6 (October 1987): 12-14. *

133. "Barber Conable's Tokyo Mission." INSTITUTIONAL INVESTOR, INTERNATIONAL ED. (May 1988): 18-19. *

134.   Barnum, Howard N., and Lyn Squire. MODEL OF
        AN AGRICULTURAL HOUSEHOLD: THEORY AND
        EVIDENCE (World Bank Staff Occasional
        Papers, 27). Baltimore, MD: Published
        for the World Bank by Johns Hopkins
        Press, 1979. xi,107 p.
        ISBN 0-8018-2225-4 (paper) LCCN 78-21397

            Based on data collected in
        Malaysia, presents a model of farm
        household behavior.

135.   Barovick, Richard. "Multilateral Development
        Banks: A Major Source of Business
        Opportunity." BUSINESS AMERICA, vol. 9,
        no. 3 (February 3, 1986): 3-9.

            Focuses on the role of the World
        Bank, IADB, African Development Bank,
        and Asian Development Bank play in
        economic development. Discusses the
        relationship of the Baker Plan to these
        multilateral development banks.

136.   Basch, A. "Financing of Economic Development
        and the International Bank."
        PROCEEDINGS OF THE ACADEMY OF POLITICAL
        SCIENCE, vol. 25, no. 2 (January 1953):
        157-170.

            Reviews the Bank's financial
        resources, and its operations (focusing
        on the financing of economic
        development). Describes how the World
        Bank provides both technical and
        financial assistance for economic
        development.

137.   Basch, Antonin. "International Bank for
        Reconstruction and Development,
        1944-1949: A Review." INTERNATIONAL
        CONCILIATION 455 (November 1949):
        787-874. *

138.   Batstone, Roger, and Wil Lepkowski.   "World
         Bank Plan to Prevent Chemical
         Disasters." TECHNOLOGY REVIEW, vol. 89
         (April 1986): 65-66.

             Discusses World Bank guidelines
             requiring chemical plant operators to
             prevent pollution and disasters.
             Describes how IBRD denies loans to
             plants with unsound equipment, and calls
             for reduction of hazardous materials as
             its way to protect the environment.

139.   Baum, Vladimir. "World Bank: Aid for Third
         World Energy Projects." PETROLEUM
         ECONOMIST,   vol. 53 (March 1986):
         87-89. *

140.   Baum, Warren C., and Stokes M. Tolbert.
         "Investing in Development: Lessons of
         World Bank Experience." FINANCE AND
         DEVELOPMENT, Vol. 22 (December 1985):
         26-36.

             Presents final chapter of Entry
             140, which summarizes the Bank's
             experience in financing development in
             member countries.

141.   Baum, Warren C., and Stokes M. Tolbert.
         INVESTING IN DEVELOPMENT.   New York:
         1985. ISBN 0-19-520475-1   LCCN 85-8830

             Provides guidelines for developing
             countries in national investment
             planning and budgeting, sector analysis
             and management.

142.   Baum, Warren C. PROJECT CYCLE. Washington,
         D.C.: World Bank, 1982.
         ISBN 0-8213-0022-9   LCCN 82-8468   *

143.   Beboeck, J. "Rural Development Policies and
        Practices of the World Bank."
        TIJDSHRIFT VOOR ECONOMISCHE MANAGEMENT,
        vol. 23 (1978): 407-426. *

144.   Beckmann, David. "World Bank and Poverty in
        the 1980s." FINANCE AND DEVELOPMENT,
        vol. 23 (September 1986): 26-29.

            Examines the role of raising the
        standard of living, in allocating
        resources to alleviate poverty.
        Highlights the Bank's effectiveness
        compared to other years. Describes
        issues for future IBRD and IDA lending.

145.   Behrman, Jere R. WILL DEVELOPING COUNTRY
        NUTRITION IMPROVE WITH INCOME? A CASE
        STUDY FOR RURAL SOUTH INDIA (CADE
        Working Paper, 85-32). Philadelphia,
        PA: Center for Analysis of Developing
        Economies, Department of Economics,
        University of Pennsylvania, 1985.
        16 p. *

            Compares "elasticity estimates"
        between major foods and nutrients in
        rural South India.

146.   Behrman, Jere R., and Anil B. Deolalikar.
        WILL DEVELOPING COUNTRY NUTRITION
        IMPROVE WITH INCOME? A CASE STUDY FOR
        RURAL SOUTH INDIA (Econometrics Working
        Paper, 85-15). Philadelphia, PA:
        Department of Economics, University of
        Pennsylvania, 1986. *

            Uses estimates for India. Argues
        that nutrient elasticities in terms of
        income may be zero, not almost one as is
        often cited by the World Bank.

147. Bello, Walden, David Kinley, and Elaine
      Elinson. DEVELOPMENT DEBACLE: THE WORLD
      BANK IN THE PHILIPPINES. San Francisco,
      CA: Published for the Philippine
      Solidarity Network by the Institute for
      Food and Development Policy, 1982.
      272 p. ISBN 0-935028-12-9 LCCN 82-9386

      Describes the fiasco in the
      Philippines -- how $3 billion (US
      dollars) was given to development
      programs, and how it caused more poverty
      and political problems. Claims the
      World Bank programs increased poverty
      and repression for the Filipino people.

148. Bennathan, Esra, and A.A. Waters. PORT
      PRICING AND INVESTMENT POLICY FOR
      DEVELOPING COUNTRIES. Baltimore, MD:
      Published for the World Bank by Oxford
      University Press, 1979. 230 p.
      ISBN 0-8018-520092-6; 0-8018-520093-4
      (paper) LCCN 78-26143

      Describes how shipping plays a
      critical role in international trade.
      LDC ports are usually owned by the
      government, and are subsidized by
      tariffs. Recommends these ports charge
      congestion levies to reflect costs.

149. Berg, Alan D. MALNOURISHED PEOPLE: A POLICY
      VIEW (Poverty and Basic Needs Series).
      Washington, D.C.: IBRD, 1981. 108 p.

      Emphasizes World Bank's view that
      investment in meeting basic needs is key
      to the reduction of poverty. Focuses on
      possible actions and costs of meeting
      basic needs (education, health,
      nutrition, housing, and clean water).

150.   Besteliu, Raluca Miga. "Procedure of
        Consensus in the Adoption of Decisions
        by the International Monetary Fund and
        the International Bank for
        Reconstruction and Development." REVUE
        ROUMAINE D'ETUDES INTERNATIONALES,
        no. 38 (1977): 517-526.

            Discusses the process of consensus
        in international organizations from
        Romania's viewpoint. Stresses the
        importance of this form of decision
        making as a means of establishing
        stability in world economy, increasing
        participation by member countries, and
        eliminating the underdevelopment process
        done by current IMF and IBRD procedures.

151.   Bhambhri, Chander Prakash. WORLD BANK AND
        INDIA. Sahibabad, India: Vikas, 1980.
        114 p.

            Examines how India has been favored
        by the World Bank due to its superior-
        subordinate relationship. India accepts
        a dependency relationship in exchange
        for foreign aid. World Bank dictates to
        the Indian government that certain
        policy conditions must be met before
        granting Bank assistance.

152.   "Big Borrower Cometh." THE ECONOMIST,
        vol. 275 (May 17, 1980): 13.

            Republic of China becomes a member
        of the World Bank and IMF. Discusses
        who benefits (India) and who loses
        (Taiwan) by their admittance.

153.   "Bigger World Bank?" JOURNAL OF COMMERCE
        (February 18, 1988): 12A. *

154.   Bing, Adotey. "Fund, the Bank and the People
        of Africa -- 2." WEST AFRICA, no. 3659
        (September 28, 1987): 1889-91.

        Reports on recent Institute for
        African Alternatives Conference in which
        four type of Bank-Fund programs were
        discussed: antipoverty growth, balance
        of payments, structural adjustment, and
        the impact of structural adjustment on
        African countries.

155.   Bird, Graham. "Less Developed Countries and
        the Reform of the International Monetary
        System." ODI REVIEW, vol. 1 (1977):
        68-91. *

156.   Birdsall, Nancy, and Frederick T. Sai.
        "Family Planning Services in Sub-Saharan
        Africa." FINANCE AND DEVELOPMENT (March
        1988): 28-31.

        Discusses the need for family
        planning policies by African
        governments, in response to rapid
        population growth during the 1970s and
        early 1980s.

157.   Black, Eugene. "International Lending as a
        Spur to Economic Development." SKAND.
        BANKEN QUARTERLY REVIEW, vol. 40, no. 2
        (April 1959): 49-53. *

158.   Black, Eugene R. "Policies and Operations of
        the World Bank." LLOYDS BANK REVIEW,
        Series 2, vol. 29 (July 1953): 17-33.

        Written while World Bank President,
        Black describes IBRD background, its
        purpose to stimulate investment,
        lending criteria, the selection of
        project, and the prospects of repayment.

159.   Black, Eugene R. "World Bank at Work."
         FOREIGN AFFAIRS, vol. 30, no. 3 (April
         1952): 402-411.

         Comments on how the World Bank
         makes loans to raise the standard of
         living and to increase productivity.
         Describes different types of projects
         (farming, transportation, electrical
         power, and industrial development).
         Indicates that the World Bank cannot
         lend more that borrowers can afford to
         repay, and borrowers must be willing to
         work with the Bank on making changes to
         improve the standard of living.

160.   Black, Eugene R. "One Type of Foreign Aid
         That Makes a Profit: Loans, Not Gifts."
         U.S. NEWS AND WORLD REPORT, vol. 30,
         no. 25 (June 22, 1956): 104-106,108,110.

         Describes how US can expand trade
         through World Bank investments in
         various countries. Asserts that instead
         of being gifts from US taxpayers, these
         loans are providing assistance to LDCs,
         while at the same time making money.

161.   Blackwood, Julian. "World Bank Experience
         with Rural Development." FINANCE AND
         DEVELOPMENT (December 1988): 12-15.

         Draws on an earlier Bank document.
         Provides a systematic review of IBRD's
         rural development experience by its
         Operations Evaluations Department.
         Identifies how clear goals are needed,
         as well as simplifying project designs
         to make them more effective.

162.   Bleicher, Samuel A. "UN vs. IBRD: a Dilemma
         of Functionalism." INTERNATIONAL
         ORGANIZATION, vol. 24, no. 1 (1970):
         31-47.

         Analyzes dispute caused by IBRD's
         refusal to deny economic privileges to
         countries with apartheid policies (i.e.,
         South Africa and Portugal).

163.   Blejer, Mario I., and Isabel Guerroro.
         "Stabilization Policies and Income
         Distribution in the Philippines."
         FINANCE AND DEVELOPMENT (December 1988):
         6-8.

         Examines the impact of adjustment.
         Abstracts the World Bank's study on
         public policy and its implications for
         the poor (1980-1986).

164.   Blitzer, Charles R., Peter B. Clark, and
         Lance Taylor (eds.). ECONOMY-WIDE
         MODELS AND DEVELOPMENT PLANNING.
         Oxford, UK: Published for the World Bank
         by Oxford University Press, 1975.
         369 p. ISBN 0-19-920073-4;
         0-19-920074-2 (paper) LCCN 74-29171

         Surveys the use of economy-wide
         planning models in LDCs, focusing on
         medium-term planning. Presents general
         planning issues, specific policy
         problems, and methodological problems.

165.   Bloch, Henry S. "Regional Development
         Financing." INTERNATIONAL ORGANIZATION,
         vol. 22, no. 1 (1968): 182-203.

         Describes role of regional
         development banks in promoting economic
         integration, using the World Bank as an
         organization model. Describes African

Development Bank, Asian Development Bank, and IADB, their relationship to the World Bank, and their role in economic integration. See Entry 166.

166.   Bloch, Henry S. "Regional Development Financing." LATIN AMERICAN REPORT, vol. 14, no. 1 (March 1969): 1-13. *

Discusses role of IBRD in regional development. Same text as Entry 165.

167.   Blough, R. "World Bank Group." INTERNATIONAL ORGANIZATION, vol. 22, no. 1 (Winter 1968): 152-81.

Examines lending policies of the World Bank Group as it impacts on the flow of capital to LDCs, and on economic development in general. Describes the methods of increasing funds for financing development efforts.

168.   Blustein, Paul. "World Bank Approves $1.25 Billion in Loans to Argentina." WASHINGTON POST (October 28, 1988): G1, G2. *

169.   Bock, David. CURRENCY SWAPS. Washington, D.C.: World Bank, 1984. ii,54 p. ISBN 0-8213-0360-0 LCCN 84-7228 *

170.   Bock, David, and Michalopoulos, Constantine. "Emerging Role of the Bank in Heavily Indebted Countries." FINANCE AND DEVELOPMENT, vol. 23 (September 1986): 22-25.

Discusses how Bank is helping to restructure economies in light of significant debt. Comments it is doing more policy-oriented lending than in the past.

171.   Bock, David R.   "Bank's Role in Resolving the
        Debt Crisis."   FINANCE AND DEVELOPMENT
        (June 1988): 6-8.

        Describes how the Bank is
        responding to its heavily indebted
        middle income member countries though
        its development financing program.

172.   Bogdanowicz-Bindert, Christine A.   "World
        Debt: The United State Reconsiders."
        FOREIGN AFFAIRS, vol. 64 (Winter
        1985/86): 259-273.

        Describes how US finally came to
        recognize the world debt crisis as a
        barrier to world economic growth.   Gives
        historical background to debt crisis.
        Examines role of IMF and World Bank, in
        light of US policy on world debt.

173.   Bogdanowicz-Bindert, Christine A., and T.
        Chris Canavan.   "World Bank and
        International Private Sector."   COLUMBIA
        JOURNAL OF WORLD BUSINESS, vol. 21 (Fall
        1986): 31-35.   *

174.   Boskey, Shirley.   PROBLEMS AND PRACTICES OF
        DEVELOPMENT BANKS.   Baltimore, MD:
        Published for the World Bank by Johns
        Hopkins Press, 1959.   xv,201 p.
        LCCN 59-15892

        Intended as a companion to William
        Diamond's DEVELOPMENT BANKS (Entry 65).
        Covers problems facing sponsors of a new
        bank, as well as issues that arise from
        daily operations.   Not an official
        statement of policies, it offers
        reference material from experience of
        other development banks.

175.   Bouvard, James. "World Bank Confidentially
             Damns Itself." WALL STREET JOURNAL
             (September 23, 1987): 34. *

176.   Bouvard, James. "Alarming Truth About the
             World Bank." READER'S DIGEST (June
             1989): 108-112.

             Condensed from the April 1989
             article in REASON MAGAZINE by the same
             author. Criticizes the Bank's lending
             policies and reforms. Argues most of
             its programs have encouraged serious
             debt rather than a healthy economy.

177.   Bowring, Philip. "Hong Kong's Bond Dilemma."
             FAR EASTERN ECONOMIC REVIEW, vol. 94,
             no. 49 (December 3, 1976): 45-47.

             Describes proposal for World Bank
             to raise $105 million (US dollars) via
             bonds without interest being taxed on
             them. Discusses the proposals' impact
             on Hong Kong.

178.   Bowring, Philip. "Hong Kong Wary of
             Controls." FAR EASTERN ECONOMIC REVIEW,
             vol. 98, no. 48 (December 2, 1977): 68.

             Based on its report on Hong Kong
             economy, the World Bank recommends that
             Hong Kong establish a central bank.

179.   Bratter, Herbert. "Fund and Bank Follow the
             Talks." BANKER, vol. 9 (September
             1949): 171-177. *

             Presents IMF and IBRD
             accomplishments and their impact on
             sterling-dollar crisis.

180.   Bratter, Herbert. "Pie in the World Bank
            Sky: Authorized to Fix Their Own Pay,
            the Governors of the New World Fund and
            World Bank Set the Level Nice and High."
            NATIONS BUSINESS, vol. 34, no. 6 (June
            1946): 64,66,68,71.

            The Bank's Board of Governors sets
            its own salary and expense funds. The
            British asked for lower salaries, while
            US staff argued for higher ones.
            Salaries for other US government and
            Latin American officials are compared.

181.   "Breeze of Economic Change Over Africa." THE
            ECONOMIST, vol. 299 (April 12, 1986):
            69.

            According to FINANCING ADJUSTMENT
            WITH GROWTH (Entry 417), the worst of
            the famine appears to be over. Income
            may rise for the first time in 6 years,
            but some African countries still have to
            face long-term economic decline.

182.   Brietzke, Paul (ed.). "World Bank's
            Accelerated Development In Sub-Saharan
            Africa: A Symposium." AFRICAN STUDIES
            REVIEW, vol. 27, no. 4 (December 1984):
            1-60.

            J.C.N. Paul, R.H. Green, and B.
            Selassie present their different views
            on the Bank's ACCELERATED DEVELOPMENT
            report (see Entry 378).

183.   Bresciani-Turroni, Costantino. "Fifth Annual
            Meeting of the International Bank for
            Reconstruction and Development." REVIEW
            OF ECONOMIC CONDITIONS IN ITALY, vol. 5
            (January 1952): 5-12. *

Summarizes the Bank's report of activities presented at the 1952 Board of Governors meeting.

184. "British Fudge is Best: IMF-World Bank Salaries." THE ECONOMIST, vol. 267 (May 13, 1978): 97-98.

Only the US Bank staff pay taxes; other nationals receives their salary tax-free. Americans did not want pay raises until the salary review was completed later in 1978, while the Europeans wanted a 7% cost of living increase now. They compromised on a 3.5% increase during the interim.

185. Brookings Institution. "World Bank at Quarter Century." BROOKINGS BULLETIN. (1973). *

186. "Brother, Can You Spare a Billion?" ECONOMIST FINANCIAL REPORT, vol. 13 (September 29, 1988): 1-2. *

187. Browne, Robert S. (ed.). REFORM OF THE INTERNATIONAL ECONOMICS SYSTEM (Ethics in Foreign Policy Series, 3). Transaction Books, 1986. 164 p. ISBN 0-88738-143-X; ISBN 0-88738-674-1 (paper) *

188. Brummer, Alex. "World Bank Wants $75bn." GUARDIAN (February 15, 1988): 10. *

189. Buchanan, Patrick. "Bankrolling Our Foes Around the Globe?" WASHINGTON TIMES (December 28, 1987): D1. *

190. Burki, Shahid Javed, and Robert L. Ayres. "Fresh Look at Development Aid." FINANCE AND DEVELOPMENT, vol. 23 (March 1986): 6-10.

Discusses effectiveness of existing
aid programs to developing countries,
and major findings of a joint IMF-IBRD
task force (the Development Committee).

191.   Burnham, James B. "Living Together: The Case
of the Bretton Woods Sisters."
WASHINGTON QUARTERLY, vol. 9 (Winter
1986): 121-135.

Examines the history of the Bank-
Fund relationship. Proposes methods of
encouraging economic policies in
developing countries that can be
administered by both IMF and World Bank.

192.   "Butcher Barber." THE ECONOMIST, vol. 306
(September 26, 1987): 94,96.   *

193.   Cairncross, Alec K. INTERNATIONAL BANK FOR
RECONSTRUCTION AND DEVELOPMENT (Essays
in International Finance, 33).
Princeton, NJ: Princeton University,
International Finance Section, 1959.
36 p.

Borrowing and lending functions of
IBRD are described, as well as its role
in the international capital market.

194.   "Call for a New IMF-Bank Unit." ECONOMIST
FINANCIAL REPORT, vol. 13 (December 8,
1988): 1.   *

195.   Camps, Miriam, and Catherine Gwin.
COLLECTIVE MANAGEMENT: THE REFORM OF
GLOBAL ECONOMIC ORGANIZATIONS. New
York: McGraw-Hill, 1982.   371 p.
ISBN 0-07-009708-9   LCCN 81-394

Argues the need for improved
intergovernmental economic institutions
on global level. Problems need to be

better managed than is possible on
individual level. Cooperation is the
key to relieving poverty, improving
trade, coordinating development and
managing international finance.
Concentrates on collective action more
than on organizational details.

196. "Canny Nomination of Barbara Who." THE
ECONOMIST, vol. 298 (March 22, 1986):
71.

Comments on Barber Conable's
nomination as World Bank president to
succeed Clausen. Hints at the influence
of friends and lack of banking
experience, but concludes that he is
someone Congress trusts.

197. Cantley, Mark F. "Report on Reports: World
Bank Series on Integrated Resource
Recovery." ENVIRONMENT, vol. 28
(October 1986): 25-9. *

198. Carter, Douglas. "Eugene Black: Banker to
the World." REPORTER: THE MAGAZINE OF
FACTS AND IDEAS (April 4, 1957): 13-16.

Describes policies and achievements
while Eugene Black was president of the
Bank. Discusses how he took the mandate
seriously (i.e., to promote private
investment) by establishing IFC, and
getting the Bank to go into the private
market to sell its own bonds.

199. Casley, Dennis J., and Krishna Kumar.
COLLECTION, ANALYSIS, AND USE OF
MONITORING AND EVALUATION DATA (joint
study of IBRD, FAO, and IFAD).
Washington, D.C.: 1988. ix,174 p.
ISBN 0-8018-3669-7 LCCN 87-46375

Presents practical methods of data collection and analysis for agricultural projects, including design of qualitative survey and methods of participant observation.

200.   Casley, Dennis J., and Denis A. Lury. MONITORING AND EVALUATION OF AGRICULTURE AND RURAL DEVELOPMENT PROJECTS. Baltimore, MD: Published for the World Bank by Johns Hopkins University Press, 1982. viii,145 p. ISBN 0-8018-2910-0 LCCN 82-7126

Describes how to design and implement monitoring systems. Presents indicators and sample methodology.

201.   Cernea, Michael M. (ed.). PUTTING PEOPLE FIRST: SOCIOLOGICAL VARIABLES IN RURAL DEVELOPMENT. New York: Published for the World Bank by Oxford University Press, 1985. xiv,430 p. ISBN 0-19-520465-4   LCCN 85-11574

Argues that social organization should be the highest priority in development policies and project design. Presents lessons from World Bank projects, and suggests practical approaches to future development projects.

202.   Chadenet, Bernard, and John A. King, Jr. "What Is 'a World Bank Project'?" FINANCE AND DEVELOPMENT, vol. 9, no. 3 (September 1972): 2-12.   *

Describes earlier IBRD and IDA lending were for physical projects (dams, power plants, etc.), but now lending has moved to education, training, and policy changes.

203.   "Challenge for Conable." BANKER, vol. 136
        (May 1986): 62+. *

204.   Chand, Sheetal K., and Reinold van Til.
        "Ghana: Toward Successful Stabilization
        and Recovery." FINANCE AND DEVELOPMENT
        (March 1988): 32-35.

        Discusses joint Bank-Fund program
        that revitalized the Ghanian economy in
        the early 1980s.

205.   Chanda, Nayan. "Vaguely Back in Financial
        Good Books." FAR EASTERN ECONOMIC
        REVIEW, vol. 138, no. 40 (October 1,
        1987): 69-70.

        Vietnam tries to get back in good
        graces with international community, by
        agreeing to pay its overdue loan and
        accepting IMF policies. World Bank has
        a "wait-and-see" attitude about future
        loans.

206.   Chauifournier, Roger. "Coming of Age."
        FINANCE AND DEVELOPMENT (June 1984):
        6-9.

        Written by the Vice President of
        the Bank's European, Middle East and
        North America Regional Office, traces
        the evolution of the Bank from the 1950s
        through 1960s. Includes personal
        observations about Eugene Black and
        George Wood, former World Bank
        presidents.

207.   Chenery, Hollis, Sherman Robinson, and Moises
        Syrquin. INDUSTRIALIZATION AND GROWTH:
        A COMPARATIVE STUDY. Washington, D.C.:
        Published for the World Bank by Oxford
        University Press, 1986. x,387 p.
        ISBN 0-19-520547-2 LCCN 86-21837

Analyzes industrial development
patterns and policy implications in
Turkey, Korea, Colombia, and Taiwan.

208.   Chenery, Hollis Burnely, and Moises Syrquin.
        PATTERNS OF DEVELOPMENT, 1950-1970
        (World Bank Research Publication). New
        York: Published for the World Bank by
        the Oxford University Press, 1975.
        xvi,234 p. ISBN 0-19-920075-0;
        0-19-920076-9 (paper) LCCN 74-29172

        Provides a description of
        structural changes, and analyzes their
        relationship to growth within developing
        countries.

209.   Chenery, Hollis, et al. REDISTRIBUTION
        WITH GROWTH: POLICIES TO IMPROVE INCOME
        DISTRIBUTION IN DEVELOPING COUNTRIES IN
        THE CONTEXT OF ECONOMIC GROWTH (A joint
        study by the World Bank's Development
        Research Center and the University of
        Sussex's IDS). Oxford, UK: Published
        for the World Bank and IDS by Oxford
        University Press, 1974. xx,304 p.
        ISBN 0-19-920069-6; 0-19-920070-X
        (paper) LCCN 75-306757

        A state-of-the-art on the design of
        policies in income distribution and
        employment. Synthesizes initial ideas
        from a 1973 conference on Redistribution
        with Growth. Describes proposed
        reorientation of development policy,
        surveys the existing planning models,
        and indicates where further research is
        needed.

210.   Chernick, Sidney Earl. COMMONWEALTH
        CARIBBEAN: THE INTEGRATION EXPERIENCE:
        REPORT OF A MISSION SENT TO THE
        COMMONWEALTH CARIBBEAN BY THE WORLD BANK
        (World Bank Country Economic Report).
        Baltimore, MD: Published for the World
        Bank by Johns Hopkins University Press,
        1978. 521 p. ISBN 0-8018-2089-8;
        0-8018-2089-8 (paper) LCCN 77-17246

             Presents an overview (not a
        detailed account) on the Bank's mission
        to the Caribbean.

211.   "Chile and the World Bank." INTER-AMERICAN
        ECONOMIC AFFAIRS, vol. 30, no. 2 (Autumn
        1976): 81-91.

             Presents a background paper in
        which the World Bank's US Director
        defines the Bank's relationship with
        Chile just prior to and throughout the
        Allende era. Presents a chronological
        listing of operations in Chile.

212.   Choe, Boum Jong. MODEL OF WORLD ENERGY
        MARKETS AND OPEC PRICING. Washington,
        D.C.: World Bank, 1984. *

213.   Chowdhury, Amitabha. "Bank Leadership is on
        Tough Probation." ASIAN FINANCE (HONG
        KONG), vol. 13 (September 15, 1987):
        55-64. *

214.   Chowdhury, Amitabha. "Lust for Profit Stirs
        A Debate." ASIAN FINANCE (HONG KONG),
        vol. 13 (September 15, 1987): 76-82. *

215.   Christoffersen, L. "Bank and Rural Poverty."
        FINANCE AND DEVELOPMENT (1980): 11-15.

             Reviews the approach to poverty
        evolved by the Bank since 1973,

contrasting it with the productive potential of the rural poor. Claims that absolute poverty is not likely to disappear in the future, and raising productivity of the rural poor areas will lead to higher growth and better distribution of income.

216.   Cilingiroglu, Ayhan. MANUFACTURE OF HEAVY ELECTRICAL EQUIPMENT IN DEVELOPING COUNTRIES (World Bank Occasional Paper, 9). Baltimore, MD: Published for the World Bank by Johns Hopkins Press, 1969. xiii,122 p. ISBN 0-8018-1097-3 LCCN 76-89962

   Analyzes growth and competitiveness of heavy electrical equipment in Argentina, Brazil, Mexico, Pakistan, and Spain. Compares prices and costs in LDCs with international markets.

217.   Clausen, A.W. DEVELOPMENT CHALLENGE OF THE EIGHTIES: MAJOR POLICY ADDRESSES, 1981-1986. Washington, D.C.: World Bank, 1986. xxvii,496 p. ISBN 0-8213-0778-9 LCCN 86-11204

   Commissioned in honor of Clausen's retirement as World Bank President. Presents addresses by Clausen focusing on promoting economic and social development.

218.   Cleave, John. "Environmental Assessments." FINANCE AND DEVELOPMENT, vol. 25 (March 1988): 44-47.

   Describes Philippine forestry, fisheries, and agricultural resources management study. Discusses why World Bank is concerned about the environment, and describes its new approaches.

219.   Clements, Jonathan.   "Seoul-searching in
        Washington."   EUROMONEY (December 1985):
        122-123+.   *

            Comments on the search for the next
        World Bank president.

220.   Coats, A.W. (ed.).   ECONOMISTS IN
        INTERNATIONAL AGENCIES: AN EXPLORATORY
        STUDY. New York: Praeger, 1986.
        xi,197 p.   ISBN 0-275-92010-0
        LCCN 85-16750

            Based on 1983 conference at
        Institute for International Economics.
        Examines the role of economists in UN,
        GATT, IMF, OECD, and the World Bank.
        See also Entry 124.

221.   Cody, John, Helen Hughes, and David Wall
        (eds.).   POLICIES FOR INDUSTRIAL
        PROGRESS IN DEVELOPING COUNTRIES
        (jointly sponsored by UNIDO and the
        World Bank).   New York: Published for
        the World Bank by Oxford University
        Press, 1980.   ix,316 p.
        ISBN 0-19-520176-0;   0-19-520177-9
        (paper)   LCCN 79-24786

            Analyzes policies that influence
        industrialization, and identifies
        practical constraints for policy making.

222.   Cohn, T.H.   "Developing Countries in the
        International Civil Service: the Case of
        the World Bank Group."   REVUE
        INTERNATIONALE DES SCIENCES
        ADMINISTRATIVES, vol. 41, no. 1 (1975):
        47-56.   *

            Presents World Bank professional
        staff recruitment process, especially
        from LDCs.

223.   Cohn, Theodore H. "Politics in the World
        Bank Group: the Question of Loans to the
        Asian Giants." INTERNATIONAL
        ORGANIZATION, vol. 28, no. 3 (1974):
        561-571.

            Argues World Bank tries to pressure
        governments to adopt certain behavior,
        and conversely, governments try to
        pressure World Bank to adopt policies
        based on other than economic aspects.
        Cites IDA loans to Asia as examples.

224.   Collins, Joseph, and Frances Moore Lappe.
        "Whom Does the World Bank Serve?"
        ECONOMIC AND POLITICAL WEEKLY, vol. 14,
        no. 19 (March 12, 1979): 853-560.

            Examines how World Bank has emerged
        as leading institution for development
        financing, and how the Bank determines
        how much other aid another country
        receives. Emphasizes that loans to
        Argentina, Chile, Philippines, and
        Uruguay (countries with repressive
        regimes) receive double the amount of
        loans to other nations. Argues that
        loans to these countries might be
        increasing poverty, instead of
        alleviating it.

225.   Commins, Stephen K. (ed.). AFRICA'S
        DEVELOPMENT CHALLENGES AND THE WORLD
        BANK: HARD QUESTIONS, COSTLY CHOICES.
        Boulder, CO: L. Rienner, 1988.
        ix,241 p. ISBN 1-55587-116-X
        LCCN 88-14875

            Examines World Bank policies and
        African dilemmas, and political and
        economic realities affecting African
        development policies. Presented at

Africa's Development Challenge and the
World Bank's Response Conference (1986).

226.   Commission on International Development.
PARTNERS IN DEVELOPMENT: REPORT OF THE
COMMISSION ON INTERNATIONAL DEVELOPMENT.
New York: Praeger, 1969. 399 p.
LCCN 73-99094

    Chaired by Lester Pearson, the
Commission analyzes development aid.
Evaluates impacts of assistance, and
provides overview of development.

227.   "Competition Pares Borrowing Rates." FAR
EASTERN ECONOMIC REVIEW, vol. 97
(September 9, 1977): 59.

    Examines rates among international
banks, and how India has taken advantage
of it. Describes how the commercial
loans in Eurodollar markets affect
borrowing throughout Asia.

228.   Comstock, Alzada. "Dollar Looks Abroad:
Bretton Woods and the Anglo-American
Loan." CURRENT HISTORY, n.s. 10 (May
1946): 393-398.

    Describes how, in contrast to
impulsive generosity after World War I,
the US wanted a more planned,
coordinated approach to aid, that US
capital was readily available after
World War II, resulting in Bretton Woods
institutions. Discusses debate between
US vs. Britain, France, and Canada over
headquarters (New York or Washington,
D.C.), and Russia's position.

229.   Conable, Barber B.   "Some World Bank Actions
        on the Environment: Extracts from a
        Speech by Barber B. Conable, President
        of the Bank." PROJECT APPRAISAL, vol.2
        (June 1987): 88-90. *

230.   "Conable Does It, at Last." ASIAN FINANCE
        (HONG KONG), vol. 14 (April 15, 1988):
        9. *

231.   "Conable Says World Bank to Study Loan
        Insurance." WALL STREET JOURNAL (April
        13, 1988): 2. *

232.   "Conable's Fig Leaves." ECONOMIST FINANCIAL
        REPORT, vol. 12 (June 23, 1988):
        1-3. *

233.   "Conable's Respite is Over." ECONOMIST
        FINANCIAL REPORT, vol. 12 (February 4,
        1988): 1-2. *

234.   "Consortium is a Club: the Distance Between
        Capitol Hill and 'H' Street is Too
        Little to Be Ignored." PAKISTAN & GULF
        ECONOMIST, vol. 6 (September 19, 1987):
        6-7.

        US attitude toward foreign
        assistance dramatically affects the
        multilateral agencies in which the US is
        a member. Contends US dominance in IBRD
        lending (vis-à-vis moratorium on US aid
        in 1987) could cause problems for
        Pakistan in terms of foreign aid.

235.   Constantino, Letizia R. WORLD BANK AND THE
        IMF. Quezon City, Philippines:
        Education Forum, 1986. 10 p.

        Although written during Marcos
        regime, explains the structure and goals
        of the economic policies endorsed by the

World Bank and IMF, and adopted by the
Aquino government. Describes how the
Philippines fell into the debt trap.
Concludes that, while there were
benefits, the Philippines lost
independence and workers' rights, and
received higher taxes as result of
development loans.

236.   "Cooperation between the World Bank and
       Non-governmental Organizations." ROLE
       OF NON-GOVERNMENTAL ORGANIZATIONS IN
       DEVELOPMENT CO-OPERATION (Liaison
       Bulletin Between Development Research
       and Training Institutes, 10, n.s.).
       Paris: Development Centre, OECD, 1983.
       p. 62-65.

       Considers complementarity between
the Bank and NGOs in development
activities. During late 1970s, NGOs
were involved with 100 Bank projects.

237.   Cox, Tom. "World Bank: Development's Foe."
       WALL STREET JOURNAL (July 29, 1988):
       14.*

238.   Crane, Barbara B., and Jason L. Finkle.
       "Organizational Impediments to
       Development Assistance: the World Bank's
       Population Program." WORLD POLITICS,
       vol. 33, no. 4 (July 1981): 516-553.

       Analyses the World Bank as one part
of a study on the role of the UN and
related agencies in field of population.
Describes how and why the World Bank
began their population program, the core
technology, and relationships with other
donor agencies.

239.   Crawford, Vincent P. INTERNATIONAL LENDING,
        LONG-TERM CREDIT RELATIONSHIPS, AND
        DYNAMIC CONTRACT THEORY (Princeton
        Studies in International Finance, 59).
        Princeton, NJ: Princeton University,
        Department of Economics, 1987. 34 p.

        Provides game theory model of
        behavior underlying contract theory.
        Suggests intervention roles for the
        World Bank and IMF to improve market
        performance.

240.   Cuca, Roberto, and C.S. Pierce. EXPERIMENTS
        IN FAMILY PLANNING: LESSONS FROM THE
        DEVELOPING WORLD. Baltimore, MD:
        Published for the World Bank by Johns
        Hopkins University Press, 1977. 261 p.
        ISBN 0-8018-2013-8; 0-8018-2014-6
        (paper) LCCN 77-4602 *

241.   Cullen, Timothy. "When Critics Speak, the
        Bank Listens." BANK'S WORLD, vol. 7
        (April 1988): 15. *

242.   Dawnay, Ivan. "Free Trade Proponents Find
        Formidable New Armoury." FINANCIAL
        TIMES (April 14, 1988): 3. *

243.   Dawnay, Ivan. "World Bank Spurns Tariffs as
        Key to Deficit Control." FINANCIAL
        TIMES (April 14, 1988): 1. *

244.   De Kock, M.H. "International Bank for
        Reconstruction and Development." SOUTH
        AFRICAN JOURNAL OF ECONOMICS, vol. 12
        (September 1944): 223-232. *

245.   De Vries, Barend A. "Public Policy and the
        Private Sector." FINANCE AND
        DEVELOPMENT (September 1981): 11-15.

Discusses how public sector
behavior affects private sector
contributions to development. Asserts
that it has such an impact on economic
growth rate that other available options
must be reviewed.

246. De Vries, Barend A. REMAKING THE WORLD BANK.
Washington, D.C.: Seven Locks Press,
1987. 184 p. ISBN 0-932020-49-6
(paper) LCCN 87-23406

Describes how World Bank must play
a larger role in responding to problems
in the world economy by adapting its
operations, taking the lead, reinforcing
the links between lending and adoption
of sound policies, and working for the
expansion of resources. Claims the
World Bank needs to be flexible, so it
can adapt to a changing environment, and
thereby improve its performance.

247. De Weille, Jan. QUANTIFICATION OF ROAD USER
SAVINGS (World Bank Staff Occasional
Paper, 2). Baltimore, MD: Distributed
for the World Bank by Johns Hopkins
Press, 1966. xiv,93 p.

Provides a basis for estimates of
road user savings resulting from road
improvements, and presents technical
relationships affecting road user costs.

248. Den Tuinder, Bastiaan A. IVORY COAST: THE
CHALLENGE OF SUCCESS -- REPORT OF A
MISSION SENT TO THE IVORY COAST BY THE
WORLD BANK. Baltimore, MD: Published
for the World Bank by Johns Hopkins
University Press, 1978. 445 p.
ISBN 0-8018-1939-3; 0-8018-2099-5
(paper) LCCN 76-47395 *

249.   "Defaulters?" THE ECONOMIST, no. 254
        (February 22, 1975): 95.

        World Bank admits some borrowers
        may be forced to reschedule the
        repayment of their loans, which has
        never happened in its 30-year history.
        Rising oil prices, falling process of
        raw materials are affecting the credit-
        worthiness of member countries.

250.   Delfs, Robert. "Policy Advice Helps the Huge
        Country." FAR EASTERN ECONOMIC REVIEW,
        vol. 138, no. 40 (October 1, 1987):
        71.

        Bank's most important success is
        its relationship with China. States
        reform and technical assistance played
        complimentary roles in economic growth
        (national income doubled).

251.   Dervis, Kemal, Jaime de Melo, and Sherman
        Robinson. GENERAL EQUILIBRIUM MODELS
        FOR DEVELOPMENT POLICY (World Bank
        Research Publication). Cambridge, UK:
        Cambridge University Press, 1982.
        xviii,526 p. ISBN 0-521-24490-0;
        0-521-27030-8 (paper) LCCN 81-12307

        Combines theoretical discussion of
        applied equilibrium models with
        practical applications to problems in
        Turkey, Israel, Korea, and others.

252.   "Development Bank Policy Analyzed in Study."
        MASS TRANSIT, vol. 12 (December 1985):
        60. *

        Discusses transportation projects
        in developing countries.

253.   Diamond, William (ed.). DEVELOPMENT FINANCE
           COMPANIES: ASPECTS OF POLICY AND
           OPERATION. Baltimore, MD: Published for
           the World Bank Group by Johns Hopkins
           Press, 1968. vi,119 p. LCCN 68-27738

               Presents essays written by E.T.
           Kuiper, D. Gustafson, and P.M. Mathew
           from a 1965 conference. Discusses the
           promotion and role of development
           finance companies, ownership of private
           securities, financial policy problems,
           and the relationship between development
           finance companies and governments.

254.   DEVELOPMENT THEORY AND PRACTICE OF THE WORLD
           BANK IN ASIA. Ohignies-Louvain-la-Neuve,
           Belgium: 1980. 29 p. LCCN 84-216516   *

255.   Dodero, Giorgio. "World Bank Updates
           Guidelines, Rules for Bidding,
           Procurement." POWER (New York),
           vol. 130 (March 1986): 51-2.   *

256.   Dogra, Bharat. "World Bank vs. the People
           of Bastar." ECOLOGIST, vol. 15, no. 1/2
           (1985): 44-48.   *

257.   Dollar, David. ECONOMIC REFORM AND
           ALLOCATIVE EFFICIENCY IN CHINA'S
           STATE-OWNED INDUSTRY (Working Paper,
           490). Los Angeles, CA: Department of
           Economics, University of California,
           1988.   *

               Demonstrates that factor
           productivity in China's industry has
           been increasing in 20 enterprises
           surveyed by the World Bank.

258.   "Dollar Diplomacy." THE ECONOMIST, vol. 300
           (September 27, 1986): 14-15.   *

Discusses 1986 annual Board of
Governors meeting.

259.   Donlan, Thomas G. "New Head for World Bank."
        BARRONS, vol. 66 (March 17, 1986): 71.*

        Comments on Conable as new World
        Bank president.

260.   "Don't Count on Congress." ECONOMIST
        FINANCIAL REPORT, vol. 12 (April 14,
        1988): 1. *

261.   Drattell, Alan. "Donald Roth: Return of the
        Native." BANK'S WORLD, vol. 7 (April
        1988): 2-4. *

262.   Drattell, Alan. "Q&A with Ian Hume on the
        Human Resource Strategy." BANK'S WORLD,
        vol. 7 (December 1988): 4-6. *

263.   Drattell, Alan. "Richard Eddy Helps to Keep
        Medical Costs Down: You're in Good Hands
        With ..." BANK'S WORLD, vol. 6
        (September 1987): 16-17. *

264.   Driscoll, David D. IMF AND THE WORLD BANK
        -- HOW DO THEY DIFFER? Washington,
        D.C.: IMF, n.d. 15 p.
        ISBN 1-55775-020-1

        Provides overview to differences
        between IMF and IBRD in staffing,
        funding, purpose, and organization.

265.   Dunne, Nancy. "Volker Warns of World Bank
        Risk." FINANCIAL TIMES (July 26, 1988):
        4. *

266.   Dunne, Nancy. "World Bank Boost Divides
        Democrats." FINANCIAL TIMES (August 16,
        1988): 3. *

267.   Dunkerley, Harold B., and Christine M.E.
        Whitehead. URBAN LAND POLICY, ISSUES
        AND OPPORTUNITIES. Oxford, UK:
        Published for the World Bank by Oxford
        University Press, 1983. *

268.   Eccles, Stephen. "Crossed Lines." BANKER,
        vol. 138 (February 1988): 10.

            Comments that Johnson's article
        (see Entry 538) misconstrues the Bank's
        capital and reserves, and ignores its
        liquidity in investments. Eccles,
        Acting World Bank Treasurer, points out
        that the Bank's equity is always
        available for its operations.

269.   Edwards, Sebastian, and Liaquat Ahamed.
        ECONOMIC ADJUSTMENT AND EXCHANGE RATES
        IN DEVELOPING COUNTRIES (NBER Conference
        Report). Chicago: University of Chicago
        Press, 1986. xiii,443 p.
        ISBN 0-226-18469-2 LCCN 87-7045

            Presented at 1984 NBER-World Bank
        conference. Claims exchange rate policy
        has significant impact on economies in
        developing nations. Examines the role
        of these policies in stabilization,
        economic liberalization, and adjustment
        processes in Colombia, Greece, Kenya,
        and West Africa.

270.   "Enter Mr. Arafat and Friends: the World Bank
        and IMF." THE ECONOMIST, vol. 276
        (August 9, 1980): 68-69.

            IMF and IBRD are caught in the
        middle. PLO wants to attend the next
        Board of Governors annual meeting. PLO
        is backed by Arab nations that supply
        significant funds to both the Bank and

the Fund. IMF stands to lose more
financially than IBRD.

271. Farnsworth, Clyde. "U.S. Backs More Funds
for the World Bank." NEW YORK TIMES
(September 24, 1987): D7. *

272. Farnsworth, Clyde H. "Dollar's Drop May Hurt
Lending by World Bank." NEW YORK TIMES
(May 5, 1987): D1. *

273. Farnsworth, Clyde H. "World Bank's Staff
Upheaval." NEW YORK TIMES (September
24, 1987): D1,D7. *

274. Feder, Ernest. "Capitalism's Last-Ditch
Effort to Save Underdeveloped
Agricultures: International
Agribusiness, the World Bank and the
Rural Poor." JOURNAL OF CONTEMPORARY
ASIA, vol. 7, no. 1 (1977): 56-78.

Describes how the World Bank vows
to reorient its strategy (vis-à-vis
President McNamara's statement to the
Board of Governors in 1973). Examines
how agribusiness operates in
agricultural sector in developing
countries, and how Bank funds usually
require matching local funds.

275. Feder, Ernest. "New World Bank Programme for
the Self-liquidation of the Third World
Peasantry." JOURNAL OF PEASANT STUDIES,
vol. 3, no. 3 (April 1976): 343-354.

Describes how World Bank financing
of agricultural estate modernization has
affected the peasants. Instead of
helping them, it has furthered poverty,
while at the same time, increases
business for feed, fertilizer, etc.

276.   Feder, Ernest. "World Bank and the Expansion
         of Industrial Monopoly Capital into
         Underdeveloped Agricultures."
         PHILIPPINE SOCIAL SCIENCES AND
         HUMANITIES REVIEW, vol. 44, no. 1-4
         (December 1980): 171-211.

             Examines the redistribution of
         wealth. Offers one major criticism: no
         one knows how much the poor are
         benefiting, not even the World Bank.
         The scheme is open only to the poor who
         have some assets and land, not to the
         poorest of the poor. Argues that policy
         makers and lenders have no knowledge
         about the needs of smallholders, and
         that some of the problems experienced by
         smallholders are exacerbated by the
         capitalist system. Rather than calling
         for improvements in World Bank
         operations, calls for replacement of
         capitalist system with more equitable
         system that does not waste human and
         physical resources. See also Entry 277.

277.   Feder, Ernest. "World Bank and the Expansion
         of Industrial Monopoly Capital Into
         Underdeveloped Agricultures." JOURNAL
         OF CONTEMPORARY ASIA, vol. 12, no. 1
         (1982): 34-60.

             Based on J. Bocobo Lecture given at
         University of Philippines Law Centre in
         1981. Essentially same as Entry 276.

278.   Feder, Ernest. "World Bank's 'Investments'
         in Third World Development, Particularly
         in Agriculture." PHILIPPINE SOCIAL
         SCIENCE AND HUMANITIES REVIEW, vol. 45,
         no. 1-4 (December 1981): 113-158.

             Describes the World Bank's role as
         coordinator of technical and financial

development assistance in funnelling
resources into LDCs (via Asian
Development Bank, African Development
Bank, and IADB). Claims that World Bank
is not accountable to any outside
agency, court, or government. Describes
how the Bank calls its loans
"investments," and the social and
political impact of these "investments"
in agriculture, especially in Mexico and
the Philippines.

279.   Federal Reserve Bank of Boston. INTERNATIONAL
        MONETARY SYSTEM: FORTY YEARS AFTER
        BRETTON WOODS (Conference Series, 28).
        Boston, MA: 1984. 275 p.

        Proceedings of a Conference Held at
        Bretton Woods, New Hampshire, May 1984,
        sponsored by the Federal Reserve Bank of
        Boston. Two themes emerged from the
        conference: floating exchange rates need
        to be reformed, and measures need to be
        taken to deal with the debt crisis.

280.   Feinberg, Richard E. "Adjustment Imperative
        and U.S. Policy." ADJUSTMENT CRISIS IN
        THE THIRD WORLD, ed. by R. Feinberg and
        V. Kallab. New Brunswick, NJ:
        Transaction Books, 1984. p. 3-15.

        Argues IBRD and IMF should adhere
        to their commitments more closely, pay
        attention to structural reforms,
        coordinate their efforts, and increase
        their external financing. See also
        Entry 282.

281.   Feinberg, Richard E. "Changing Relationship
        Between the World Bank and the
        International Monetary Fund."
        INTERNATIONAL ORGANIZATION, vol. 42
        (Summer 1988): 545-560. *

282.   Feinberg, Richard E., and Kallab, Valeriana
        (eds.). ADJUSTMENT CRISIS IN THE THIRD
        WORLD (U.S.-Third World Policy
        Perspectives, 1). New Brunswick, NJ:
        Published for Overseas Development
        Council by Transaction Books, 1984.
        x,186 p. ISBN 0-87855-988-4
        LCCN 84-8690

        Examines reform in developing
        countries, arguing that constructive
        change is necessary. Better
        combinations of old and new solutions
        are offered. See also Entries 280, 286,
        669, and 698.

283.   Feinberg, Richard E., et al. BETWEEN
        TWO WORLDS: THE WORLD BANK'S NEXT DECADE
        (U.S.-Third World Policy Perspectives,
        7). New Brunswick, NJ: Published for
        Overseas Development Council by
        Transaction Books, 1986. viii,184 p.
        ISBN 0-88738-123-5; 0-88738-665-2
        (paper) LCCN 86-50513

        Examines the policy issues facing
        the Bank's new leadership (Conable).
        See also Entries 283, 284, 341, 641,
        660, 920, and 995.

284.   Feinberg, Richard E. "Open Letter to the
        World Bank's New President." BETWEEN
        TWO WORLDS: THE WORLD BANK'S NEXT
        DECADE, by R. Feinberg, et al. New
        Brunswick, NJ: Transaction Books, 1986.
        p. 3-30.

        Letter addressed to Conable
        expressing the critical roles for the
        World Bank: coordinator, mediator,
        stabilizer, and intellectual center.
        See also Entry 286.

285.   Feinberg, Richard E., and Kallab, Valeriana
        (eds.). UNCERTAIN FUTURE: COMMERCIAL
        BANKS IN THE THIRD WORLD (U.S.-Third
        World Policy Perspectives, 2). New
        Brunswick, NJ: Published for Overseas
        Development Council by Transaction
        Books, 1984. 144 p. ISBN 0-88738-041-7;
        0-87855-989-2 (paper)

        Discusses changing relationship
        between IMF, World Bank, and commercial
        banks, as well as the politics of
        international lending.

286.   Fishlow, Albert. "Debt Crisis: Round Two
        Ahead?" ADJUSTMENT CRISIS IN THE THIRD
        WORLD, ed. by R. Feinberg and V. Kallab.
        New Brunswick, NJ: Transaction Books,
        1984. p. 31-58.

        Warns that forecasts have
        overstated responsiveness of developing
        countries' economies, and debt should be
        viewed as a long-term development
        problem. See also Entry 282.

287.   Fitzgerald, Sarah Gates. "World Bank Pledges
        to Protect Wildlands." BIOSCIENCES,
        vol. 36 (December 1986): 712-5.   *

288.   Fleming, Stewart. "Dollar Fall Threatens
        World Bank Plan on Global Debt Crisis."
        FINANCIAL TIMES (April 27, 1987): 1,20.*

289.   Fleming, Stewart. "U.S. Supports Expansion
        at World Bank." FINANCIAL TIMES
        (September 24, 1987): 4.   *

290.   Fleming, Stewart. "World Bank President
        Defends Reorganization." FINANCIAL
        TIMES (September 24, 1987): 6.   *

291.   Francis, David R. "Slimmed-down World Bank
        Plots Strategy Against Global Poverty."
        CHRISTIAN SCIENCE MONITOR (September 30,
        1987): 3-4. *

292.   Frank, C.R., Jr., and M. Baird. "Foreign
        Aid: Its Speckled Past and Future
        Prospects." INTERNATIONAL ORGANIZATION,
        vol. 29 (Winter 1975): 133-167. *

293.   Fraser, Robert (ed.). WORLD FINANCIAL
        SYSTEM. Phoenix, AZ: Oryx Press, 1987.
        500 p. ISBN 0-582-90278-9 *

        Directory of international
        financial organizations (IMF, IBRD,
        etc.), as well as historical information
        on world finance.

294.   Fried, Edward R., and Henry D. Owen (eds.).
        FUTURE ROLE OF THE WORLD BANK:
        ADDRESSES, by Robert S. McNamara , et
        al. (Brookings Dialogue on Public
        Policy). Washington, D.C.: 1982.
        ix,91 p. ISBN 0-8157-2929-4
        LCCN 82-71296

        Presented at 1982 conference at the
        Brookings Institution on the role of
        bilateral and multilateral aid
        financing the World Bank. Discusses the
        World Bank and the private sector,
        developing countries and the World Bank
        in the 1980s, the future role of the
        World Bank Group, and the World Bank and
        energy investments.

295.   Friedland, Jonathan. "Turmoil at the World
        Bank." INSTITUTIONAL INVESTOR,
        INTERNATIONAL ED. (September 1987):
        77-87. *

296.   Friedland, Jonathan. "Unrest at the World
             Bank." INSTITUTIONAL INVESTOR, vol. 21
             (September 1987): 333-336+. *

297.   Friedland, Jonathan, and Melvyn Westlake.
             "Guru's Parting Shot." SOUTH, no. 83
             (September 1987): 11-12.

             Refers to Anne Kreuger, senior
         economist who left the Bank in late
         1986. She was responsible for carrying
         out the Bank's free market philosophy.

298.   Friedland, Jonathan. "Inside Job at the
             World Bank." SOUTH (September 1987):
             9-10.

             Describes how US is calling the
         shots to Barber Conable (because US is
         the biggest shareholder), and US is
         pushing protectionism to alleviate its
         trade deficit.

299.   Gamba, Julio R., David A. Caplin, and John J.
             Mulckhuyse. INDUSTRIAL ENERGY
             RATIONALIZATION IN DEVELOPING COUNTRIES.
             Baltimore, MD: Published for the World
             Bank by Johns Hopkins University Press,
             1986. ISBN 0-8018-337-X LCCN 85-45926

             Suggests balanced approach to
         industrial energy efficiency. Describes
         implementation of national energy
         rationalization program. Claims
         increasing efficiency and decreasing
         consumption, especially in industrial
         sector, is better than increasing
         supply.

300.   Galang, Jose. "Domestic Chores Prevent
             Pursuit of Development." FAR EASTERN
             ECONOMIC REVIEW, vol. 138, no. 40
             (October 1, 1987): 75-76.

The Philippines' financial and
political problems prevent them from
appropriating the full amount of World
Bank assistance available. Steady
economic growth is predicted despite
political problems. First resident
mission was established in Manila.

301.   Gavin, Michael. INCOME EFFECTS OF STRUCTURAL
        ADJUSTMENT TO TERMS OF TRADE DISTURBANCE
        ASYMMETRIES IN THE LAURSEN-MELTZER
        RELATION? (Department of Economics
        Working Paper, 375). New York, NY:
        Columbia University, 1988. *

        Discusses implications of
        structural adjustment to external
        shocks, with relation to trade
        disturbances.

302.   George, Morallina F. "Res Reps Come Home for
        Meeting: 'the Most Wonderful Job in the
        Bank'." BANK'S WORLD, vol. 6 (November
        1987): 5-8. *

303.   Ghosh, Arun. "World Bank and the Attack on
        Poverty: from the Ivory Tower."
        ECONOMIC AND POLITICAL WEEKLY, vol. 22
        (October 31, 1987): 1844-46.

        Examines the total volume of World
        Bank lending, the amount of interest
        paid, and how this impacts on the World
        Bank's objectives (especially on
        alleviating world poverty).

304.   Gilbert, Christopher L. IMPACT OF EXCHANGE
        RATES AND DEVELOPING COUNTRY DEBT ON
        COMMODITY PRICES (Applied Economics
        Discussion Paper, 30). Oxford, UK:
        Institute of Economics and Statistics,
        Oxford University, 1987. 56 p.

Uses World Bank commodity indexes as models to show elasticity of commodity prices.

305. Gilbert, Nick. "Barber Set to Change Style." EUROMONEY (September 1986): 66-67+. *

306. Girling, Robert Henriques. MULTINATIONAL INSTITUTIONS AND THE THIRD WORLD: MANAGEMENT, DEBT, AND TRADE CONFLICTS IN THE INTERNATIONAL ECONOMIC ORDER. Praeger, 1985. xxi,212 p. ISBN 0-03-001003-9; 0-03-003004-7 (paper) LCCN 84-18131 *

Surveys the World Bank, IMF, and other multinationals such as GATT.

307. Gittinger, J. Price, Joanne Leslie, and Caroline Hoisington (eds.). FOOD POLICY: INTEGRATING SUPPLY, DISTRIBUTION, AND CONSUMPTION. Baltimore, MD: Published for the World Bank by Johns Hopkins University Press, 1987. *

308. Givant, Marlene. "World Bank Sets Up Crossing Network." PENSIONS & INVESTMENT AGE, vol. 15 (June 15, 1987): 2+. *

309. Gold, Sonia S. NATIONAL DEVELOPMENT PROGRAMS OF THE INTERNATIONAL BANK FOR RECONSTRUCTION AND DEVELOPMENT, WITH SPECIAL REFERENCE TO THE ROLES OF GOVERNMENT AND PRIVATE ENTERPRISE. Ann Arbor, MI: University Microfilm International, 1957. vii,363 p. (collation of original) *

310.   Gold, Sonia S. "Shifting Emphasis on
        Macro- and Micro- Levels in Development
        Planning: the IBRD Experience,
        1946-1973." JOURNAL OF DEVELOPING
        AREAS, vol. 11, no. 1 (October 1976):
        13-38.

            Examines development planning in
        early part of World Bank's history, and
        the shift from national to project
        levels in the Bank's general philosophy.

311.   Goldsmith, Edward. "Editorial: Open Letter
        to Mr. Conable, President of the World
        Bank: You Can Only Be Judged on Your
        Record." ECOLOGIST, vol. 17 (March/June
        1987): 58-61. *

312.   Goodland, Robert. "Management of Cultural
        Property in Bank Projects." FINANCE AND
        DEVELOPMENT (March 1988): 48-49.

            Describes the World Bank's policy
        on preserving cultural property, using
        Kenya, Turkey, and Brazil, as examples
        of the Bank's safeguarding cultural
        sites.

313.   Goodland, Robert. TRIBAL PEOPLES AND
        ECONOMIC DEVELOPMENT. Washington, D.C.:
        World Bank, 1982. ISBN 0-8213-0010-5
        LCCN 82-11192   *

314.   Gordon, David. "World Bank -- New Directions
        in Africa." COMMONWEALTH JOURNAL,
        vol. 12, no. 2 (April 1969):
        51-56,87-89.

            Describes the work of IDA and World
        Bank in Africa, and the trend of
        increasing involvement in rural
        development, industrial sector,
        commodity markets (through IFC

financing), education, and population
programs. See also Entry 315.

315.   Gordon, David. "World Bank -- New Directions
       in Africa." AFRICAN AFFAIRS, vol. 68,
       no. 272 (July 1969): 232-244.

       Talk given at joint meeting of
       Royal African Society and Royal
       Commonwealth Society (1969).
       Essentially the same text as Entry 314.

316.   Gordon, David, and Joan Parker. "World Bank
       and its Critics: the Case of Sub-Saharan
       Africa." (CRED Discussion Paper, 108).
       Ann Arbor, MI: Center for Research on
       Economic Development, University of
       Michigan 1984. vii,43 p.

       Discusses controversies surrounding
       ACCELERATED DEVELOPMENT (Entry 378), and
       evaluates the differences between the
       authors and their critics. Concludes
       that critics overstate the problems in
       the report. Highlights the narrow focus
       on exchange rate policy as an instrument
       to recovery.

317.   Gray, A. "World Bank: More Capital May Mean
       More Trouble." BANKERS MONTHLY,
       vol. 105 (March 1988): 90.   *

318.   Gray, Andrew. "Washington Report: Financing
       Underdevelopment." BANKERS MAGAZINE,
       vol. 171 (March/April 1988): 76-77.   *

319.   Green, Nancy. "Administration Puts Fresh
       Focus on World Bank: Reagan Policy Shift
       Prompts Skepticism." CONGRESSIONAL
       QUARTERLY WEEKLY REPORT, vol. 43
       (October 5, 1985): 1999-2003.

Presents links between balance of
trade and the debt crisis, and the role
of the World Bank in trade imbalance.
Illustrates how major international
banks (IADB, African Development Bank,
Asian Development Bank, IFC, IDA, and
IBRD) help developing countries.

320.   Green, Reginald Herbold.   "Consolidation and
Accelerated Development of Africa
Agenda: What Agenda for Action?"
AFRICAN STUDIES REVIEW, vol. 27, no. 4
(December 1984): 17-34.

Evaluates agenda in ACCELERATED
DEVELOPMENT (Entry 378). Criticizes the
lack of research on smallholder
agriculture, and its limited
understanding of differing physical and
social aspects. Claims the report
oversimplifies problems and solutions,
and lacks understanding and involvement
of smallholders and women.

321.   Gregory, Peter.   MYTH OF MARKET FAILURE:
EMPLOYMENT AND THE LABOR MARKET IN
MEXICO. Baltimore, MD: Published for
the World Bank by Johns Hopkins
University Press, 1986. viii,299 p.
ISBN 0-8018-3343-4 LCCN 85-45927

Studies the Mexican labor market.
Argues employment conditions have
steadily improved for workers at end of
wage spectrum, and rural-urban migration
has caused an increase in migrants'
earnings. Concludes with future
employment policy recommendations.

322.   Grimes, Orville F., Jr. HOUSING FOR LOW-
       INCOME URBAN FAMILIES: ECONOMICS AND
       POLICY IN THE DEVELOPING WORLD.
       Baltimore, MD: Published for the World
       Bank by Johns Hopkins Press, 1976. xiv,
       176 p. ISBN 0-8018-1853-2;
       0-8018-1854-0 (paper) LCCN 76-4934

            Describes workings of urban housing
       market, and argues for improved use of
       resources for housing. Surveys the
       conditions in Mexico, Hong Kong, Kenya,
       Colombia, India, and Pakistan for low
       income groups. Suggest cheapest new
       housing being built is still not
       affordable for these groups.

323.   Grosse, Martha. AS THE WORLD BANKS. New
       York, NY: Rowman, 1988. 320 p.
       ISBN 0-8476-7565-3 *

324.   Gupta, S., A. Schwartz, and R. Padula.
       "World Bank Model for Global
       Interdependence: A Quantitative
       Framework for the World Development
       Report." JOURNAL OF POLICY MODELLING,
       vol. 1, no. 2 (March 1979): 179-200.

            Describes the structure of the
       Global Model used by the World Bank in
       preparing the WORLD DEVELOPMENT REPORT.
       Presents different aspects of model
       structure and relevance of each
       exercise, in view of the model's results
       between 1975 and 1985.

325.   Gupta, Syamaprasad P., assisted by Ellen
         Anderson and Ronald Padula. MODEL FOR
         INCOME DISTRIBUTION, EMPLOYMENT, AND
         GROWTH: A CASE STUDY OF INDONESIA (World
         Bank Staff Occasional Paper, 24).
         Baltimore, MD: Published for the World
         Bank by Johns Hopkins University Press,
         1977. xvii,121 p. ISBN 0-8018-1950-4
         LCCN 76-53909

              Based on a model initially prepared
         for the World Bank's 1974 economic
         mission to Indonesia. Demonstrates the
         tradeoff between growth and equity
         depends on specific policies adopted.
         Bridges the gap between models and
         policies.

326.   Hajnal, Peter I. "IGO Documents and
         Publications: Volume, Distribution,
         Recent Development and Sources of
         Information." GOVERNMENT PUBLICATIONS
         REVIEW, vol. 9, no. 2 (March/April
         1982): 121-130.

              Discusses the publications and
         documentation programs of IGOs, their
         efforts to reduce the increasing volume
         of information, their distribution
         characteristics (limited, restricted,
         and general), and their sources for
         bibliographic control. Focuses on UN
         and its spinoffs (FAO, ILO, World Bank),
         as well as OECD.

327.   Hajnal, Peter I. (ed.). INTERNATIONAL
         INFORMATION: DOCUMENTS, PUBLICATIONS,
         AND INFORMATION SYSTEMS OF INTERNATIONAL
         GOVERNMENTAL ORGANIZATIONS. Englewood,
         CO: Libraries Unlimited, 1988.
         xxix,339 p. ISBN 0-87287-501-6
         LCCN 88-2236

Focuses on bibliographic control,
publishing function, collection
development, and electronic formats of
IGOs in general, using the UN as the
primary example.

328.   Hajnal, Peter I. "Sales Catalogues of the UN
System of Organizations." GOVERNMENT
PUBLICATIONS REVIEW, vol. 6, no. 4
(1979): 401-404.

Annotated bibliography of sales
catalogues for United Nations and
related agencies (World Bank Group, FAO,
ILO, IMF, GATT, and others).

329.   Harbison, Ralph W., and Aklilu Habte.
"External Aid for African Education."
FINANCE AND DEVELOPMENT (March 1988):
24-24.

Addresses how donor community could
aid educational development in Sub-
Saharan Africa. Offers suggestions for
improving the impact of educational
assistance.

330.   Hariharan, A. "Poor Returns from Industry."
FAR EASTERN ECONOMIC REVIEW, vol. 97
(September 16, 1977): 50-51.

Discusses World Bank report on
economy in India. Admits return-on-
investment was poor compared to other
LDCs. States that investment rate
slowed in recent years and absorption of
forced savings was low. Growth in
agriculture and industry were
unsatisfactory, but industrial
productivity has been rising since 1975.

331.   Harriman, J. "Burma's First Steps to
          Capitalism." FAR EASTERN ECONOMIC
          REVIEW, vol. 94 (December 24, 1976):
          100-102.

                Calls for economic reform as a
          condition for foreign aid, and
          acceptance for foreign capital in Burma.
          Suggests a reorienting of priorities
          towards agriculture and export sectors,
          and a compromise between socialism and
          capitalism. Describes Bank's efforts to
          make the reforms, especially in
          investment policies for capital.

332.   Harris, Anthony. "International Agencies: An
          Appraisal -- Two Plumbers Seek a Brief."
          FINANCIAL TIMES (May 18, 1988): III,
          sect. III. *

333.   Havrylyshyn, Oli. EXPORTS OF DEVELOPING
          COUNTRIES: HOW DIRECTION AFFECTS
          PERFORMANCE. Washington, D.C.: World
          Bank, 1987. 168 p.

                Papers from a 1983 conference on
          South-South vs. North-South trade.
          Presents a variety of viewpoints on
          nature of trade among developing
          countries.

334.   Hasan, Muzaffar. "IMF/World Bank Meeting:
          the Mood in Berlin." PAKISTAN & GULF
          ECONOMIST, vol. 7, no. 41 (October
          8-14, 1988): 12-14.

                Describes atmosphere at Board of
          Governors meeting in West Berlin. No
          major decisions are expected due to the
          upcoming US elections. The mood for
          developed nations was upbeat while that
          of LDCs was anxious.

335.   Hasan, Parvez, and D.C. Rao. KOREA: POLICY
        ISSUES FOR LONG-TERM DEVELOPMENT: THE
        REPORT OF A MISSION SENT TO THE REPUBLIC
        OF KOREA BY THE WORLD BANK. Baltimore,
        MD: Published for the World Bank by
        Johns Hopkins University Press, 1979.
        xx,538 p. ISBN 0-8018-2228-9;
        0-8018-2229-7 (paper) LCCN 78-21399 *

336.   Hasan, Parvez. KOREA: PROBLEMS AND ISSUES IN
        A RAPIDLY GROWING ECONOMY (World Bank
        Country Economic Report). Baltimore,
        MD: Published for the World Bank by
        Johns Hopkins University Press, 1976.
        xv,277 p. ISBN 0-8018-1864-8
        LCCN 76-17238

            Based on 1973 economic mission but
        with updated information. Describes the
        problems Korea has faced and will likely
        face, as it sustains a high rate of
        economic expansion and structural
        changes in the economy. Focuses on
        resource mobilization, allocation, and
        income distribution. Calls for export
        expansion as the key to Korea's
        development.

337.   Havnevik, Kjell J. (ed.). IMF AND THE WORLD
        BANK IN AFRICA: CONDITIONALITY, IMPACT
        AND ALTERNATIVES (Seminar Proceedings,
        18). Uppsala, Sweden: Scandinavian
        Institute of African Studies, 1987.
        179 p. ISBN 91-7106-264-5

            Based on the proceedings of a 1987
        conference. Presents different
        positions of the IMF and World Bank in
        Africa. In addition, the impact of
        conditionality is traced through various
        case studies, and alternatives are
        discussed.

338.   Hayter, Teresa. AID AS IMPERIALISM.
        Baltimore, MD: Penguin Books, 1971.
        213 p. *

                Commissioned by ODI. Alleges that
        the capitalist system was preserved
        through efforts of IBRD, IMF, and AID in
        Colombia, Chile, Brazil and Peru.

339.   Heilbroner, Robert L. THIS GROWING WORLD:
        ECONOMIC DEVELOPMENT AND THE WORLD BANK
        (Public Affairs Pamphlet, 237). New
        York: Public Affairs Committee, 1956.
        28 p.

                Describes how the World Bank
        revolutionized the Third World. Argues
        that if the Bank makes no further loans,
        it has shown that improvements in the
        standard of living are possible.
        Explains that pouring money into LDCs is
        not the answer, but other obstacles need
        also to be addressed (for example,
        population, basic needs). Describes how
        World Bank makes its money go as far as
        it does, and its role in economic
        development.

340.   Hellinger, Stephen, Douglas Hellinger, and
        Fred O'Regan. AID FOR JUST DEVELOPMENT:
        REPORT ON THE FUTURE OF FOREIGN
        ASSISTANCE. Boulder, CO: L. Rienner,
        1988.   275 p.   ISBN 1-55587-121-6;
        1-55587-122-4 (paper)

                Traces history of foreign aid,
        while claiming that it has not served
        the poor in developing nations.
        Recommends reorganization of aid
        structure.

341.   Helleiner, G.K.   "Policy-Based Program
       Lending: A Look at the Bank's New Role."
       BETWEEN TWO WORLDS: THE WORLD BANK'S
       NEXT DECADE, by R. Feinberg, et al.
       New Brunswick, NJ: Transaction Books,
       1986. p. 47-66.

       Recommends the Bank increase
       structural adjustment lending to more
       than 15% of total lending. See also
       Entry 283.

342.   Helmore, Kristin.   "World Bank and the
       World's Poor." CHRISTIAN SCIENCE
       MONITOR (March 23, 1988): 16-17.   *

343.   Henderson, Patrick David.   INDIA: THE ENERGY
       SECTOR. Baltimore, MD: Published for
       the World Bank by Oxford University
       Press, 1976. ix,191 p.
       ISBN 0-19-560653-1 LCCN 75-315900

       Summarizes the review of the energy
       sector in India from a 1974 unpublished
       report on the economic situation in
       India. Presents the technical,
       historical, and statistical background.
       Analyzes the current situation and its
       future prospects.

344.   Henke, Cliff.   "World Bank: Much Bigger Game,
       Same Rule." MASS TRANSIT, vol. 13
       (April 1986): 16+.   *

345.   "Hey, Big Lender." THE ECONOMIST, no. 256
       (August 2, 1975): 84.

       Interviews R. McNamara, World Bank
       President who wants to see an 8% growth
       in lending in the next five years. He
       has sought more money from OPEC
       countries, and wants to give them a
       bigger voice at the Bank (i.e., raise

their voting rights). This would affect
the disbursement of funds.

346. Heywood, Peter. "U.S. Seeks Harder Terms for
Bank's Softest Loans (World Bank)."
ENGINEERING NEWS-RECORD, vol. 216
(February 6, 1986): 13. *

347. Hill, Hortensia. "Cofinancing With the World
Bank." JOURNAL OF COMMERCIAL BANK
LENDING, vol. 68 (July 1986): 2-11. *

348. Hill, M.R. "International Bank." AUSTRALIAN
OUTLOOK, vol. 6, no. 4 (December 1952):
202-210. *

349. Hino, Hiroyuki. "IMF-World Bank
Collaboration." FINANCE AND DEVELOPMENT,
vol. 23 (September 1986): 10-14.

Discusses how economic
stabilization (IMF) and structural
adjustment (IBRD) are linked. Describes
how IBRD and IMF collaborate in
sponsoring conferences, publishing
FINANCE AND DEVELOPMENT, and sharing a
library (shared by IBRD, IFC, and IMF).

350. Hirschman, Albert O. DEVELOPMENT PROJECTS
OBSERVED. Washington, D.C.: Brookings
Institution, 1967. xiv,197 p.
LCCN 67-27683

Studies capital assistance program
in Pakistan, Peru, Nigeria, and other
countries. Examines the ways decision
making was shaped or hindered by type of
project observed.

351. Hitchens, Christopher. "McNamara's Bank."
NEW STATESMAN, vol. 88 (October 25,
1974): 564.

Discusses US strategy in World Bank
in past few years, especially in
relation to Saigon, and the opposition
of other member countries who view South
Vietnam as a bad short-term risk. US
made their IDA replenishment conditional
on Bank assistance for Saigon. Argues
against the use of the Bank as an
instrument of US foreign policy.

352.   Hodd, Michael. "Africa, the IMF and the
World Bank." AFRICAN AFFAIRS, vol. 86,
no. 344 (July 1987): 331-342.

Reviews control of IMF and World
Bank operations, and their involvement
in Africa. Explains the evolution of
their policies and the impact on
political power in African countries,
especially as more Africans in political
service have been educated and gain
competency as advisors to rulers.

353.   Holden, Constance. "World Bank Launches New
Environment Policy." SCIENCE, no. 236
(May 15, 1987): 769.

Bank President Conable announces
more attention will be given to
environmental aspects of development.
Describes how IBRD will be reorganized
to do this (creating Environment
Department). Announces environment,
population growth, and women in LDCs are
his top concerns.

354.   Holden, Constance. "World Bank, U.S. at Odds
on Population." SCIENCE, no. 225 (July
27, 1984): 396.

Comments on WORLD DEVELOPMENT
REPORT 1984 (see Entry 502) stating that
rapid population growth is hindering

development. US administration claims
it will no longer support NGOs that
promote abortions. Emphasizes that
better health care means fewer children
die. With increasing population and
lack of voluntary family planning, there
is a concern that some countries will
turn to mandatory measures including
coercive abortions.

355.   Holden, Dennis W. "Conable and the World
         Bank." UNITED STATES BANKER, vol. 97
         (September 1986): 60. *

356.   Holloway, Nigel. "Planning to Plough Back
         the Profits." FAR EASTERN ECONOMIC
         REVIEW, vol. 138, no. 40 (October 1,
         1987): 66-67.

         Japan is in the best position to
         fill the gap in leadership for economic
         and political reasons. States Japan is
         the world's largest creditor and
         supports the Bank (unlike the US in
         recent years). Argues Japan is holding
         back because it does not want to offend
         the US.

357.   Holloway, Nigel. "Willingness to Play
         Greater Role." FAR EASTERN ECONOMIC
         REVIEW, vol. 138, no. 40 (October 1,
         1987): 66-67.

         Interviews Vice Minister for
         International Affairs at the Ministry of
         Finance (Japan) on Japan's relationship
         with the World Bank.

358.   Honadle, George, and Rudi Klaus (eds.).
         INTERNATIONAL DEVELOPMENT
         ADMINISTRATION: IMPLEMENTATION ANALYSIS
         FOR DEVELOPMENT PROJECTS. New York:
         Praeger, 1979. 240 p.
         ISBN 0-03-051041-4 LCCN 79-65182

              Describes views on development
         administration and project
         implementation, especially in rural
         development projects.

359.   Hopkins, Antony G. "World Bank in Africa:
         Historical Reflections on the African
         Present." WORLD DEVELOPMENT, vol. 14
         (December 1986): 1473-1787

              Comments on ACCELERATED DEVELOPMENT
         report (see Entry 378) in historical
         context. Illustrates how Africa's past
         impacts on its future by linking the
         economic history to its continuing
         development problems.

360.   "How to Make the Poor Richer." THE
         ECONOMIST, vol. 272 (August 18, 1979):
         57-58.

              Comments on WORLD DEVELOPMENT
         REPORT 1978 (see Entry 496) which states
         development is possible, given enough
         time and the right policies. Examines
         the contrasts between growth and
         equality, asserting that an alliance
         between them can reinforce economic
         development.

361.   Howe, Geoffrey. "International Monetary Fund
         and the World Bank: the British
         Approach." INTERNATIONAL AFFAIRS,
         vol. 58, no. 2 (Spring 1982): 199-209.

Based on his address to the Board
of Governors 1981 annual meeting (he is
UK governor for IMF). Discusses the
roles of private sector, government,
IMF, and the World Bank, as well as
Special Drawing Rights and UK
assistance. Concludes with lessons
learned from past years. Calls for
continuing movement of economic
liberalization, and strengthening
stability and order.

362.   Htun, Kyaw. "Somalia's Drought
Rehabilitation." FINANCE AND
DEVELOPMENT, vol. 13 (September 1976):
6.

Describes Somalia's efforts to
recover from the 1973-74 drought (with
IDA funding).

363.   Hu, Yao-Su. "World Bank and Development
Finance Companies." JOURNAL OF GENERAL
MANAGEMENT, vol. 7, no. 1 (Autumn 1981):
46-57. *

364.   Hudson, Michael, and Dennis Goulet. MYTH OF
AID: THE HIDDEN AGENDA OF DEVELOPMENT
REPORTS. New York: Prepared by the
Center for the Study of Development and
Social Change, IDOC North America, 1971.
135 p. *

Argues that aid is not a cure to
changing inequities between nations.
Discusses political aspects of IBRD
programs.

365.   Humphreys, Charles, Dan Swanson, et al.
AFRICAN ECONOMIC AND FINANCIAL DATA.
Washington, D.C.: UNDP, and World Bank,
1989. xiii,204 p.

Provides 1980-1987 provisional data on national economic indicators, external sector, debt, government finance, agriculture, public enterprise, and aid flows.

366. Hunter, C.E. "International Bank: An Appraisal for Investors." TRUSTS AND ESTATES: THE JOURNAL OF CAPITAL MANAGEMENT, vol. 80 (February 1945): 142-144. *

367. Hurni, Bettina S. LENDING POLICY OF THE WORLD BANK IN THE 1970S: ANALYSIS AND EVALUATION (Westview Special Studies in International Economics and Business). Boulder, CO: Westview Press, 1980. ISBN 0-89158-681-4   LCCN 79-16385

Evaluates World Bank as a model for international investment and development lending.

368. Hurni, Bettina. "'New Style' Lending Policy of the World Bank." JOURNAL OF WORLD TRADE LAW, vol. 13 (November/December 1979): 523-34. *

369. "If OPEC Pays the Piper." THE ECONOMIST, vol. 276 (September 6, 1980): 17.

Describes the tension between western countries and OPEC, as well as discusses who is doing most harm in Third World countries. Comments that World Bank is approaching OPEC for funding developing in LDCs on energy projects, but there is a debate of who owns the oil rights.

370. "IMF/World Bank: Into Africa." THE ECONOMIST, vol. 299 (April 5, 1986): 91.

Describes how money is being
earmarked for Ghana, Zaire, and Zambia
in a joint IBRD-IMF three-year economic
program where economic benchmarks,
instead of performance criteria, are
being used.

371.   "IMF/World Bank: Meeting In New
        Circumstances." THE ECONOMIST, vol. 299
        (April 12, 1986): 68+.

        Debt and international economic
        coordination were topics at 1985 annual
        meeting in Seoul. However cheaper oil
        prices will affect development funding
        (means lower inflation, lower interest
        rate, and lighter debt burden).

372.   "IMF-IBRD: Working Together." BANKER,
        vol. 136 (October 1986): 6. *

373.   "India Needs More Foreign Assistance, Says
        World Bank." COMMERCE WEEKLY (INDIA),
        vol. 155, no. 3986 (October 10, 1987):
        14-21.

        Focuses on India's need of more
        World Bank and IDA lending. Examines
        past IBRD lending projects and IDA
        credits in agriculture and rural
        development, telecommunications,
        transportation, urban development, and
        water supply and sewerage.

374.   "India: World Bank Sees Some Remedies." FAR
        EASTERN ECONOMIC REVIEW, vol. 87, no. 1
        (January 3, 1975): 38.

        World Bank offers suggestions to
        India's energy problems (raise coal and
        petroleum prices, and raise cost of
        transport services). Some are not

acceptable to a government committed to
socialism (i.e., too capitalist).

375. Institute of International Finance.
INTERNATIONAL BANK FOR RECONSTRUCTION
AND DEVELOPMENT. New York: 1947. *

376. "Intelligence: Private Sector." FAR EASTERN
ECONOMIC REVIEW, vol. 140 (April 14,
1988): 11. *

377. International Bank for Reconstruction and
Development. ABSTRACTS OF CURRENT
STUDIES: THE WORLD BANK RESEARCH PROGRAM
1981- . Washington, D.C.: 1981- .
210 p. ISBN 0-8213-0052-0

Published annually. Provides brief
description of research projects in
progress. See also Entries 453, 493,
and 535.

378. International Bank for Reconstruction and
Development. ACCELERATED DEVELOPMENT IN
SUB-SAHARAN AFRICA: AN AGENDA FOR
ACTION, written by the African Strategy
Review Group (led by Elliot Berg).
Washington, D.C.: 1981. viii,198 p.
LCCN 81-16828

Stresses that more efficient use of
resources is needed for improvement of
Africa's economic conditions. A number
of public sector improvements are
suggested. See also Entries 417, 456,
and 465.

379. International Bank for Reconstruction and
Development. ADDRESS TO THE BOARD OF
GOVERNORS, BY A.W. CLAUSEN, SEPTEMBER
27, 1983. Washington, D.C.: 1983.
26 p. ISBN 0-8213-0281-7

World Bank President's remarks to
Board of Governors are published
annually. Here Clausen sums up World
Bank and IFC activities during 1982/83
in 2 words: innovation and progress.

380. International Bank for Reconstruction and
Development. ANNUAL REPORT, 1945/46- .
Washington, D.C.: 1946- .

Reviews IBRD and IDA activities on
fiscal basis. Highlights significant
ventures.

381. International Bank for Reconstruction and
Development. ASSAULT ON WORLD POVERTY,
PROBLEMS OF RURAL DEVELOPMENT, EDUCATION
AND HEALTH. Baltimore, MD: Published
for the World Bank by Johns Hopkins
Press, 1975. 425 p.
ISBN 0-8018-1745-5; 0-8018-1746-3
(paper) LCCN 75-7912 *

Presents nature of rural
development projects, and analyses
rural poverty. Outlines the World
Bank's programs to alleviating them.

382. International Bank for Reconstruction and
Development. AUTONOMOUS REGIONAL
CORPORATION OF THE CAUCA AND THE RECENT
DEVELOPMENT OF THE UPPER CAUCA VALLEY:
REPORT OF A MISSION ORGANIZED BY THE
BANK AT THE REQUEST OF THE REPUBLIC OF
COLOMBIA AND THE AUTONOMOUS REGIONAL
CORPORATION OF THE CAUCA. Washington,
D.C.: 1955. vii,145 p.

Studies the Cauca Region to make
recommendations to stimulate economic
progress. Addresses role that
Autonomous Regional Corporation of

the Cauca would play in regional development.

383. International Bank for Reconstruction and Development. BASIS OF A DEVELOPMENT PROGRAM: REPORT OF A MISSION HEADED BY LAUCHLIN CURRIE AND SPONSORED BY THE BANK, IN COLLABORATION WITH THE GOVERNMENT OF COLOMBIA (IBRD Special Publication, 1950.2). Washington, D.C.: 1950. xxxviii,642 p. LCCN 50-11983
      Republished in Baltimore, MD: Johns Hopkins Press, 1952. LCCN 52-3061

      Describes the problems and economic conditions in Colombia (a comprehensive report based on a 1949 economic mission). Recommends a development program to raise the standard of living for Colombians (first World Bank economic mission). See also Entry 384.

384. International Bank for Reconstruction and Development. BASIS OF A DEVELOPMENT PROGRAM IN COLOMBIA: THE SUMMARY -- REPORT OF A MISSION HEADED BY LAUCHLIN CURRIE AND SPONSORED BY THE BANK, IN COLLABORATION WITH THE GOVERNMENT OF COLOMBIA (IBRD Special Publication, 1950.1). Washington, D.C.: 1950. xv,76 p. LCCN 51-5891
      Republished in Baltimore, MD: Johns Hopkins Press, 1952. xviii,98 p. LCCN 52-28239

      Summarizes the major conclusions and recommendations of economic mission to Colombia. See also Entry 383.

385. International Bank for Reconstruction and Development. BELIZE: ECONOMIC REPORT. Washington, D.C.: 1984. xxxiv,111 p. ISBN 0-8213-0308-2 LCCN 83-25970

Based on the findings of a 1982 economic mission to Belize headed by Carlos Elbirt. Describes Belize's economy, and analyzes the current economic policies and public sector investment program. Assesses economic prospects and credit-worthiness.

386.   International Bank for Reconstruction and Development. BORROWING AND LENDING TERMINOLOGY. Washington, D.C.: 1984. vii, 56 p. ISBN 0-8213-0365-1 LCCN 84-25684 *

387.   International Bank for Reconstruction and Development. BRAZIL: INTEGRATED DEVELOPMENT OF THE NORTHWEST FRONTIER (World Bank Country Study). Washington, D.C.: 1981. vi,101 p.

Based on findings of the 1979 mission led by Dennis J. Mahar. Focuses on Brazil's Northwest Frontier, an area with great potential for agricultural development.

388.   International Bank for Reconstruction and Development. CHAD: DEVELOPMENT POTENTIAL AND CONSTRAINTS (World Bank Country Study). Washington, D.C.: 1974. xv,133 p.

Based on a 1972 mission led by Richard Westebbe. Identifies potentials (livestock, cotton) and constraints (public finance, transportation, human resources).

389.   International Bank for Reconstruction and Development. COMMODITY TRADE AND PRICE TRENDS. Baltimore, MD: Published for the World Bank by Johns Hopkins University Press.

Statistical handbook issued annually. Presents commodity prices and trade, historical as well as current, for 55 commodities.

390.   International Bank for Reconstruction and Development. COPING WITH EXTERNAL DEBT IN THE 1980S. Washington, D.C.: 1985. xxxiv,7 p. ISBN 0-8213-0508-5 LCCN 85-3225 *

391.   International Bank for Reconstruction and Development. CURRENT ECONOMIC POSITION AND PROSPECTS OF ECUADOR (World Bank Country Study). Washington, D.C.: 1973. xiv,200 p.

Based on the work of a 1972 economic mission led by R. Echeverria, and drawing on the findings of 1980 IBRD Agricultural Sector Review mission. Has statistical annex on national accounts and long-term projections.

392.   International Bank for Reconstruction and Development. ECONOMIC DEVELOPMENT AND THE PRIVATE SECTOR. Washington, D.C.: 1981. 39 p.

Articles reprinted from FINANCE AND DEVELOPMENT. Emphasizing that the public sector and private sector relationship should be complementary, because it has a significant impact on development.

393.   International Bank for Reconstruction and Development. ECONOMIC DEVELOPMENT OF BRITISH GUIANA: A REPORT OF A MISSION ORGANIZED BY THE BANK AT THE REQUEST OF THE GOVERNMENT OF BRITISH GUIANA. Baltimore, MD: Johns Hopkins Press, 1953. xix,366 p. LCCN 53-13267

Report of 1953 mission led by E.
Harrison Clark. Presents structure of
proposed Five-Year Development Plan,
recommendations of the mission, as well
as sector reports on agriculture,
transport, forestry, and industry.

394.   International Bank for Reconstruction and
Development. ECONOMIC DEVELOPMENT OF
CEYLON: REPORT OF A MISSION ORGANIZED BY
THE BANK AT THE REQUEST OF THE
GOVERNMENT OF CEYLON. Washington, D.C.:
1952. xiii,131 p. LCCN 52-4217
Published by Baltimore, MD: Johns
Hopkins Press, 1953. xxxii,829 p.
LCCN 53-1066

Surveys development potential
especially in agriculture, minerals,
industrial development, vocational
training, and health. Led by Sydney
Crain and Paul Ellsworth, the 1951
mission advises on the Five-Year
Development Plan. Suggests investment
programs and changes in government
policy.

395.   International Bank for Reconstruction and
Development. ECONOMIC DEVELOPMENT OF
GUATEMALA: REPORT OF A MISSION ORGANIZED
BY THE BANK AT THE REQUEST OF THE
GOVERNMENT OF GUATEMALA (IBRD Special
Publication, 1951.2). Washington, D.C.:
1951. xviii,305 p. LCCN 51-14496

Led by George Britnell in 1950, the
mission analyzes the economy and its
problems. Examines agriculture,
industry, mining, transport, power, and
telecommunications sectors. Appraises
resources available for development
programs, and offers some alternatives.

396.   International Bank for Reconstruction and
         Development. ECONOMIC DEVELOPMENT OF
         IRAQ: REPORT OF A MISSION ORGANIZED BY
         THE BANK AT THE REQUEST OF THE
         GOVERNMENT OF IRAQ. Baltimore, MD:
         Johns Hopkins Press, 1952. xix,463 p.
         LCCN 52-2530

              Based on 1951 mission led by Ivar
         Rooth and John de Wilde. Recommends
         investment priorities in different
         sectors, the rate of investment that is
         appropriate, as well as economic and
         fiscal policies to accelerate
         development.

397.   International Bank for Reconstruction and
         Development. ECONOMIC DEVELOPMENT OF
         JAMAICA: REPORT OF A MISSION OF THE
         BANK. Baltimore, MD: Johns Hopkins
         Press, 1952. 288 p. LCCN 53-136

              Led by John de Wilde in 1952, this
         mission examines the agriculture,
         manufacturing, mining, transport, and
         social services sectors. Recommends
         financing programs and takes into
         account projects already included in
         Jamaica's Ten-Year Development Plan.

398.   International Bank for Reconstruction and
         Development. ECONOMIC DEVELOPMENT OF
         JORDAN: REPORT OF A MISSION ORGANIZED BY
         THE BANK AT THE REQUEST OF THE
         GOVERNMENT OF JORDAN. Baltimore, MD:
         Johns Hopkins Press, 1957. xvi,488 p.
         LCCN 57-9517

              Recommendations by the 1955 mission
         led by Pieter Lieftinck for organizing
         and financing government programs over
         ten years. Recommends long-term
         development programs for raising the

standard of living, and reducing
dependency on foreign aid.

399.   International Bank for Reconstruction and
Development. ECONOMIC DEVELOPMENT OF
KENYA: REPORT OF A MISSION ORGANIZED BY
THE BANK AT THE REQUEST OF THE
GOVERNMENT OF KENYA. Baltimore, MD:
Johns Hopkins Press, 1963. xv,380 p.
LCCN 63-15811

        Based on 1961 mission led by Edmond
Leavey and C.H. Thompson. Reviews
economic potential of Kenya. Makes
recommendations to assist government in
development planning, and to formulate
policies to stimulate economy during
time of political change as Kenya moves
toward independence.

400.   International Bank for Reconstruction and
Development. ECONOMIC DEVELOPMENT OF
KUWAIT: REPORT OF A MISSION ORGANIZED BY
THE BANK AT THE REQUEST OF THE
GOVERNMENT OF KUWAIT. Baltimore, MD:
Johns Hopkins Press, 1965. xiii,194 p.
LCCN 65-11664   *

401.   International Bank for Reconstruction and
Development. ECONOMIC DEVELOPMENT OF
LIBYA: REPORT OF A MISSION ORGANIZED BY
THE BANK AT THE REQUEST OF THE
GOVERNMENT OF LIBYA. Baltimore, MD:
Johns Hopkins Press, 1960. xvii,524 p.
LCCN 60-12910

        Economic mission in 1958/59 led by
P.S. Narayan Prasad to appraise the
economic development since independence,
and to submit a proposal of priorities
for future development. Notes economic
impact of discovery of oil (minimal).

Examines agriculture, fisheries, and tourism sectors.

402.   International Bank for Reconstruction and Development. ECONOMIC DEVELOPMENT OF MALAYA: REPORT OF A MISSION ORGANIZED BY THE BANK AT THE REQUEST OF THE GOVERNMENTS OF THE FEDERATION OF MALAYA, THE CROWN COLONY, AND THE UNITED KINGDOM. Baltimore, MD: Johns Hopkins Press, 1955. xix,707 p. LCCN 55-12042
        Republished in New York: Oxford University Press, 1956. 2 v. x,857 p. LCCN 56-61479

        General survey mission led by Louis Chick to assess the resources available for development, and how they contributed to Malaya's economic and social development. Presents recommendations for future development.

403.   International Bank for Reconstruction and Development. ECONOMIC DEVELOPMENT OF MEXICO: REPORT OF THE COMBINED MEXICAN WORKING PARTY, compiled by Paul Ortiz Mena, et al. Baltimore, MD: Johns Hopkins Press, 1953. xxiv,329 p. LCCN 53-6495

        Combined working team from IBRD and Mexican government (led by Raul Ortiz Mena, Victor Urquidi, Albert Waterson, and Jonas Haralz) to assess long-term trends in economy with relation to foreign investment. Reviews investment from 1939-50, and assesses national income and balance of payments.

404.   International Bank for Reconstruction and
         Development. ECONOMIC DEVELOPMENT OF
         MOROCCO: REPORT OF A MISSION ORGANIZED
         BY THE BANK AT THE REQUEST OF THE
         GOVERNMENT OF MOROCCO. Baltimore, MD:
         Johns Hopkins Press, 1966. xiv,356 p.
         LCCN 66-24215

              Mission led by Johan Beyen in 1965
         to assess the development potential of
         the economy. Recommends economic,
         political, and investment programs to
         accelerate growth.

405.   International Bank for Reconstruction and
         Development. ECONOMIC DEVELOPMENT OF
         NICARAGUA: REPORT OF A MISSION ORGANIZED
         BY THE BANK AT THE REQUEST OF THE
         GOVERNMENT OF NICARAGUA. Washington,
         D.C.: 1952. xxvii,108 p. LCCN 52-4752
              Republished in Baltimore, MD: 1953.
         424 p. LCCN 53-6788

              E. Harrison Clark and Walter
         Armstrong were posted in Nicaragua in
         1951/52 to help the government to plan
         long-term development, and to give
         advice on economic policies.

406.   International Bank for Reconstruction and
         Development. ECONOMIC DEVELOPMENT OF
         NIGERIA: REPORT OF A MISSION ORGANIZED
         BY THE BANK AT THE REQUEST OF THE
         GOVERNMENTS OF NIGERIA AND THE UNITED
         KINGDOM. Baltimore, MD: Published for
         IBRD by Johns Hopkins Press, 1955.
         xxii,686 p. LCCN 55-7216

              Mission led by A. Broches and John
         Adler in 1953 to assess the resources
         available for future development, and to
         study the possibility of development in

economy. Recommends practical steps for development.

407. International Bank for Reconstruction and Development. ECONOMIC DEVELOPMENT OF SPAIN: REPORT OF A MISSION ORGANIZED BY THE BANK AT THE REQUEST OF THE GOVERNMENT OF SPAIN. Baltimore, MD: Johns Hopkins Press, 1963. 416 p. LCCN 63-8811

Mission led by Hugh Ellis-Rees and Benjamin King to assist in preparation of long-range development program to modernize economy, raise the standard of living, and maintain financial stability.

408. International Bank for Reconstruction and Development. ECONOMIC DEVELOPMENT OF SYRIA: REPORT OF A MISSION ORGANIZED BY THE BANK AT THE REQUEST OF THE GOVERNMENT OF SYRIA. Washington, D.C.: 1953. xxii,686 p. LCCN 55-7216
Republished in Baltimore, MD: Johns Hopkins Press, 1955. 486 p. LCCN 55-9741

Led by Pieter Lieftinck and John de Wilde, reviews the economy's potential. Makes recommendations to help to prepare a long-term development program, increase productive resources, and raise the standard of living.

409. International Bank for Reconstruction and Development. ECONOMIC DEVELOPMENT OF TANGANYIKA: REPORT OF A MISSION ORGANIZED BY THE BANK AT THE REQUEST OF THE GOVERNMENTS OF TANGANYIKA AND THE UNITED KINGDOM. Baltimore, MD: Johns Hopkins Press, 1961. xviii,548 p. LCCN 61-9915

Assesses available resources, and makes recommendations for practical measures to further development. The mission team led by William Stevenson and Svend Laursen indicates the consequences in Tanganyika's economy of their recommendations.

410.   International Bank for Reconstruction and Development. ECONOMIC DEVELOPMENT OF THE TERRITORY OF PAPUA AND NEW GUINEA: REPORT OF A MISSION ORGANIZED BY THE BANK AT THE REQUEST OF THE GOVERNMENT OF THE COMMONWEALTH OF AUSTRALIA. Baltimore, MD: Johns Hopkins Press, 1965. xvii,468 p. LCCN 65-817079

Mission led by Kenneth Iverson and Marinus van del Mel reviews potential of economy. Makes recommendations to Australia to assist in the preparation of a development program to raise the standard of living, and to stimulate economic growth.

411.   International Bank for Reconstruction and Development. ECONOMIC DEVELOPMENT OF THAILAND: REPORT OF A MISSION ORGANIZED BY THE BANK AT THE REQUEST OF THE GOVERNMENT OF THAILAND. Washington, D.C.: 1959. 301 p. *

412.   International Bank for Reconstruction and Development. ECONOMIC DEVELOPMENT OF UGANDA: REPORT OF A MISSION ORGANIZED BY IBRD AT THE REQUEST OF THE GOVERNMENTS OF UGANDA AND THE UNITED KINGDOM. Baltimore, MD: Published for the World Bank by Johns Hopkins Press, 1962. xviii,475 p. LCCN 62-10309

Reports priorities for public investment, and major public policy

priorities for the first five years
following Uganda's independence.

413.   International Bank for Reconstruction and
         Development. ECONOMIC DEVELOPMENT OF
         VENEZUELA: REPORT OF A MISSION ORGANIZED
         BY THE BANK AT THE REQUEST OF THE
         GOVERNMENT OF VENEZUELA. Baltimore, MD:
         Johns Hopkins Press, 1961. xviii,494 p.
         LCCN 61-11502

         Economic survey mission in 1959
         (led by Henry Labouisse and Gerald
         Alter) to assess resources and major
         sectors in economy. Recommends
         investment and development priorities
         for five years.

414.   International Bank for Reconstruction and
         Development. ECONOMIC GROWTH OF
         COLOMBIA: PROBLEMS AND PROSPECTS --
         REPORT OF A MISSION SENT TO COLOMBIA IN
         1970 BY THE WORLD BANK. Baltimore, MD:
         Johns Hopkins Press, 1972. xx,509 p.
         ISBN 0-8018-1389-1; 0-8018-1397-2
         (paper) LCCN 78-186501

         Based on 1970 mission led by
         Dragoslav Avramovic, analyzes major
         sectors (agriculture, transport,
         telecommunications, tourism, social
         sectors). Discusses employment,
         investment, and public finance projects
         in Colombia.

415.   International Bank for Reconstruction and
         Development. ENVIRONMENT AND
         DEVELOPMENT, written by the Office of
         Environmental Affairs (Albert Wall,
         principal author). Washington, D.C.:
         1975. 33 p.

Provides overview of environmental problems, lessons from the Bank's experience, and future action.

416. International Bank for Reconstruction and Development. ENVIRONMENTAL, HEALTH AND HUMAN ECOLOGIC CONSIDERATIONS IN ECONOMIC DEVELOPMENT PROJECTS. Washington, D.C.: 1974. ix,142 p.

Identifies environmental considerations for 16 development projects financed by the Bank, with 35 pages of resource materials.

417. International Bank for Reconstruction and Development. FINANCING ADJUSTMENT WITH GROWTH IN SUB-SAHARAN AFRICA, 1986-90. Washington, D.C.: 1986. x,120 p. ISBN 0-8213-0767-3 LCCN 86-7754

Argues that, although progress has been made, medium-term programs are essential to reverse the mistakes of the past. Six ways to improve coordination of donor assistance are suggested. See also Entries 378, 456, and 465.

418. International Bank for Reconstruction and Development. GAMBIA: BASIC NEEDS IN THE GAMBIA (World Bank Country Study). Washington, D.C.: 1981. xi,142 p.

Based on the 1978 economic mission led by Heinz B. Bachmann. Assesses basic needs in Gambia to guide in future policy decisions.

419. International Bank for Reconstruction and Development. GUIDELINES FOR PROCUREMENT UNDER WORLD BANK LOANS AND IDA CREDITS. Washington, D.C.: 1975- . 22 p.

Describes guidelines to providing goods and services under Bank projects.

420. International Bank for Reconstruction and Development. GUIDELINES FOR THE USE OF CONSULTANTS BY WORLD BANK BORROWERS AND BY THE WORLD BANK AS EXECUTING AGENCY. Washington, D.C.: 1981. v, 38 p. ISBN 0-8213-9000-7

Explains policies and procedures for using consulting firms. Updates Entry 468.

421. International Bank for Reconstruction and Development. HUNGARY: ECONOMIC DEVELOPMENTS AND REFORMS. Washington, D.C.: 1984. *

422. International Bank for Reconstruction and Development. INAUGURAL MEETING OF THE BOARD OF GOVERNORS OF THE INTERNATIONAL BANK FOR RECONSTRUCTION AND DEVELOPMENT (Savannah, GA, March 8-18, 1946; selected documents). Washington, D.C.: 1946. 78 p. *

See also Entry 380.

423. International Bank for Reconstruction and Development. INDONESIA: EMPLOYMENT AND INCOME DISTRIBUTION IN INDONESIA (World Bank Country Study). Washington, D.C.: 1980. xiii, 187 p.

Based on a 1978 mission led by Mark Leiserson. Examines demographic and employment trends, and impact on past development efforts to address long-term development strategy.

424.   International Bank for Reconstruction and
        Development. INTERNATIONAL BANK FOR
        RECONSTRUCTION AND DEVELOPMENT,
        1946-1953. Baltimore, MD: Johns Hopkins
        Press, 1954. 273 p. LCCN 54-11252

            Discussion of origins and financial
        structure, operations and policies.
        Summarizes Bank activities within each
        country.

425.   International Bank for Reconstruction and
        Development. KENYA: INTO THE SECOND
        DECADE -- REPORT OF A MISSION SENT TO
        KENYA BY THE WORLD BANK. Baltimore, MD:
        Published for the World Bank by Johns
        Hopkins University Press, 1975. 533 p.
        ISBN 0-8018-1754-4; 0-8018-1755-2
        (paper) LCCN 75-10895

            Reviews operations of Kenya's
        economy, based on 1973 mission led by
        John Burrows. Reviews successes and
        failures, assesses prospects, and
        identifies major issues in Kenya's
        development.

426.   International Bank for Reconstruction and
        Development. KENYA: POPULATION AND
        DEVELOPMENT (World Bank Country Study).
        Washington, D.C.: 1980. 213 p.

            Based on a field mission led by
        Rashid Faruquee and Bank research on
        Kenya demographic trends.

427.   International Bank for Reconstruction and
        Development. KOREA: DEVELOPMENT IN A
        GLOBAL CONTEXT. Washington, D.C.:
        1984.*

428.   International Bank for Reconstruction and
        Development. LEARNING BY DOING: WORLD
        BANK LENDING FOR URBAN DEVELOPMENT,
        1972-1982. Washington, D.C.: 1983.
        vi,55 p. ISBN 0-8213-0158-6
        LCCN 83-1277

            Reviews performance of the Bank's
        urban lending program which began in
        1972. Project types (shelter,
        transport, regional and urban
        development) are presented.
        Implementation experience, internal
        management, and operation objectives are
        also described.

429.   International Bank for Reconstruction and
        Development. LIST OF NATIONAL
        DEVELOPMENT PLANS, 2nd ed. Washington,
        D.C.: 1968. 658 p.

            Reprinted from DEVELOPMENT PLANNING
        (Entry 86). Lists plans compiled or
        prepared as of July 1st. Updated by
        Entries 430 and 431.

430.   International Bank for Reconstruction and
        Development. LIST OF NATIONAL
        DEVELOPMENT PLANS, 3rd rev. ed. by
        Elizabeth W. Edwards. Washington, D.C.:
        1971.

            See also Entries 429 and 431.

431.   International Bank for Reconstruction and
        Development. LIST OF NATIONAL
        DEVELOPMENT PLANS, 4th ed. completed by
        Naomi L. Solomon. Washington, D.C.:
        1973. *

            See also Entries 429 and 430.

432.   International Bank for Reconstruction and
            Development. LOANS AT WORK.
            Washington, D.C.: 1952. LCCN 52-60086
            36 p.

                Arranged by geographic region.
            Summarizes the amount and types of loans
            made by the Bank.

433.   International Bank for Reconstruction and
            Development. THE MALDIVES: AN
            INTRODUCTORY ECONOMIC REPORT (World Bank
            Country Study). Washington, D.C.: 1980.
            vi,172 p.

                Based on a 1979 mission to the
            Maldives led by K. Sarwar Lateef.
            Provides basic data for this island
            group in the Indian Ocean which became
            an IBRD member in 1978.

434.   International Bank for Reconstruction and
            Development. MULTILATERAL INVESTMENT
            INSURANCE (WORLD BANK STAFF REPORT).
            Washington, D.C.: 1962. 51 p.

                Identifies issues involved in
            multilateral investment scheme.
            Discusses its impact on foreign private
            investment, and the advantages and
            disadvantages of this scheme.

435.   International Bank for Reconstruction and
            Development. PARAGUAY: REGIONAL
            DEVELOPMENT IN EASTERN PARAGUAY (World
            Bank Country Study). Washington, D.C.:
            1978. viii,50 p.

                Based on a 1977 mission led by
            Alfredo Gutierrez. Examines expansion
            of agricultural production and impact of
            hydroelectric projects.

436.   International Bank for Reconstruction and
        Development. PERU: MAJOR DEVELOPMENT
        POLICY ISSUES AND RECOMMENDATIONS (World
        Bank Country Study). Washington, D.C.:
        1980. vii,220 p.

        Based on findings of the 1980
        economic mission led by Ulrich Thumm
        during Peru's transition from military
        to civilian rule in 1980 and following
        the 1977-1978 severe economic crisis.

437.   International Bank for Reconstruction and
        Development. THE PHILIPPINES:
        INDUSTRIAL DEVELOPMENT STRATEGY AND
        POLICIES (World Bank Country Study).
        Washington, D.C.: 1980. ix,301 p.

        Based on a 1979 mission led by
        Barend A. de Vries. Reviews industrial
        objectives and policies with the aim of
        increasing efficiency in specific
        industries.

438.   International Bank for Reconstruction and
        Development. THE PHILIPPINES:
        PRIORITIES AND PROSPECTS FOR DEVELOPMENT
        -- REPORT OF A MISSION SENT TO THE
        PHILIPPINES BY THE WORLD BANK.
        Baltimore, MD: Published for the World
        Bank by Johns Hopkins Press, 1976.
        xx,573 p. ISBN 0-8018-1893-1
        LCCN 76-17243

        Based on 1975 mission led by
        Russell Cheetham and Edward Hawkins.
        Identifies areas crucial to development
        prospects. Discusses financial
        implication of growth and development.

439.   International Bank for Reconstruction and
        Development. POLAND: REFORM,
        ADJUSTMENT, AND GROWTH. Washington,
        D.C.: 1987. 2 v. ISBN 0-8213-0972-2
        (v.1); ISBN 0-8213-0973-0 (v.2)
        LCCN 87-28016

            Studies the attempts to reform
        Poland's economic system, and to bring
        about internal and external adjustment
        during the 1978-1982 severe economic
        crisis. Reviews overall economy and the
        principal sectors (agriculture, energy,
        manufacturing, transport, and housing).

440.   International Bank for Reconstruction and
        Development. POLICIES AND OPERATIONS:
        THE WORLD BANK GROUP. Washington, D.C.:
        1974. 112 p.

            Describes the origin and nature of
        the World Bank, IDA, IFC, and ICSID.
        Summarizes the basic data (member
        countries, staff members, lending
        commitments), as well as World Bank and
        IDA lending operations. See also
        Entries 487, 491, and 492.

441.   International Bank for Reconstruction and
        Development. POPULATION CHANGE AND
        ECONOMIC DEVELOPMENT. Oxford, UK:
        Published for the World Bank by Oxford
        University Press, 1985. *

442.   International Bank for Reconstruction and
        Development. POPULATION GROWTH AND
        ECONOMIC AND SOCIAL DEVELOPMENT:
        ADDRESSES BY A.W. CLAUSEN. Washington,
        D.C.: 1984. 36 p.

            Addresses to the National Leaders'
        Seminar on Population and Development,
        and International Population Conference,

emphasizing the Bank's interest in
population aspects of development.

443.   International Bank for Reconstruction and
        Development. POPULATION POLICIES AND
        ECONOMIC DEVELOPMENT (World Bank Staff
        Report). Baltimore, MD: Published for
        the World Bank by Johns Hopkins Press,
        1974. 214 p. ISBN 0-8018-1675-0;
        0-8018-1676-9 (paper) LCCN 74-12786 *

        Study on population policies by
        Timothy King and Roberto Cuca.

444.   International Bank for Reconstruction and
        Development. POVERTY AND BASIC NEEDS.
        Washington, D.C.: 1980. 34 p.

        Articles reprinted from FINANCE AND
        DEVELOPMENT, discussing the design of
        public services to transform poverty.
        Asserts that providing better access to
        essential public services (education,
        health care, and clean water) is the key
        to enhancing human achievement.

445.   International Bank for Reconstruction and
        Development. POVERTY AND HUMAN
        DEVELOPMENT. New York: Published for
        the World Bank by Oxford University
        Press, 1980. vi,90 p.
        ISBN 0-19-520389-5

        Provides an overview of alleviating
        poverty. Examines one approach (human
        development), and draws conclusions from
        experience with human development
        programs. Reprinted from WORLD
        DEVELOPMENT REPORT 1980, written by Paul
        Isenman, et al. See Entry 498.

446.   International Bank for Reconstruction and
         Development. POVERTY AND HUNGER: ISSUES
         AND OPTIONS FOR FOOD SECURITY IN
         DEVELOPING COUNTRIES (World Bank Policy
         Study). Washington, D.C.: 1986.
         ix,69 p. ISBN 0-8213-0678-2
         LCCN 86-1583

              Argues that global food production
         has increased faster than population
         growth, but lack of food security
         (access to enough food) is the problem.
         Identifies key issues and policy options
         available.

447.   International Bank for Reconstruction and
         Development. PROGRAM TO ACCELERATE
         PETROLEUM PRODUCTION IN THE DEVELOPING
         COUNTRIES. Washington, D.C.: 1979.
         31 p.

              In 1977 the Bank recognized a need
         to finance petroleum (oil and natural
         gas) product projects, in order to aid
         LDCs in exploiting their energy
         resources. Summarizes recent Bank work
         in the energy sector, problems and
         prospects faced, and proposals for
         future lending.

448.   International Bank for Reconstruction and
         Development. PROPOSAL FOR AN INCREASE
         IN THE AUTHORIZED CAPITAL OF THE BANK:
         REPORT OF THE EXECUTIVE DIRECTOR TO THE
         BOARD OF GOVERNORS. Washington, D.C.:
         1958. 18 p.

              Board of Governors proposes an
         increase in the resources of the IMF and
         in the capital of the World Bank.

449.   International Bank for Reconstruction and
         Development. PUBLIC DEVELOPMENT PROGRAM
         FOR THAILAND: REPORT OF A MISSION
         ORGANIZED BY THE BANK AT THE REQUEST OF
         THE GOVERNMENT OF THAILAND. Baltimore,
         MD: Johns Hopkins Press, 1959.
         xv,301 p. LCCN 59-14230

              Mission led by Paul Ellsworth and
         William Gilmartin during 1957-58.
         Assesses public development program
         funds available. Suggests allocation in
         light of development priorities to
         assist government planning during next
         few years.

450.   International Bank for Reconstruction and
         Development. QUESTIONS AND ANSWERS.
         Washington, D.C.: 1947. 28 p.   *

451.   International Bank for Reconstruction and
         Development. REPORT ON CUBA: FINDINGS
         AND RECOMMENDATIONS OF AN ECONOMIC AND
         TECHNICAL MISSION ORGANIZED BY THE BANK,
         IN COLLABORATION WITH THE GOVERNMENT OF
         CUBA IN 1950 (IBRD Special Publication,
         1951.3). Washington, D.C.: 1951.
         xxiv,1049 p. LCCN 51-14869   *

              Reports the findings of a Bamk team
         led by Francis Adams Truslow in 1951.

452.   International Bank for Reconstruction and
         Development. RECOVERY IN THE DEVELOPING
         WORLD: LONDON SYMPOSIUM ON THE WORLD
         BANK'S ROLE. Washington, D.C.: 1986.
         vi,122 p. ISBN 0-8213-0776-2
         LCCN 86-13211

              World Bank called a symposium of
         100 development experts (London,
         February 1985) to assess the Bank's
         activities and future directions.

453.   International Bank for Reconstruction and
        Development. RESEARCH PROGRAM OF THE
        WORLD BANK. Washington, D.C.: 1981.
        ii,64 p. LCCN 81-187367

            Provides an overview to World Bank
            research (dimensions, impact, new
            directions, and content). See also
            Entries 377, 493, and 535.

454.   International Bank for Reconstruction and
        Development. SOCIAL INDICATORS OF
        DEVELOPMENT 1988. Baltimore, MD:
        Published for the World Bank by Johns
        Hopkins University Press, 1988.
        ISBN 0-8018-3831-2   273 p.

            Assesses overall impact of
            development policies. Social indicators
            (labor force, housing, education,
            income, and population) provide
            guidelines for formulating more
            effective economic programs. See also
            Entry 512.

455.   International Bank for Reconstruction and
        Development. SOME ASPECTS OF THE
        ECONOMIC PHILOSOPHY OF THE WORLD BANK.
        Washington, D.C.: 1968. 51 p.

            Lectures by World Bank economists
            (I.S. Friedman, D. Avramovic, A.M.
            Kamarck, and J.H. Adler) at a Seminar
            for Brazilian Professors of Economics in
            Rio de Janeiro (September 1967).

456.   International Bank for Reconstruction and
        Development. SUB-SAHARAN AFRICA:
        PROGRESS REPORT ON DEVELOPMENT PROSPECTS
        AND PROGRAMS. Washington, D.C.: 1983.
        v,32 p.

Highlights major problems faced by
African governments in designing reform
efforts. Examines World Bank's
effectiveness of giving priority to
Africa. See also Entries 378, 417, and
465.

457. International Bank for Reconstruction and
Development. SUPPLEMENTARY FINANCIAL
MEASURES: A STUDY REQUESTED BY THE
UNCTAD, 1964. Washington, D.C: 1965.
125 p.

Studies the feasibility of dealing
with problems arising from adverse
export movements in LDCs. Proposes a
scheme for supplementary aid (not a
substitute for existing aid).

458. International Bank for Reconstruction and
Development. SUPPLIERS' CREDITS FROM
INDUSTRIALIZED TO DEVELOPING COUNTRIES:
A STUDY REQUESTED BY THE UNITED NATIONS
CONFERENCE ON TRADE AND DEVELOPMENT.
Washington, D.C: 1967. iv,72 p.

Discusses the use of suppliers'
credits and credit insurance as a means
of financing imports. Advocates
effective international coordination to
reduce costs resulting from previous use
of suppliers' credits.

459. International Bank for Reconstruction and
Development. SURINAM: RECOMMENDATIONS
FOR A TEN-YEAR DEVELOPMENT PROGRAM --
REPORT OF A MISSION ORGANIZED BY THE
BANK AT THE REQUEST OF THE GOVERNMENTS
OF THE NETHERLANDS AND OF SURINAM.
Baltimore, MD: Johns Hopkins Press,
1952. xxvi,271 p. LCCN 52-2215

Based on economic survey mission of
Surinam led by Richard Denuth in 1951.
Presents suggestions for development
priorities for the Ten-Year Plan.

460.   International Bank for Reconstruction and
         Development. THAILAND: INDUSTRIAL
         DEVELOPMENT STRATEGY IN THAILAND (World
         Bank Country Study). Washington, D.C.:
         1980. x,59 p.

Based on the work of a 1979
industrial policy mission led by Bela
Balassa. Summarizes four studies on
industrial policy.

461.   International Bank for Reconstruction and
         Development. THAILAND: INDUSTRIAL
         GROWTH AND POVERTY ALLEVIATION (World
         Bank Country Study). Washington, D.C.:
         1980. viii,56 p.

Based on the work of a 1979 mission
led by John Shilling. Synthesizes the
four special studies on poverty.

462.   International Bank for Reconstruction and
         Development. THAILAND: RURAL GROWTH AND
         DEVELOPMENT. Washington, D.C.: 1983.   *

463.   International Bank for Reconstruction and
         Development. THAILAND: TOWARD A
         DEVELOPMENT STRATEGY OF FULL
         PARTICIPATION (World Bank Country
         Study). Washington, D.C.: 1980.
         xiv,232 p.

Based on a 1977 mission led by E.
R. Lim and J. D. Shilling. Presents
statistical annex and summaries of eight
background working papers (human
resources, development problems,
industrial policy, etc.).

464.   International Bank for Reconstruction and
            Development.   THIRD WORLD DEBT AND
            GLOBAL RECOVERY, by A.W. Clausen.
            Washington, D.C.:   1983.   22 p.
            ISBN 0-8213-0170-5

            Text of the 1983 Jodidi Lecture at
            the Center for International Affairs,
            Harvard University (February 1983).
            Clausen explains the problems of Third
            World debt.   Offers why they are
            manageable if both developed and
            developing nations, development banks,
            and international agencies cooperate.

465.   International Bank for Reconstruction and
            Development.   TOWARD SUSTAINED
            DEVELOPMENT IN SUB-SAHARAN AFRICA: A
            JOINT PROGRAM FOR ACTION, written by a
            World Bank team led by Stanley Please.
            Washington, D.C.:   1984.   ix,102 p.
            ISBN 0-8213-0423-2   LCCN 84-19696

            Argues that better coordination is
            needed between developing countries and
            international institutions to provide
            consistent support to reform efforts.
            See also Entries 378, 417 and 456.

466.   International Bank for Reconstruction and
            Development.   TRENDS IN DEVELOPING
            COUNTRIES: ECONOMIC GROWTH,
            INTERNATIONAL DEVELOPMENT FINANCE, AND
            INTERNATIONAL TRADE.   Washington, D.C.:
            1968.   25 p.

            Charts economic trends affecting
            LDCs.   Highlights global economic
            growth, international capital flows and
            trade.

467.   International Bank for Reconstruction and
        Development. TURKEY: POLICIES AND
        PROSPECTS FOR GROWTH (World Bank Country
        Study). Washington, D.C.: 1980.
        xxxi,316 p.

            Based on a 1979 special economic
        mission led by Vinod Dubey and Shakil
        Faruqi. Examines patterns of
        development (1962-78) and foreign trade
        policy. Identifies the potential for
        sustainable growth.

468.   International Bank for Reconstruction and
        Development. USE OF CONSULTANTS BY THE
        WORLD BANK AND ITS BORROWERS.
        Washington, D.C.: 1974. 19 p.

            Explains use of consultants and
        consulting firms. Updated by Entry 420.

469.   International Bank for Reconstruction and
        Development. WATER AND POWER RESOURCES
        OF WEST PAKISTAN: A STUDY IN SECTOR
        PLANNING. Baltimore, MD: Published for
        the World Bank as administrator of the
        Indus Basin Development Fund, by Johns
        Hopkins Press, 1968-69. 3 v.
        LCCN 68-28008

            Prepared by a World Bank study
        group headed by P. Lieftinck, R. Sadove,
        and T.C. Creyke. Covers methodology and
        development of irrigation and
        agriculture.

470.   International Bank for Reconstruction and
        Development. WORLD BANK. Washington,
        D.C.: 1981. 12 p.

            Briefly explains IBRD and IDA
        (operating methods, technical
        assistance, etc.).

471.   International Bank for Reconstruction and
        Development. WORLD BANK ACTIVITIES IN
        LATIN AMERICA. Washington, D.C.: 1957.
        52 p.

            Presents report for the Economic
        Conference of the OAS (1957). See also
        Entries 490, 485, and 521.

472.   International Bank for Reconstruction and
        Development. WORLD BANK AND JAPAN.
        Washington, D.C.: 1967. 33 p. *

            Focuses on Japan's position (during
        the late 1950s to early 1960s) in
        providing assistance to LDCs, as well as
        its role as a user of development
        assistance for its own economy.

473.   International Bank for Reconstruction and
        Development. WORLD BANK AND THE WORLD'S
        POOREST. Washington, D.C: 1979. 32 p.

            A series of articles appearing in
        FINANCE AND DEVELOPMENT (June 1978
        through September 1979). Focuses on the
        Bank's experience in working towards the
        alleviation of poverty.

474.   International Bank for Reconstruction and
        Development. WORLD BANK ATLAS.
        Washington, D.C.: 1989.
        ISBN 0-8213-1354-1 29 p.

            Graphically presents current
        economic and social indicators. Reveals
        per capita income rose for most
        countries and improved the standard of
        living.

475.   International Bank for Reconstruction and
        Development. WORLD BANK GLOSSARY.
        Washington, D.C.: 1986. 2 v.
        ISBN 0-8213-0819-X (vol. 1,
        English/French); 0-8213-0820-3 (vol. 2
        English/Spanish) LCCN 86-15872

            Written to assist World Bank
        translators and interpreters. Lists
        acronyms frequently used, as well as
        international, regional, and national
        organizations.

476.   International Bank for Reconstruction and
        Development. WORLD BANK GROUP.
        Washington, D.C.: 1969. 33 p.

            Describes the World Bank Group and
        its lending activities in agriculture,
        education, transportation, utilities,
        and industry. See also Entries 470, and
        486.

477.   International Bank for Reconstruction and
        Development. WORLD BANK GROUP IN
        AFRICA. Washington, D.C.: 1963. 20 p.

            Describes work of IFC, IDA, and
        IBRD in Africa. See also Entry 488.

478.   International Bank for Reconstruction and
        Development. WORLD BANK GROUP IN
        COLOMBIA. Washington, D.C.: 1967.
        18 p. LCCN 77-350880 *

479.   International Bank for Reconstruction and
        Development. WORLD BANK GROUP IN
        ETHIOPIA. Washington, D.C.: 1967.
        15 p. LCCN 76-369061 *

480.   International Bank for Reconstruction and
        Development. WORLD BANK GROUP IN IRAN.
        Washington, D.C.: 1967. 10 p.
        LCCN 76-377255 *

481.   International Bank for Reconstruction and
        Development. WORLD BANK GROUP IN
        MALAYSIA. Washington, D.C.: 1967.
        17 p. LCCN 77-352157 *

482.   International Bank for Reconstruction and
        Development. WORLD BANK GROUP IN
        MEXICO. Washington, D.C.: 1967. 13 p.
        LCCN 78-300778

483.   International Bank for Reconstruction and
        Development. WORLD BANK GROUP IN
        MOROCCO. Washington, D.C.: 1967. 9 p.
        LCCN 77-352749 *

484.   International Bank for Reconstruction and
        Development. WORLD BANK GROUP IN
        TUNISIA. Washington, D.C.: 1967. 9 p.
        LCCN 76-380692 *

485.   International Bank for Reconstruction and
        Development. WORLD BANK GROUP IN THE
        AMERICAS: A SUMMARY OF ACTIVITIES.
        Washington, D.C.: 1963. 94 p. *

            Describes IFC, IDA, and IBRD in
        economic development in member countries
        in the Western Hemisphere. See Entries
        471, 490, and 521.

486.   International Bank for Reconstruction and
        Development. WORLD BANK GROUP --
        PROFILES OF DEVELOPMENT. Washington,
        D.C.: 1971. 32 p.

            Illustrates World Bank-financed
        projects in Tunisian education,
        Afghanistan agriculture, Indus Waters

development, Ethiopian highways, Mexican energy, and Philippine industries.

487.   International Bank for Reconstruction and Development. WORLD BANK, IFC AND IDA: POLICIES AND OPERATIONS. Washington, D.C.: 1962-. 132 p.

Covers origin, relationships, and other factors relating to the World Bank Group's operations and policies. See also Entry 440.

488.   International Bank for Reconstruction and Development. WORLD BANK IN AFRICA. Washington, D.C.: 1961-. 30 p. *

See also Entry 477.

489.   International Bank for Reconstruction and Development. WORLD BANK IN ASIA. Washington, D.C.: 1967. 34 p. *

490.   International Bank for Reconstruction and Development. WORLD BANK IN THE AMERICAS. Washington, D.C.: 1967. 30 p.

See also Entry 471.

491.   International Bank for Reconstruction and Development. WORLD BANK OPERATIONS: SECTORAL PROGRAMS AND POLICIES. Baltimore, MD: Published for the World Bank by Johns Hopkins Press, 1972. 513 p.   ISBN 0-8018-1448-0   LCCN 72-4032

Examines operations by activity (industry, transportation, etc.) to determine primary problems facing the Bank. Economic and developmental characteristics, and the scale of

operations are covered. See also
Entries 440, 487, and 492.

492. International Bank for Reconstruction and
Development. WORLD BANK, POLICIES AND
OPERATIONS. Washington, D.C.: 1957.
139 p.

Presents Bank's activities and
policies. See also Entries 440, 487,
and 491.

493. International Bank for Reconstruction and
Development. WORLD BANK RESEARCH
PROGRAM: ABSTRACTS OF CURRENT STUDIES.
Washington, D.C.: 1980. 146 p.

Summarizes research undertaken by
World Bank excluding short-term studies.
See also Entries 377, 453, and 535.

494. International Bank for Reconstruction and
Development. WORLD BANK'S ROLE IN
SCHISTOSOMIASIS CONTROL. Washington,
D.C.: 1978. 15 p.

Explains schistosomiasis and the
Bank's approach to this problem.

495. International Bank for Reconstruction and
Development. WORLD DEBT TABLES:
EXTERNAL PUBLIC DEBT OF LDCs.
Washington, D.C.: World Bank, 1974.
309 p.

Presents data on the external debt
of developing countries.

496. International Bank for Reconstruction and
Development. WORLD DEVELOPMENT REPORT
1978. Washington, D.C.: 1978.
ix,121 p. LCCN 78-67086

Provides comprehensive evaluation
of global development. Presents
statistical annex on social and economic
aspects of development. Updated
annually. See also Entries 497-507.

497.   International Bank for Reconstruction and
         Development. WORLD DEVELOPMENT REPORT
         1979. New York: Published for the
         World Bank by Oxford University Press,
         1979. ix,188 p. ISBN 0-19-502637-3;
         0-19-502638-1 (paper)

         Covers development prospects,
         international policy issues, structural
         change, and individual country's
         development experience. Presents 24
         tables of development indicators.

498.   International Bank for Reconstruction and
         Development. WORLD DEVELOPMENT REPORT
         1980. Washington, D. C.: 1980.
         viii,166 p. ISBN 0-19-502833-3;
         0-19-502834-1 (paper)

         Discusses economic policies,
         adjustment and growth, poverty and human
         development.

499.   International Bank for Reconstruction and
         Development. WORLD DEVELOPMENT REPORT
         1981. New York: Published for the
         World Bank by Oxford University Press,
         1981. viii,192 p. ISBN 0-19-502997-6;
         0-19-502998-4 (paper)

         Examines national and international
         development, and analyzes national
         adjustments. Presents social and
         economic aspects of development.

500.   International Bank for Reconstruction and
         Development. WORLD DEVELOPMENT REPORT
         1982. New York: Published for the
         World Bank by Oxford University Press,
         1982. x,172 p. ISBN 0-19-503224-1;
         0-19-503225-X (paper)

              Presents international development
         trends. Examines agriculture and
         development. Presents 25 tables and 5
         maps.

501.   International Bank for Reconstruction and
         Development. WORLD DEVELOPMENT REPORT
         1983. New York: Published for the
         World Bank by Oxford University Press,
         1983. x,214 p. ISBN 0-19-520431-X;
         0-19-520432-8 (paper)

              Focuses on world economic trends
         and management aspects in development.
         Presents 27 tables and 5 maps on social
         and economics aspects.

502.   International Bank for Reconstruction and
         Development. WORLD DEVELOPMENT REPORT
         1984. New York: Published for the
         World Bank by Oxford University Press,
         1984. xi,286 p. ISBN 0-19-520459-X;
         0-19-520460-3 (paper)

              Assesses population change and its
         links with development. Reviews global
         economic development.

503.   International Bank for Reconstruction and
         Development. WORLD DEVELOPMENT REPORT
         1985. New York: Published for the
         World Bank by Oxford University Press,
         1985. xii,243 p. ISBN 0-19-520481-6;
         0-19-520482-4 (paper)

Focuses on international capital and its impact on economic development. Highlights development in Sub-Saharan Africa.

504.   International Bank for Reconstruction and Development. WORLD DEVELOPMENT REPORT 1986. New York: Published for the World Bank by Oxford University Press, 1986. x,256 p. ISBN 0-19-520517-0; 0-19-520518-9 (paper)

Examines trade and pricing policies in world agriculture, and prospects for sustained growth.

505.   International Bank for Reconstruction and Development. WORLD DEVELOPMENT REPORT 1987. New York: Published for the World Bank by Oxford University Press, 1987. xii,285 p. ISBN 0-19-520562-6; 0-19-520563-4 (paper)

Reviews recent trends in world economy and implications for future prospect of development. Examines role of foreign trade.

506.   International Bank for Reconstruction and Development. WORLD DEVELOPMENT REPORT 1988/89. New York: Published for the World Bank by Oxford University Press, 1988. xii,307 p. ISBN 0-19-520649-5; 0-19-5206650-9 (paper)

Reviews economic trends in world economy noting: (1) industrial countries need to reduce external payment imbalances, (2) developing countries need to persevere in restructuring their domestic economic policies, and (3) resource transfers must be trimmed to encourage growth and investment.

507.   International Bank for Reconstruction and
        Development. WORLD DEVELOPMENT REPORT
        1989. New York: Published for the
        World Bank by Oxford University Press,
        1989. xii,251 p. ISBN 0-19-520784-4;
        0-19-520788-2 (paper)

            Provides selected social and
        economic data for over 100 countries.
        Reviews trends in world economy.
        Forecasts implications for developing
        countries (economic growth, decline in
        foreign capital, and inflows approach to
        private sector).

508.   International Bank for Reconstruction and
        Development. WORLD ECONOMIC AND SOCIAL
        INDICATORS. Washington, D.C.: 1977- .
        monthly *

509.   International Bank for Reconstruction and
        Development. WORLD ENVIRONMENT AND THE
        WORLD BANK. [Washington, D.C.:] 1972.
        14 p. LCCN 74-185051 *

510.   International Bank for Reconstruction and
        Development. WORLD TABLES, 2ND ED.,
        1980 -- FROM THE DATA FILES OF THE WORLD
        BANK. Baltimore, MD: Published for the
        World Bank by Johns Hopkins University
        Press, 1980. vii,474 p.
        ISBN 0-8213-2389-7; 0-8018-2390-0
        (paper) LCCN 79-3649

            Presents economic, demographic and
        social data used in analysis of economic
        and social conditions. Updated by
        Entries 511 and 512.

511. International Bank for Reconstruction and
      Development. WORLD TABLES, 3RD ED.,
      FROM THE DATA FILES OF THE WORLD BANK,
      Vol. 1 -- ECONOMIC DATA. Baltimore, MD:
      Published for the World Bank by Johns
      Hopkins University Press, 1983.
      xxxv,585 p. ISBN 0-8213-3200-4;
      0-8213-3201-2 (paper) LCCN 83-25609

      Presents time-series of basic
      economic variables for 140 countries and
      country groups. Updates Entry 510. See
      also Entry 512.

512. International Bank for Reconstruction and
      Development. WORLD TABLES, 3RD ED.:
      FROM THE DATA FILES OF THE WORLD BANK,
      Vol. 2 -- SOCIAL DATA. Baltimore, MD:
      Published for the World Bank by Johns
      Hopkins University Press, 1983.
      xxi,161 p. ISBN 0-8213-3202-0;
      0-8213-3203-9 (paper) LCCN 83-25609

      Presents time series data for
      social variables. Updates Entry 510.
      See also Entries 454, and 511.

513. International Bank for Reconstruction and
      Development. WORLD TABLES 1987: FROM
      THE DATA FILES OF THE WORLD BANK, 4th
      ed. Baltimore, MD: Published for the
      World Bank and IFC by Johns Hopkins
      University Press, 1988. 521 p.
      ISBN 0-8213-1035-6 LCCN 88-5596

      Provides core economic indicators
      used to compile global aggregates in
      WORLD DEVELOPMENT REPORT. Omits
      detailed socio-economic indicators from
      earlier editions. See also Entries 511,
      and 512.

514.   International Bank for Reconstruction and
        Development. WORLD TABLES 1988-89: FROM
        THE DATA FILES OF THE WORLD BANK.
        Baltimore, MD: Published for the World
        Bank by Johns Hopkins University Press,
        1989. iv,653 p. ISBN 0-8018-3855-X

            Updates the indicators from the
        WORLD TABLES 1987 (Entry 513). Covers
        137 member countries and Switzerland by
        providing time series to measure tends.

515.   International Bank for Reconstruction and
        Development. YOUNG PROFESSIONALS
        PROGRAM OF THE WORLD BANK GROUP.
        Washington, D.C.: 1975. 26 p.

            Explains Young Professional Program
        (qualifications and recent recruits).
        Offers thumbnail sketch of IFC, IBRD,
        ICSID, and IDA.

516.   International Bank for Reconstruction and
        Development. YUGOSLAVIA: ADJUSTMENT
        POLICY AND DEVELOPMENT PERSPECTIVES
        (WORLD BANK COUNTRY STUDY). Baltimore,
        MD: 1983. xiv,435 p. ISBN 0-8213-0189-6
        LCCN 83-6551

            Reviews Yugoslavia during 1970s in
        light of high energy prices, recession,
        and shifts in international capital
        flow. Focuses on 1976-80 adjustment
        efforts in agriculture and industry.

517.   International Bank for Reconstruction and
        Development. YUGOSLAVIA: DEVELOPMENT
        WITH DECENTRALIZATION -- REPORT OF A
        MISSION SENT TO YUGOSLAVIA BY THE WORLD
        BANK. Baltimore, MD: Published for the
        World Bank by Johns Hopkins Press, 1975.
        490 p. ISBN 0-8018-1702-1;
        0-8018-1715-3 (paper) LCCN 74-24404

Discusses the development problems
and prospects. Identifies the sectors of
potential growth. Based on findings of
1972 economic mission led by V. Dubey.

518.   International Bank for Reconstruction and
Development, and International
Development Association. RECENT
ECONOMIC TRENDS - CEYLON. Ceylon:
Ministry of Planning and Economic
Affairs, 1966. 95 p.

Prepared by E. Bevan Waide,
describes economic condition in Ceylon
during 1964-1965.

519.   International Bank for Reconstruction and
Development, and International
Development Association. FOREIGN
EXCHANGE PROBLEM OF CEYLON. Ceylon:
Ministry of Planning and Economic
Affairs, 1966. 82 p.

Discusses causes of foreign
exchange crisis in Ceylon. Examines
possible actions in order to correct it.

520.   International Bank for Reconstruction and
Development, and International
Development Association. WORLD BANK AND
IDA IN ASIA. Washington, D.C.: 1962.
54 p.

Summarizes work in Asia countries
(from Japan, to the Philippines, to
Pakistan) which comprises 50% of all IDA
credits.

521.   International Bank for Reconstruction and
        Development, and International
        Development Association. WORLD BANK AND
        IDA IN THE AMERICAS: A SUMMARY OF
        ACTIVITIES. Washington, D.C.: 1962.
        103 p. *

        See also Entries 471, 485, and 490.

522.   International Bank for Reconstruction and
        Development, and International Finance
        Corporation. WORLD BANK AND
        INTERNATIONAL FINANCE CORPORATION.
        Washington, D.C.: 1983. 65 p.

        Describes lending criteria,
        IBRD-IFC complementarity, ownership,
        types of projects assisted, project
        cycle, finances, organization and
        management.

523.   International Bank for Reconstruction and
        Development, International Development
        Association, and International Finance
        Corporation. ROLE OF NATIONAL
        DEVELOPMENT FINANCE COMPANIES IN
        INDUSTRIAL DEVELOPMENT (Information
        Paper). Washington, D.C.: n.d. 22 p.

        Prepared for International
        Symposium on Industrial Development
        (UNIDO: Athens, December 1967). Reviews
        experience of World Bank Group with
        development finance companies,
        especially those created recently.

524.   International Bank for Reconstruction and
        Development, International Development
        Association, and International Finance
        Corporation. SUMMARY PROCEEDINGS:
        ANNUAL MEETINGS OF THE BOARDS OF
        GOVERNORS. Washington, D.C.: 1946- .

Annual meetings of IDA and IFC are held at the same time as IBRD annual meetings. These proceedings record the statements by the Governors on IBRD, IDA, and IFC activities. See also Entries 379, and 380.

525.   Ipsen, Erik. "Can the Baker Plan Work?" INSTITUTIONAL INVESTOR, vol. 19 (December 1985): 278-280+. *

Comments on the international debt crisis and Baker's plan for changing it.

526.   Ipsen, Erik. "Great $75 Billion Giveaway?" INSTITUTIONAL INVESTOR, INTERNATIONAL ED. (September 1988): 84-94. *

527.   "It's the World Bank." THE ECONOMIST, vol. 267 (April 22, 1978): 19-20.

Emphasizes IBRD is a "world" bank, not an US bank. Discusses US politics (especially the current Congress), and its role in trying to influence World Bank loan operations.

528.   "Japan and the World Bank: Voter Power." THE ECONOMIST, vol. 299 (April 19, 1986): 82,87.

Japan seeks to increase its voting power in the Bank. Argues that Japan's votes do not adequately reflect its IDA contributions.

529.   Javetski, Bill, Steve Baker, and Frank J. Comes. "Conable's Year of Living Dangerously at the World Bank." BUSINESS WEEK (July 20, 1987): 118-119.

Describes Conable's first year as Bank president and the changes he made

(tightening controls, reduction of
staff, etc.). He is generally given
high marks for putting the Bank back on
a more businesslike footing.

530.   "Jaw Jaw: Rich Countries and Poor." THE
ECONOMIST, vol. 260 (September 18,
1976): 113.

Discusses the dialogue between poor
and rich countries. Notes the apparent
deadlock that will probably be delayed
until after the US elections.

531.   Jawed, Tufail. "World Bank and the Indus
Basin Dispute (1)." PAKISTAN HORIZON,
vol. 18, no. 3 (3rd Quarter 1965):
226-237.

In addition to financing
reconstruction, the Bank offers to act
as a mediator in international economic
disputes among its member countries.
Describes the background to the Indus
Basin dispute involving Pakistan and
India. See also Entries 532, and 533.

532.   Jawed, Tufail. "World Bank and the Indus
Basin Dispute (2)." PAKISTAN HORIZON,
vol. 19, no. 1 (1st Quarter 1966):
34-44.

Discusses the mediation by the Bank
in the Indus Basin dispute. See also
Entries 531, and 533.

533.   Jawed, Tufail. "World Bank and the Indus
Basin Dispute (3)." PAKISTAN HORIZON,
vol. 19, no. 2 (2nd Quarter 1966):
133-142.

Describes the Indus Waters Treaty.
See also Entries 531, and 532.

534.   Jaycox, Edward V.K.   "Africa: Development
        Challenges and the World Bank's
        Response."   FINANCE AND DEVELOPMENT,
        vol. 23 (March 1986): 21-22.

            Excerpts Jaycox's speech (World
        Bank's Vice President of Eastern and
        Southern Africa Region) at Woodrow
        Wilson International Center for
        Scholars, the Smithsonian Institution
        (August 1985).   Discusses how 34
        countries have been afflicted by
        drought, and emergency assistance is not
        enough. Describes the Special Facility
        for Sub-Saharan Africa and other World
        Bank programs.

535.   Jessup, Francesca.   ABSTRACTS OF CURRENT
        STUDIES 1984: WORLD BANK RESEARCH
        PROGRAM.   Washington, D.C.: World Bank,
        1984. *

            Summarizes current research.   See
        also Entry 377.

536.   Jha, L.K.   "Do Outward-oriented Policies
        Really Favor Growth?"   FINANCE AND
        DEVELOPMENT, vol. 24 (December 1987):
        44-46.

            Argues different conclusions from
        those presented can be drawn from the
        WORLD DEVELOPMENT REPORT 1987 data
        (Entry 505), especially in the area of
        trade orientation.   Presents a rejoinder
        by Sarath Rajapatirana, leader of the
        WORLD DEVELOPMENT REPORT team.

537.   Jimenez, Emmanuel. PRICING POLICY IN THE
        SOCIAL SECTORS: COST RECOVERY FOR
        EDUCATION AND HEALTH IN DEVELOPING
        COUNTRIES. Baltimore, MD: Published for
        the World Bank by Johns Hopkins
        University Press, 1987.
        ISBN 0-8018-3501-1 LCCN 86-27590

            Evaluates pricing policy in
        providing social services. Education
        and health are primary investments in
        LDCs. Based on paper presented at 1984
        conference. Discusses efficiency,
        equity in price policy, and feasibility
        of policy change.

538.   Johnson, Christopher. "Capital Markets: In
        Search of Max Headroom." BANKER,
        vol. 137, no. 741 (November 1987):
        117-118.

            Discusses the current balance and
        proposed funding increase for the World
        Bank. Comments that problems of delayed
        repayments are causing the Bank to seek
        a General Capital Increase to create a
        margin of safety. See also Entry 268.

539.   Johnson, Christopher. "Fleshing Out the
        Baker Plan for Third World Debt."
        BANKER, vol. 135 (December 1985):
        15-16+. *

540.   Johnson, Lyndon B. "World Bank and
        International Monetary Fund." WEEKLY
        COMPILATION OF PRESIDENTIAL DOCUMENTS,
        vol. 4 (October 7, 1968): 1425-1419.

            US President Johnson's address
        before the Board of Governors meeting in
        Washington, D.C. (September 1968).
        Calls on expansion of activities for

African Development Bank, Asian
Development Bank, and IADB. Urges
cooperation and strengthening of
international financial organizations.

541.   Johnston, Brian. "New Direction of World
         Bank Policy." JOURNAL OF SOCIAL AND
         POLITICAL STUDIES, vol. 3, no. 4 (Winter
         1978): 347-352.

              Points out that purpose and
         direction of Bank has changed over 30
         years. Initially loans were made for
         reconstruction of Europe, but the focus
         changed to assistance to underdeveloped
         countries. Now the focus is on more
         support for the poor within those LDCs.

542.   Joint Library of International Monetary Fund,
         and International Bank for
         Reconstruction and Development. CURRENT
         LIST OF PERIODICALS RECEIVED.
         Washington, D.C.: 1976. *

543.   Joint Library of International Monetary Fund,
         and International Bank for
         Reconstruction and Development.
         DEVELOPING AREAS: A CLASSIFIED
         BIBLIOGRAPHY OF THE JOINT BANK-FUND
         LIBRARY. Boston: G. K. Hall, 1976.
         3 vol. ISBN 0-8161-0023-3

              Arranged by country and by Dewey
         classification numbers, shelflist
         represents 40% of Joint Bank-Fund
         Library collection.

544.   Joint Library of International Monetary Fund,
         and International Bank for
         Reconstruction and Development.
         ECONOMICS AND FINANCE: INDEX TO
         PERIODICAL ARTICLES, 1947-1971, compiled
         by the staff of the Joint Bank-Fund
         Library. Washington, D.C.

Arranged by main entry, presents
subject access to articles indexed by
library staff. See also Entry 545.

545.   Joint Library of International Monetary Fund,
        and International Bank for
        Reconstruction and Development.
        ECONOMICS AND FINANCE: INDEX TO
        PERIODICAL ARTICLES, 1ST-2ND SUPPLEMENT:
        1972/74-1975/77, compiled by the staff
        of the Joint Library. Washington, D.C.:
        1976-1979, 2 v. x,423 p.
        ISBN 0-8161-1064-6

        Divided into theoretical and
        general literature, and geographic
        regions. Presents classification
        schedule. Arranged alphabetically by
        main entry. Actually a copy of their
        card catalog of articles indexed by the
        staff. See also Entry 544.

546.   Joint Library of International Monetary Fund,
        and International Bank for
        Reconstruction and Development. LIST OF
        PERIODICAL ARTICLES, 1947- .
        Washington, D.C.: 1947- .

        Indexes working papers, newspaper
        articles and periodical articles
        received by the Joint Library. Arranged
        by subject and country.

547.   Joint Library of International Monetary Fund,
        and International Bank for
        Reconstruction and Development. LIST OF
        RECENT ADDITIONS, 1947- . Washington,
        D.C.: 1947- .

        Items added to the Joint Library.
        Arranged by reference works, general
        works, geographic regions, and then by
        Library of Congress classification.

548.   Joint Ministerial Committee of the Boards of
        Governors of the World Bank and the
        International Fund on the Transfers of
        Real Resources to Developing Counties
        (Development Committee). DEVELOPMENT
        COMMITTEE: ITS FIRST TEN YEARS 1974-1984
        (Development Committee, 1). Washington,
        D.C.: 1984. v,79 p.

            Describes the Development
        Committee's origins, achievements, and
        special features.

549.   Joint Ministerial Committee of the Boards of
        Governors of the World Bank and the
        International Fund on the Transfers of
        Real Resources to Developing Counties
        (Development Committee). TWELFTH ANNUAL
        REPORT OF THE DEVELOPMENT COMMITTEE,
        JULY 1985-JUNE 1986 (Development
        Committee Publication, 12). Washington,
        D.C.: 1987. 89 p. ISBN 0-8213-0837-8

            Discusses current development
        issues. Reports Development Committee's
        activities to the Board of Governors of
        the World Bank and IMF (September 1986).

550.   Joyce, Christopher. "World Bank Gives Green
        Light to Ecology." NEW SCIENTIST,
        vol. 114 (May 14, 1987): 26.

            Barber Conable, World Bank
        President, agrees to set up
        environmental watch, and to create
        ecological awareness in the World Bank
        with a country-by-country assessment of
        developing nations' environments.

551.   Kakonen, J. "World Bank: a Bridgehead of
        Imperialism." INST. RESEARCH ON PEACE
        AND VIOLENCE, vol. 5, no. 3 (1975):
        150-164. *

552.   Kamaluddin, S. "Second Thoughts on Aid."
        FAR EASTERN ECONOMIC REVIEW, vol. 108,
        no. 19 (May 2, 1980): 47-48.

            World Bank is ready to give more
        help to Bangladesh more, now that it has
        made improvements in the disbursement of
        foreign aid. Project implementation,
        especially in food grain production,
        appears to have helped changed World
        Bank President Robert McNamara's mind.

553.   Kamarck, A.M. "Allocation of Aid by the
        World Bank Group." FINANCE AND
        DEVELOPMENT, vol. 9, no. 3 (September
        1972): 22-24.

            Examines aid to LDCs over past ten
        years and the increase in amount, as
        well as disbursement of funds.
        Describes complex nature of decision
        making involved in allocating funds.

554.   Kamarck, Andrew Martin. TROPICS AND
        ECONOMIC DEVELOPMENT: A PROVOCATIVE
        INQUIRY INTO THE POVERTY OF NATIONS.
        Baltimore, MD: Published for the World
        Bank by Johns Hopkins University Press,
        1976. 113 p. ISBN 0-8018-1891-5;
        0-8018-1903-2 (paper) LCCN 76-17242

            Argues that developing nations in
        the tropics need more funds to achieve
        similar results as industrialized
        nations in the northern climate. Both
        the climate and the environment should
        be considered in economic development.

555.   Kamarck, Andrew M. "World Bank Development:
        A Personal Perspective." FINANCE AND
        DEVELOPMENT (DECEMBER 1984): 18-20.

Reflects on Bank's efforts to promote development and evolution of lending, as well as its impact on future lending.

556.   Karasz, A.   "World Bank and the Third World." REVIEW OF POLITICS, vol. 32, no. 4 (October 1970): 476-489.

Comments on origins of foreign aid, and present situation at the World Bank. Makes suggestions for improving procedures and enlarging income sources. Discusses global strategy for international cooperation proposed in PARTNERS IN DEVELOPMENT (Entry 226).

557.   Kavalsky, Basil.   "Reviewing Public Investment Programs."   FINANCE AND DEVELOPMENT, vol. 23 (March 1986): 37-40.

Governments under pressure to reduce public expenditures turn to the World Bank for investment advice.   The Bank assists government in preparing and revising their public investment programs.

558.   Kaye, Lincoln.   "Harsh Medicine Prescribed for a Big Borrower."   FAR EASTERN ECONOMIC REVIEW, vol. 138, no. 40 (October 1, 1987): 72-73.

Biggest customer for World Bank credit is India, but the amount available will decrease (20% of IDA credit authorization in 1987, down from 40% from 1970s).   World Bank warns India to reduced its commercial lending, and to slash the average import tariff in half (two of the 10 recommendations).

559.   Keith, J.R. "World Bank Director."
        CANADIAN BUSINESS (December 1946):
        70-71+. *

           Describes Robert Bryce, World
        Bank's Canadian director.

560.   King, Benjamin B. NOTES ON THE MECHANICS OF
        GROWTH AND DEBT (World Bank Staff
        Occasional Paper, 6). Baltimore, MD:
        Distributed for the World Bank by Johns
        Hopkins Press, 1968. x,59 p.

           Explores the flow of capital into a
        country and its effect on the economy's
        growth, focusing on the savings gap.

561.   Knight, Peter T., Michael Crowe, and Alan H.
        Gelb. BRAZIL: FINANCIAL SYSTEMS REVIEW.
        Washington, D.C.: World Bank, 1984.

           Financial reform was key to
        Brazil's stabilization during the 1960s,
        but growth slowed by the mid-1970s.
        Analyzes financial system up to 1978.
        Concludes with policy recommendations
        (remove credit subsidies, phase out
        agricultural controls, etc.).

562.   Kolko, Gabriel. "United States Effort to
        Mobilize World Bank Aid to Saigon."
        JOURNAL OF CONTEMPORARY ASIA, vol. 5,
        no. 1 (1975): 42-52.

           Discusses how the US has tried
        using US-dominated World Bank and Asian
        Development Bank for planning in
        Vietnam. Multilateral aid via these
        agencies was desirable because of the
        economic consequences of US involvement
        in the Vietnam war. Congressional
        hostility is increasing, and the Saigon
        economy is disintegrating.

563.   Kolle, Hans Martin. "Assessing the World
         Bank: A Sweet Deal for the United
         States." NEW YORK TIMES (September 20,
         1987): F2. *

564.   Kolle, Hans Martin. "Changing Course on the
         Environment: the World Bank Reacts to
         Its Critics." D & C: DEVELOPMENT AND
         COOPERATION (GERMANY), no. 5 (1988):
         14-16.

             Argues the World Bank should be
         grateful to critics of environmental
         disasters caused by the Bank's projects
         in India's river basin, Botswana,
         Nigeria, Brazil, and Indonesia.
         Criticism has led to a review of the
         Bank's environmental policy. World Bank
         is moving towards a more environment-
         friendly economic reforms.

565.   Kravis, Irving B., Alan Heston, and Robert
         Summers. INTERNATIONAL COMPARISONS OF
         REAL PRODUCT AND PURCHASING POWER (UN
         International Comparison Project, Phase
         2), produced by the UN Statistical
         Office. Baltimore, MD: Published for
         the World Bank, and by Johns Hopkins
         University Press, 1978. 264 p.
         ISBN 0-8018-2019-7; 0-8018-2020-0
         (paper)   LCCN 77-17251

             UN program to develop reliable
         system to estimate GDP among countries.
         Presents comparison of real GDP and
         purchasing power of currency. Phase 2
         was joint responsibility of World Bank,
         UN, and University of Pennsylvania. See
         also Entry 566.

566.   Kravis, Irving B., Zoltan Kenessey, Alan
        Heston, and Robert Summers. SYSTEM OF
        INTERNATIONAL COMPARISONS OF GROSS
        PRODUCT AND PURCHASING POWER (UN
        International Comparison Project: Phase
        1), produced by the UN Statistical
        Office, the World Bank, and the
        University of Pennsylvania International
        Comparison Unit. Baltimore, MD:
        Published for the World Bank by Johns
        Hopkins Press, 1975. xi,294 p.
        ISBN 0-8018-1606-8; 0-8018-1609-6
        (paper) LCCN 73-19352

        Presents methodology for
        establishing a system of international
        comparisons that could be applied to
        various countries. Purpose was to
        develop methods for international,
        multilateral and bilateral comparisons.
        See Entry 565.

567.   Kuczynski, Pedro-Pablo. "Teller-vision at
        the World Bank." INTERNATIONAL ECONOMY,
        vol. 2 (November-December 1988): 40-45.*

568.   "Kuwaitis Blaze a Trail -- Again." BANKER,
        vol. 137 (August 1987): 74.   *

569.   Lahart, K. "Last Resort." FINANCIAL WORLD,
        vol. 157, no. 13 (June 14, 1988): 18-20.

        Interviews the Bank's chief
        financial officer, Ernest Stern, on the
        political aspects of the World Bank and
        development financing. Describes fund
        rating and other financial aspects of
        managing a multilateral development
        organization.

142

570.   Lal, Deepak. METHODS OF PROJECT ANALYSIS; A
       REVIEW. Baltimore, MD: Published for
       the World Bank by Johns Hopkins Press,
       1974. *

571.   Lal, Deepak, and Martin Wolf. STAGFLATION,
       SAVINGS, & THE STATE PERSPECTIVES ON THE
       GLOBAL ECONOMY. New York: Published for
       the World Bank by Oxford University
       Press, 1986. *

572.   Lanyi, Anthony. "Issues in Capital Flows to
       Developing Countries." FINANCE AND
       DEVELOPMENT, vol. 24 (September 1987):
       27-30.

            Describes supply and demand for
       external finance (public and private
       sector, donor coordination, etc.) in the
       1980s. Based on paper presented at
       Netherlands Ministry of Development
       Cooperation-sponsored conference on
       North-South cooperation.

573.   Lawrence, Richard. "More Help Likely for
       Debtor Nations." JOURNAL OF COMMERCE
       (April 18, 1988): 3a. *

574.   Lawrence, Richard. "World Bank Urges Bold
       Moves to Cope With Third World Debt."
       JOURNAL OF COMMERCE (January 19, 1988):
       3a. *

575.   Lee, James A. ENVIRONMENT, PUBLIC HEALTH,
       AND HUMAN ECOLOGY: CONSIDERATIONS FOR
       ECONOMIC DEVELOPMENT. Baltimore, MD:
       Published for the World Bank by Johns
       Hopkins University Press, 1985.
       ISBN 0-8018-2911-9 LCCN 82-6574

            Focuses on sustainable development.
       Describes Bank policy. Presents
       considerations for detection and

assessment of human, ecological, and environmental effects in development.

576. Lee, James A. "World Bank." ENVIRONMENT, vol. 26 (December 1984): 2-4.

James Lee, Director of the Bank's Office of Environmental and Social Affairs, describes World Bank experience that environment and economic development can occur as interdependent and supportive objectives.

577. Lee, James, and Robert Goodland. "Economic Development and the Environment." FINANCE AND DEVELOPMENT, vol. 23 (December 1986): 36-39.

Discusses how management of the environment is essential to "sustainable" development. Describes the Bank's environment policy and various projects.

578. Lee, P. "World Bank Gets the Accolade." EUROMONEY (September 1987): 1129+. *

579. Lee, Peter. "Borrower of the Year: World Bank Gets the Accolade." EUROMONEY (September 1987): 129-37. *

580. Leff, Nathaniel H. DISJUNCTION BETWEEN POLICY RESEARCH AND PRACTICE (First Boston Series of Money, Economics and Finance, FB-85-02). New York, NY: Graduate School of Business, Columbia University, 1985. *

Uses World Bank's social benefit-cost analysis for investment choices, as the basis for analyzing the causes of disjunction between policy research and practice.

581.   Leff, Nathaniel H.   "Use of Policy-Science
        Tools for Decision-Making in the Public
        Sector: Social Benefit-Cost Analysis in
        the World Bank."   KYKLOS, vol. 38, no. 1
        (1985): 60-76.

            Focuses on general topic of
        adoption and utilization. Examines the
        World Bank's use of social benefit-cost
        analysis for selecting for investment in
        LDCs as an example. Raises questions
        concerning the relationship between
        political science and decision making in
        the public sector.

582.   Lele, Uma J.   DESIGN OF RURAL DEVELOPMENT:
        LESSONS FROM AFRICA.   Baltimore, MD:
        Published for the World Bank by Johns
        Hopkins University Press, 1975.
        xiii,246 p.   ISBN 0-8018-1756-0;
        0-8018-1769-2 (paper)   LCCN 76-4934

            Studies 17 rural development
        projects in Sub-Saharan Africa to
        identify the basic constraints and
        potential. Analyzes the efficiency of
        policies on programs. Draws on them to
        aid planning for future programs.

583.   Lemarchand, Rene.   WORLD BANK IN RWANDA.
        Bloomington, IN: 1982.   ii,77 p.
        ISBN 0-941934-39-X   LCCN 82-70681   *

584.   Lepkowski, Wil.   "World Bank May Eliminate
        its Technology Advisory Function."
        CHEMICAL & ENGINEERING NEWS, vol. 62
        (August 6, 1984): 15-17.   *

585.   Leslie, Winsome J.   WORLD BANK AND STRUCTURAL
        TRANSFORMATION IN DEVELOPING COUNTRIES:
        THE CASE OF ZAIRE.   Boulder, CO: L.
        Reinner, 1987.   208 p.
        ISBN 1-55587-036-8   *

Analyzes effectiveness of
assistance in Zaire since 1975.
Examines how political factors play a
role in structural reform.

586.   Levitsky, Jacob. WORLD BANK LENDING TO SMALL
        ENTERPRISES. Washington, D.C.: World
        Bank, 1986. viii,53 p.
        ISBN 0-8213-0814-9 LCCN 86-15790 *

587.   Lewis, John P., and Valeriana Kallab (eds.).
        DEVELOPMENT STRATEGIES RECONSIDERED.
        New Brunswick, NJ: Transaction Books,
        1986. 208 p. ISBN 0-88738-044-1;
        0-88855-991-4 (paper) *

        Proposes reconsideration of goals
        of equity, growth, and adjustment,
        especially in large low-income
        countries.

588.   Lewis, John P. and Ishan Kapur. WORLD BANK
        GROUP, MULTILATERAL AID, AND THE 1970S.
        Lexington, MA: D.C. Heath, 1973. 168 p.
        ISBN 0-669-90555-0 LCCN 73-10365

        Based on 1971 seminar at Princeton.
        Covers formal structure, lending terms,
        debt, and relationships with other
        multilateral agencies.

589.   Lindemann, Terrance L. "Evaluating the
        Depository Library System of the World
        Bank." AREAS OF COOPERATION IN LIBRARY
        DEVELOPMENT IN ASIAN AND PACIFIC REGIONS
        by Chinese-American Libraries
        Association, 1985. p. 28-32.
        ISBN 0-930691-00-8 LCCN 84-71808

        Presented at 1983 joint program of
        Asian/Pacific American Librarians
        Association, and Chinese-American

Libraries Association. Describes World
Bank Depository Library Program.
Surveys depository libraries in 1982 to
identify inactive depositories.

590.   Linn, Johannes F. CITIES IN THE DEVELOPING
WORLD: POLICIES FOR THEIR EQUITABLE AND
EFFICIENT GROWTH. New York: Published
for the World Bank by Oxford University
Press, 1983. ISBN 0-19-520382-8;
0-19-520383-6 (paper) LCCN 82-22401

Background paper for WORLD
DEVELOPMENT REPORT 1979 (Entry 497).
Discusses problems of adapting to growth
in cities, as well as the policies to
increasing efficiency and equity of
urban development. Evaluates policies
on pricing, taxation, and public
investment, focusing on urbanization
policies at the municipal level.

591.   Linn, Johannes F. ECONOMIC AND SOCIAL
ANALYSIS OF PROJECTS IN THE WORLD BANK:
PRINCIPLES AND APPLICATIONS (Occasional
Paper, 1). Bradford, UK: Project
Planning Centre for Developing
Countries, University of Bradford, n.d.
23 p. ISBN 0-901945-32-3

Reviews past and present practice
in the economic analysis of Bank
projects. Reports on how the Bank has
implemented the new social project
analysis methodology proposed by L.
Squire and H. van de Tak.

592.   Lohman, P. H. "Investors in Bretton Woods:
Prospects of World Bank Loan Policy and
Repayment." TRUSTS AND ESTATES: THE
JOURNAL OF CAPITAL MANAGEMENT, vol. 79
(September 1944): 195-199. *

593.   Lonaeus, Hakan. "How the Bank Finances its
        Operations." FINANCE AND DEVELOPMENT,
        vol. 25 (September 1988): 40-42.

           Discusses how flexibility and
        financial management have aided the Bank
        to finance its lending operations from
        international financial markets.
        Describes how risk management and volume
        of lending affect funding.

594.   Ludlow, Nicholas H. "Future of Urban
        Transport Lending at the Development
        Banks." MASS TRANSIT, vol. 13
        (September 1986): 56+. *

595.   Ludlow, Nicholas H. "Urban Transit Winner in
        World Bank's 1987 Funding Plans." MASS
        TRANSIT, vol. 14 (January-February
        1987): 60+. *

596.   McDiarmid, Orville John. UNSKILLED LABOR FOR
        DEVELOPMENT: ITS ECONOMIC COST.
        Baltimore, MD: Published for the World
        Bank by Johns Hopkins University Press,
        1977. xii,206 p. ISBN 0-8018-1949-0;
        0-8018-1838-5 (paper) LCCN 76-47398

           Estimates the costs of using
        unskilled agricultural labor in economic
        development projects in Asia. Explores
        labor market in LDCs. Examines economic
        pricing of labor.

597.   McNamara, Robert S. MCNAMARA YEARS AT THE
        WORLD BANK: MAJOR POLICY ADDRESSES OF
        ROBERT S. MCNAMARA, 1968-1981.
        Baltimore, MD: Johns Hopkins University
        Press, 1981. xv,675 p.
        ISBN 0-8018-2685-3 LCCN 81-3743

           Presents McNamara's thoughts on
        development policy issues in support of

economic development and international
understanding. Commemorated his
retirement after 13 years as World Bank
President.

598.   McNamara, Robert S. ONE HUNDRED COUNTRIES,
        TWO BILLION PEOPLE: THE DIMENSIONS OF
        DEVELOPMENT. New York: Praeger, 1973.
        140 p. ISBN 0-269-28313 LCCN 73-165486

            Public statements on development
        policy presented as McNamara his second
        term as World Bank President. Sees a
        need to increase development assistance,
        citing population growth is aggravating
        malnutrition and unemployment.

599.   McWilliam, Michael. "World Bank and the
        Transfer in Kenya." JOURNAL OF
        COMMONWEALTH POLITICAL STUDIES, vol. 2,
        no. 2 (May 1964): 165-169.

            Describes Bank's economic survey
        mission to Kenya. Analyzes the report
        (Entry 399), its strengths, and its
        deficiencies. Concludes that, although
        the report produced a wealth of
        information, it was hindered by the
        brevity of the mission.

600.   Manning, Robert. "Hostility Still Runs
        Strong on the Hill." FAR EASTERN
        ECONOMIC REVIEW, vol. 138, no. 40
        (October 1, 1987): 67-69.

            Describes continuing debate in
        Congress over foreign aid, and the
        effect on IFC and MIGA (both promote
        free enterprise in Third World nations).

601.   Marion, Larry. "World Bank Enters the High-
        Tech Age." INSTITUTIONAL INVESTOR,
        vol. 20 (September 1986): 293-294.   *

602.   Marsh, David. "IMF and World Bank Urge
        Resources Shift to Developing Nations."
        FINANCIAL TIMES (September 24, 1988):
        1,24. *

603.   Mason, Edward S., and Robert E. Asher. WORLD
        BANK SINCE BRETTON WOODS. Washington,
        D.C.: Brookings Institution, 1973.
        915 p. ISBN 0-8157-5492-2 LCCN 73-1089

             Written in honor of the Bank's 25th
        anniversary. Presents a historical
        narrative and performance appraisal.
        Describes principal functions of the
        Bank Group, its relationship with IMF
        and other international organizations,
        as well as its future role as a
        development institution.

604.   Mathov, Mauricio J. "World Bank: Choosing a
        Path to Interconnection." DATA
        COMMUNICATIONS, vol. 15 (January 1986):
        119-127. *

605.   Mattern, William. "Burma Eyes the Aid
        Lifebelt." FAR EASTERN ECONOMIC REVIEW,
        vol. 94 (November 26, 1976): 44,47.

             Describes McNamara's recent visit
        to Burma, and how the Bank is seeking
        financing for development projects.
        Burma is trying to maintain a balance
        between its socialist economy and the
        World Bank's call for liberal reforms.

606.   Mauritius Ministry of Finance. LETTERS TO
        THE MANAGING DIRECTOR, INTERNATIONAL
        MONETARY FUND, AND TO THE PRESIDENT,
        INTERNATIONAL BANK FOR RECONSTRUCTION
        AND DEVELOPMENT. Port Louis, Mauritius:
        1983. ii,34 p. LCCN 85-980044 *

607.   May, Donald H.   "World Bank OK's $80 Million
        for Ecuador." WASHINGTON TIMES (May 7,
        1987): 9C. *

608.   May, Donald H.   "World Bank Reorganization
        Set." WASHINGTON TIMES (May 5, 1987):
        12C. *

609.   May, Donald H.   "World Bank Unveils
        Environment Protection Plan."
        WASHINGTON TIMES (May 6, 1987): 7C. *

610.   Measham, Anthony R.   "Health and Development:
        the Bank's Experience." FINANCE AND
        DEVELOPMENT, vol. 23 (December 1986):
        26-29.

            Describes the lessons learned from
        various health projects, pointing out
        that nutrition and health are important
        social indicators. Describes evolving
        role, future work, and past lending
        experiences.

611.   Meier, Gerald M. (ed.).   PRICING POLICY FOR
        DEVELOPMENT MANAGEMENT. Baltimore, MD:
        Published for EDI by Johns Hopkins
        University Press, 1983.
        ISBN 0-8018-2803-1; 0-8018-2804-X
        (paper) LCCN 82-7716

            Examines the role of prices in
        development process on three levels:
        theory, application, and policy.
        Discusses the elements in pricing
        systems, their functions, and the
        consequences of pricing policies.
        Concludes with the relationship of price
        analysis to project appraisal.

612.   Mendelsohn, M.S.   "Changes at the World
        Bank." BANKER, vol. 132, no. 678 (August
        1982): 35-41.   *

613.   Meyer, Eugene. "International Bank for
        Reconstruction and Development."
        PROCEEDINGS OF THE ACADEMY OF POLITICAL
        SCIENCE, vol. 22 (January 1957):
        148-156.

            World Bank President Meyer defines
        the functions of the World Bank,
        emphasizing that it is to stimulate
        private investment, not hinder it.
        Remarks that modernization of industrial
        technology leads to increased trade.

614.   Meyer, Eugene. "World Bank and U.S.-Canadian
        Cooperation." COMMERCIAL AND FINANCIAL
        CHRONICLE, vol. 165, no. 4560 (January
        16, 1947): 274,306-7.

            Presents his reasons for resigning
        as World Bank President (i.e., he was
        made president to get World Bank
        organized and operational). Explains
        lending policy and objectives, and cites
        US-Canada as a model of economic
        cooperation.

615.   Michaelis, A. "International Bank Activities
        in the Middle East." MIDDLE EASTERN
        AFFAIRS, vol. 8, no. 5 (May 1957):
        180-185. *

616.   Michalopoulos, Constantine. "World Bank
        Lending for Structural Adjustment."
        FINANCE AND DEVELOPMENT, vol. 24 (June
        1987): 7-10.

            Reviews World Bank support of
        reform efforts in member countries.
        Identifies five categories of Bank
        lending: specific investment loans,
        sector operations, structural adjustment
        loans, technical assistance, and
        emergency reconstruction loans.

617.   Mikkelsen, Randall. "Trade Bill Provision
        Threatens U.S. Participation in World
        Bank." JOURNAL OF COMMERCE (October 29,
        1987): 10A. *

618.   Miller, Morris. COPING IS NOT ENOUGH! THE
        INTERNATIONAL DEBT CRISIS, AND THE ROLES
        OF THE WORLD BANK AND THE INTERNATIONAL
        MONETARY FUND. Homewood, IL: Dow Jones-
        Irwin, 1986. xiii,268 p.
        ISBN 0-87094-933-0 LCCN 86-71358 *

            Former World Bank Executive
        Director Miller discusses the debt
        crisis in 1983 and 1984, and the role of
        the World Bank in the global debt
        situation. Discusses the roots of
        crisis, and proposes a new "Bretton
        Woods" system. Also discusses impact of
        US change from a creditor to debtor
        national, as well as the World Bank's
        prospects for the future.

619.   Miller, Sarah. "Re-assessing the Nuclear
        Bill." FAR EASTERN ECONOMIC REVIEW,
        vol. 99, no. 1 (January 6, 1978): 25.

            World Bank is encouraging LDCs to
        consider nuclear power, implying that
        funds will be available for these
        projects. But heavy capital is required
        and the advantages are questionable.
        Calls for consideration of appropriate
        technology alternatives.

620.   Milne, Roger. "World Bank Reforms Its Green
        Policies." NEW SCIENTIST, vol. 114
        (April 9, 1987): 20.

            Describes how environmental aspects
        are being considered. References a
        paper by Jeremy Warford which stresses
        environment plays a major role in

economic growth. Countries with World Bank financing should be required to manage their natural resources, and to include the environmental aspect in their development programs.

621.   Mirza, Aziz. "Developing Countries and the International Financial Institutions." AFRO-ASIAN ECONOMIC REVIEW, vol. 4, no. 38 (November 1962): 1-8.

Describes how LDCs are disappointed with 1962 annual meeting of Board of Governors, because they keep hoping that measures will be adopted to alleviate their problems. Discusses the 1961 GATT report on international trade (which stated trade has slowed dramatically), and how the report should have impacted the Board of Governors. LDCs had expected IMF and IBRD to do a reappraisal in light of the GATT report.

622.   Mohan, Rakesh. URBAN ECONOMIC AND PLANNING MODELS: ASSESSING THE POTENTIAL FOR CITIES IN DEVELOPING COUNTRIES (World Bank Staff Occasional Paper, 25). Baltimore, MD: Published for the World Bank by Johns Hopkins University Press, 1979. 180 p. ISBN 0-8018-2141-X LCCN 78-8437

Surveys operational and analytic urban models to find suitable approaches for understanding cities in LDCs. Concludes that operational models are more useful than analytical models, which require large sets of data.

623.   "Money at a Price: Fund-Bank Meeting." ECONOMIC AND POLITICAL WEEKLY, vol. 22, no. 42/43 (October 17-24, 1987): 1774-5.

Reviews the September 1987 annual
IMF-IBRD meeting. Emphasizes the IMF's
role in structural adjustment facility
and Third World debt.

624.   Moock, Peter R., and Dean T. Jamison.
        "Educational Development in Sub-Saharan
        Africa: Prospects and Policy Options."
        FINANCE AND DEVELOPMENT (March 1988):
        22-24.

        Discusses experience in Africa with
        investment in educational programs 1960-
        1983 (adult literacy and primary school
        enrollment increased). But economic
        difficulties may lead to a reduction in
        education spending. Argues continued
        investment in education and training
        will yield economic returns.

625.   Moore, Frederick T. "World Bank and Its
        Economic Missions." REVIEW OF ECONOMICS
        AND STATISTICS, vol. 42, no. 1 (February
        1960): 81-93.

        Describes economic mission to 15
        countries. Claims the mission reports
        receive high marks for historical and
        descriptive summaries, but low marks for
        not being documents on which development
        programs can be based.

626.   Moore, Maureen. "World Bank Statistical
        Publications." GOVERNMENT PUBLICATIONS
        REVIEW, vol. 9 (1982): 185-188.

        Surveys the World Bank publications
        designed to provide statistical data.
        Describes Joint Library, and Debt
        Reporting System (specialized
        statistical reporting system used to
        collect data on external debt). Major
        statistical publications are summarized.

627. Moore, Mick. "Institutional Development, the World Bank, and India's New Agricultural Extension Programme." JOURNAL OF DEVELOPMENT STUDIES, vol. 20, no. 4 (July 1984): 303-317.

   States little or no change in quality of extension despite increased investment. Claims failures of previous extension systems were not analyzed. Criticizes new World Bank Training and Visit Program in India (agricultural extension).

628. Moran, Theodore H., et al. INVESTING IN DEVELOPMENT: NEW ROLES FOR PRIVATE CAPITAL? New Brunswick, NJ: Transaction Books, 1984. ISBN 0-88738-044-3; 0-88738-644-X (paper) *

   Assesses the impact of multinational corporate operations on development. Analyzes the link between Bank co-financing and international companies to reduce risk.

629. Morawetz, David. TWENTY-FIVE YEARS OF ECONOMIC DEVELOPMENT, 1950-1975. Baltimore, MD: Published for the World Bank by Johns Hopkins Press, 1977. xi,126 p. ISBN 0-8018-2134-7; 0-8018-2092-8 (paper)

   Examines objectives of development after 25 years. Concludes growth has happened but poverty still exists.

630. "More Bunce." THE ECONOMIST, vol. 268 (September 30, 1978): 82,86.

   Robert McNamara spoke about the "roaring tide to protectionism" at the 1978 annual meeting, and called for

doubling of capital while IMF increases
its total resources.

631.   Morris, James. ROAD TO HUDDERSFIELD: A
        JOURNEY TO FIVE CONTINENTS. New York:
        Pantheon Books, 1963. xi,235 p.
        LCCN 63-7350

            Commissioned by the Bank.
        Describes the Bank and its work in
        Ethiopia, Thailand, Italy, Colombia, and
        the Indus Basin. Focuses on the Bank
        under World Bank President E. Black.

632.   Morris, James. WORLD BANK: A PROSPECT.
        London: Faber & Faber, 1963. 195 p.
        LCCN 63-4762

            Comments by the World Bank
        (previously published in journals)
        commemorating the last month of Eugene
        Black's presidency.

633.   Mosley, Paul. "Politics of Economic
        Liberalization: USAID and the World Bank
        in Kenya: 1980-84." AFRICAN AFFAIRS,
        vol. 85, no. 338 (January 1986):
        107-119.

            Originally presented at 1984
        African Studies Association (UK)
        conference. Discusses the ACCELERATED
        DEVELOPMENT report (see Entry 378),
        which called for lifting of exchange
        rate and agricultural price controls.
        Points out how political opposition to
        conditions requested by World Bank and
        AID caused failure of plans.

634.   Mosley, Paul. "Politics of Evaluation: A
         Comparative Study of World Bank and
         UKODA Evaluation Procedures."
         DEVELOPMENT AND CHANGE, vol. 14, no. 4
         (October 1983): 593-608.

              Examines the evaluation procedures
         of UK Overseas Development
         Administration (UKODA) and World Bank,
         as well as how they differ, the criteria
         used, and the value in their evaluating
         aid projects. ODA tends to evaluate
         earlier in the project cycle.

635.   Mosley, Paul. CONDITIONALITY AS BARGAINING
         PROCESS: STRUCTURAL ADJUSTMENT LENDING
         1980-1986 (Essays in International
         Finance, 168). Princeton, NJ:
         International Finance Section, 1987.
         36 p. ISBN 0-88165-075-7 LCCN 87-25806

              Presents the history of supply-side
         conditionality, its effectiveness in
         inducing change, and implications for
         donor policies.

636.   Mossberg, Walter S. "World Bank is Seen
         Taking New Debt Role -- Agency is
         Expected to Push Measures Such as Swaps
         to Loosen Loan Burden." WALL STREET
         JOURNAL (September 29, 1987): 35.   *

637.   Mossberg, Walter S. "World Bank Chief Calls
         for Weighting New Approaches in Fighting
         Debt Crisis." WALL STREET JOURNAL
         (April 6, 1988): 11.   *

638.   Moulton, Anthony D. "On Concealed Dimensions
         of Third World Involvement in
         International Economic Organizations."
         INTERNATIONAL ORGANIZATIONS, vol. 32,
         no. 4 (Autumn 1978): 1019-35.

Based on research in India during early 1970s. Describes effect of membership on Third World nations in international organizations. Analyzes assistance-investment relationship, its influence on national policy, and benefits from participation for both multilateral development banks and LDCs.

639.   Nations, Richard. "Poor Inherit the Dearth." FAR EASTERN ECONOMIC REVIEW, vol. 123, no. 4 (January 26, 1984): 52-53.

As result of US refusal to pay more IDA funds, China and India will receive less in interest-free loans. European countries are adamant that the US share is at least 25%, and the US refuses to pick up the difference, causing an overall reduction in IDA's budget. Both countries will borrow on commercial markets to make up the deficit.

640.   Neikirk, William. "World Bank: Can It Overcome Conable's Debacle?" INTERNATIONAL ECONOMY (US), vol. 1 (October/November 1987): 28-35.   *

641.   Nelson, Joan M. "Diplomacy of Policy-Based Lending." BETWEEN TWO WORLDS: THE WORLD BANK'S NEXT DECADE, by R. Feinberg, et al. New Brunswick, NJ: Transaction Books, 1986. p. 67-88.

Emphasizes the Bank needs to stress sustained commitment to reform, rather than specific measures at certain times. See also Entry 283.

642.   "New Broom." BANKER, vol. 137 (January 1987): 13.   *

Discusses impact of Conable coming on board as new World Bank president.

643. Nicholl, Alexander. "Greater Effort Urged to Ease Debt Problem." FINANCIAL TIMES (September 18, 1987): 3. *

644. Nichols, Alan B. "Wastewater Treatment Meets Third World Needs." JOURNAL OF WATER POLLUTION CONTROL FEDERATION, vol. 59 (August 1987): 739-45. *

645. "Not Impossible Dream." THE ECONOMIST, vol. 268 (August 19, 1978): 63-65.

Shows progress made in LDCs and the problems still remaining. Based on WORLD DEVELOPMENT REPORT 1977 (Entry 496) which illustrated progress in agriculture, industry, foreign trade, and financial flows. Problems still exist in food supply, population growth, protectionism, and debt.

646. Nsekela, Amin J. "World Bank and the New International Economic Order." DEVELOPMENT DIALOGUE, vol. 1 (1977): 75-84. *

647. O'Brien, Catherine P.A. BIBLIOGRAPHY ON MONEY, BANKING AND FINANCE IN DEVELOPING COUNTRIES (Bibliography Series, 1). Washington, D.C.: Joint Bank-Fund Library, 1981. 196 p.

Covers books and articles on economic development, monetary and financial policies related to LDCs.

648. "One-Handed Clap for Washington (editorial)." REVIEW OF THE RIVER PLATE (ARGENTINA), no. 4373 (October 9, 1987): 278-279. *

649.   Oppenheim, V.H.   "Whose World Bank?"
        FOREIGN POLICY, vol. 19 (Summer 1975):
        99-108.

        Discusses the tense relationship
        between World Bank and OPEC nations.
        Describes how Bank depends on OPEC
        funding, and the relationship between
        which countries receive assistance and
        oil prices. Argues that in an effort to
        break a dependence on US, the World Bank
        has become more dependent on OPEC.

650.   Organization for Economic Co-operation and
        Development. EXTERNAL DEBT: DEFINITION,
        STATISTICAL COVERAGE AND METHODOLOGY --
        A REPORT BY AN INTERNATIONAL WORKING
        GROUP ON EXTERNAL DEBT STATISTICS OF THE
        WORLD BANK, IMF, BANK FOR INTERNATIONAL
        SETTLEMENTS, AND OECD. Paris: OECD,
        1988. 178 p. ISBN 92-64-13039-X

        Presents the background to the
        creation of this international working
        group, as well as its progress. An
        agreement on a definition of external
        debt is the most important step made.

651.   Owen, Henry. "... Or Development's Friend?"
        WALL STREET JOURNAL (August 29, 1988):
        14. *

652.   "Palestine is Not a Money Matter." THE
        ECONOMIST, vol. 276 (September 27,
        1980): 14-15.

        Discusses Palestine at 1980 Board
        of Governors meeting. Argues that IMF
        and IBRD should not be distracted (by
        PLO's presence) from agreeing to finance
        more development and provide more aid.

653.   Paul, James C.N. "World Bank's Agenda for
       the Crisis in Agriculture and Rural
       Development in Africa: An Introduction
       the Debate." AFRICAN STUDIES REVIEW,
       vol. 27, no. 4 (December 1984): 1-8.

           Introduces the agenda recommended
       by ACCELERATED DEVELOPMENT (Entry 378).
       Debate took place at the 1983 African
       Studies Association meeting. Summarizes
       each of the issues raised, and the
       implications.

654.   Paul, Samuel. "Community Participation in
       World Bank's Projects." FINANCE AND
       DEVELOPMENT, vol. 24 (December 1987):
       20-23.

           Describes community participation
       used in Bank projects in Bangladesh,
       Zimbabwe, and Mexico. Argues that,
       while it takes time and funds for
       sustaining and organizing, it is
       essential to programs where building
       organizational capacity is an objective.

655.   Paul, Samuel. COMMUNITY PARTICIPATION IN
       DEVELOPMENT PROJECTS: THE WORLD BANK
       EXPERIENCE (World Bank Discussion Paper,
       6). Washington, D.C.: World Bank, 1987.
       ix,37 p. ISBN 0-8213-0886-6
       LCCN 87-2183

           Reviews the Bank's experience with
       community participation in urban
       housing, irrigation, and health sectors.

656.   Payer, Cheryl. TANZANIA AND THE WORLD BANK.
       Bergen, Norway: 1982. 32 p.
       LCCN 85-219560 *

657.   Payer, Cheryl. WORLD BANK: A CRITICAL
          ANALYSIS. NY: Monthly Review, 1982.
          414 p. ISBN 0-85345-601-1
          LCCN 81-84738 *

658.   Payer, Cheryl. "World Bank and the Small
          Farmer." JOURNAL OF PEACE RESEARCH,
          vol. 16, no. 4 (1979): 293-312.

                    Argues that rural poor do not need
          large doses of foreign capital -- they
          need freedom from creditors and new
          forms of land tenure. Describes World
          Bank's new emphasis on smallholder
          lending as a means of increasing
          participation in market economy.
          Settlement projects, price manipulation,
          and changes in tenure systems are being
          used to achieve this objective.

659.   Payer, Cheryl. "World Bank and the Small
          Farmer." MONTHLY REVIEW, vol. 32, no. 6
          (November 1980): 30-46.

                    Argues World Bank poses as champion
          of small farmers but it contributes to
          total poverty. Development means that
          peasants are forced from their land to
          make way for roads, dams, etc., financed
          by the Bank. Argues projects are not
          designed for the poorest of the poor,
          and they destroy subsistence farming.

660.   Peck, Howard. "Technological Impact of World
          Bank Operations." BETWEEN TWO WORLDS:
          THE WORLD BANK'S NEXT DECADE, by R.
          Feinberg, et al. New Brunswick, NJ:
          Transaction Books, 1986. 161-177 p.

                    Recommends the Bank increase
          lending to small-scale industrial
          projects, encourage productivity
          programs, and generate innovations

useful in small-scale sector. See also
Entry 283.

661.   Perkins, Dwight Heald, and Shahid Yusuf.
RURAL DEVELOPMENT IN CHINA. Baltimore,
MD: Published for the World Bank by
Johns Hopkins University Press, 1984.
ISBN 0-8018-3261-6   LCCN 83-49366

Examines agricultural production,
distribution of income, and health and
education in rural China. Attempts to
measure effectiveness of various
programs in rural areas. Examines
overall development strategies and rate
of growth in agricultural output.

662.   Perret, Heli. USING COMMUNICATION SUPPORT IN
PROJECTS. Washington, D.C.: World Bank,
1982. 68 p. ISBN 0-8213-0119-5
LCCN 82-20023 *

663.   Phaup, E. Dwight. WORLD BANK: HOW IT CAN
SERVE U.S. INTERESTS. Washington, D.C.:
Heritage Foundation, 1984. vi,57 p.
ISBN 0-89195-213-0   LCCN 84-82165 *

664.   Ping, Ho Kwon. "End of the McNamara Era ...
But the Vietnam Legacy Continues to
Haunt Him." FAR EASTERN ECONOMIC
REVIEW, vol. 109, no. 39 (September 19,
1980): 106-110.

Robert McNamara retired to a chorus
of dissent over his battles (especially
regarding aid to Vietnam). He led the
Bank through a growth phase, made
friends and enemies, and doubled the
staff. He wrote a letter promising to
withhold aid to UN, touching off a
controversy among the management.

665.   Ping, Ho Kwon. "World Bank Blueprint for
        Economic Reform." FAR EASTERN ECONOMIC
        REVIEW, vol. 108 (May 23, 1980): 43-45.*

            Presents the World Bank's plans for
        Thailand.

666.   Pingali, Prabhu L., Yves Bigot, and Hans P.
        Binswanger. AGRICULTURAL MECHANIZATION
        AND THE EVOLUTION OF FARMING SYSTEMS IN
        SUB-SAHARAN AFRICA. Baltimore, MD:
        Published for the World Bank by Johns
        Hopkins University Press, 1987. *

667.   Plavcic, Sanja. "Dutch Speaks Out On the
        Bank: an Encounter in The Hague."
        BANK'S WORLD, vol. 7 (October 1988):
        2-3. *

668.   Please, Stanley. HOBBLED GIANT: ESSAYS ON
        THE WORLD BANK. Boulder, CO: Westview,
        1984. 100 p. ISBN 0-86531-872-7;
        0-86531-872-7 LCCN 84-51211

            Argues World Bank is prevented from
        exercising its strengths in promoting
        faster development in LDCs due to
        constraints (legal restrictions and
        division of responsibility between IMF
        and Bank are major ones). Argues for
        greater cooperation between IMF and
        Bank, and greater involvement by Bank in
        formulation of national policy on
        economic assistance.

669.   Please, Stanley. "World Bank: Lending for
        Structural Adjustment." ADJUSTMENT
        CRISIS IN THE THIRD WORLD, by R.
        Feinberg and V. Kallab. New Brunswick,
        NJ: Transaction Books, 1984. p. 83-98.

            Argues that the structural
        adjustment lending is a major watershed

for the Bank in present and future research. See also Entry 282.

670.   Please, Stanley, and K.Y. Amoako. "World Bank's Report on Accelerated Development in Sub-Sahara Africa: A Critique of Some of the Criticism." AFRICAN STUDIES REVIEW, vol. 27, no. 4 (December 1984): 47-58.
         Also published in AFRICA IN ECONOMIC CRISIS, by John Ravenhill (ed.) New York: Macmillan, 1963.

         Argues the World Bank is concerned with the immediate crisis, not long range planning. Solving food crisis must be done first, or there is no reason to expect success with long-term plans.

671.   "Policy Framework Approach." FINANCE AND DEVELOPMENT, vol. 24 (December 1987): 7.

         Describes how a comprehensive three-year "policy framework paper" will be prepared annually by the Joint Bank-Fund staff under the structural adjustment fund program.

672.   "Politics Holds Up World Bank Loans: Governments are Hampered in Their Work by Trouble Abroad Between the US and Nations in the Soviet Orbit." WORLD REPORT: THE MAGAZINE OF WORLD AFFAIRS (October 22, 1946): 28.

         Describes how political differences between Russian-dominated nations and the US are hampering the World Bank loan program. US is opposed to relief programs (as opposed to reconstruction projects) in the Eastern Bloc countries,

and US international policy affects loan
decisions.

673.   Pouliquen, Louis Y.   RISK ANALYSIS IN PROJECT
        APPRAISAL (World Bank Staff Occasional
        Paper, 11).   Baltimore, MD: Published
        for the World Bank by Johns Hopkins
        Press, 1970.   ISBN 0-8018-1155-4
        LCCN 79-120739

            Describes three case studies using
        risk analysis in the project appraisals:
        the Port of Mogadiscio (Somalia), the
        Tanzanian portion of the TanZam highway,
        and the Great East Road preproject study
        (Zambia).   Summarizes the advantages and
        cautions of risk analysis.

674.   "Profile: Barber Conable and Michael
        Camdessus."   TIME (UK) (September 19,
        1987): 10.   *

675.   "Progress of the World Bank."   BANK REVIEW,
        vol. 28, no. 3 (August 1953): 52-3.   *

676.   Psacharopoulos, George, and William A.
        Loxley.   DIVERSIFIED SECONDARY EDUCATION
        AND DEVELOPMENT: EVIDENCE FROM COLOMBIA
        AND TANZANIA.   Baltimore, MD: Published
        for the World Bank by Johns Hopkins
        University Press, 1985.
        ISBN 0-8018-3119-9   LCCN 85-45103

            Evaluates secondary school system
        in Colombia and Tanzania, comparing
        students in conventional (just academic
        or just vocational) with those in
        diversified (both academic and
        vocational).   Examines equity and cost
        effectiveness, labor market experience,
        and cognitive learning.

677.   Psacharopoulos, George, and Maureen Woodhall.
        EDUCATION FOR DEVELOPMENT: AN ANALYSIS
        OF INVESTMENT CHOICES. Oxford, UK:
        Oxford University Press, 1985.
        ix,337 p. ISBN 0-19-520477-8;
        0-19-520478-6 (paper) LCCN 85-13782

            Draws on World Bank experience with
        education projects, focusing on analysis
        of educational investment. Reviews
        results of earlier unpublished studies
        by the Bank on lending for education.

678.   Rahill, Michael. "Joint Bank-Fund Library:
        World Bank and International Monetary
        Fund." SPECIAL COLLECTIONS, vol. 2,
        no. 3 (Spring 1983): 105-108.

            Briefly introduces the Joint
        Library, and its unique collection of
        materials on finance and economic
        development.

679.   "Qualified Gloom: World Bank." THE
        ECONOMIST, vol. 276 (August 23, 1980):
        62-63.

            Summarizes WORLD DEVELOPMENT REPORT
        1980 (Entry 498) in which Bank sees
        world trade slowing in early 1980s but
        picking up in late 1980s. States five
        "lean" years in the world economy, will
        be followed by sharp recovery, provided
        the right policies are adopted now.

680.   Rama Rao, G.J. INDIA AND THE TWO PYTHONS:
        IMF AND WORLD BANK (Communist Party
        Publication, 12). New Delhi, India:
        Communist Party of India, 1982.
        xi,99 p.

            Presents Marxist view of the Bank's
        and IMF's influence on India's economy.

Claims India has been adversely affected
by IMF conditionality and IBRD
structural adjustment.

681.   Ravenhill, John (ed.). AFRICA IN ECONOMIC
        CRISIS. London: Macmillan Press, 1986.
        xiii,359 p. ISBN 0-333-37173-9;
        0-333-37174-7 (paper)

        Examines issues (agriculture, and
        debt, for example). Assesses different
        proposals to solve Africa's economic
        problems, especially the Lagos Plan of
        Action (OAU) and the Bank's ACCELERATED
        DEVELOPMENT (see Entry 378).

682.   Ray, Anandarup. COST-BENEFIT ANALYSIS:
        ISSUES AND METHODOLOGIES. Baltimore,
        MD: Published for the World Bank by
        Johns Hopkins University Press, 1984.
        ISBN 0-8018-3068-0; 0-8018-3069-9
        (paper) LCCN 83-49367

        Evolved from a series of workshops
        conducted on different approaches to
        cost-benefit analysis. Discusses social
        evaluation, issue of distributed
        weights, valuation of traded/nontraded
        goods, and capital market.

683.   "Reconstruction Loans Held Up as World Bank
        Runs Into Snags: Financial, Political
        and Personnel Difficulties Force
        Curtailment and Delay in Aiding Member
        Countries." WORLD REPORT: THE MAGAZINE
        OF WORLD AFFAIRS (February 11, 1947):
        29-30.

        Describes how loans for 1947 are
        smaller due to several difficulties.
        Organizational problems like vacant
        presidential position, which direction
        the Bank should take, and lack of

coordination in lending program are
causing financial difficulties.
Russia's absence as a charter member,
and where the headquarters should be
located are additional problems.

684.   Reid, Escott. FUTURE OF THE WORLD BANK: AN
        ESSAY. Washington, D.C.: World Bank,
        1965. v, 71 p.

        Summarizes some of problems faced
        by George Wood, as well as some of his
        achievements as president of the World
        Bank. Discusses the Bank's record,
        staff, diplomacy, and future
        development.

685.   Reid, Escott. "McNamara's World Bank."
        FOREIGN AFFAIRS, vol. 51, no. 4 (July
        1973): 794-810.

        Discusses Robert McNamara's
        accomplishments at the end of 5 years as
        Bank president (doubled volume of
        lending and number of staff, changed
        administrative structure). Suggests
        NcNamara's goals for next 5 years (make
        administration more efficient, and
        stronger Bank through member governments
        having larger share in decision making).

686.   Reid, Escott. STRENGTHENING THE WORLD BANK.
        Chicago: Adlai Stevenson Institute,
        1973. xviii, 289 p.   *

        Discusses future direction of
        development activities, through stronger
        participation by developing countries
        and more effective methods of
        eradicating poverty.

687.   "Reports of the International Monetary Fund
        and the International Bank for
        Reconstruction and Development."
        FEDERAL RESERVE BULLETIN,   vol. 32
        (October 1946): 1123-1139.

            Text of the first annual report
        deals with the progress and development
        since the inaugural meeting (March
        1946). Describes operations,
        investments, organization, policies,
        membership, and financial statements.

688.   "Requiem for the World's Banks Postponed."
        THE ECONOMIST, Vol. 284 (September 11,
        1982): 61-62.

            Mexican debt problem is casting a
        shadow over IMF and IBRD annual meeting
        in Toronto. Due to Mexican two-tier
        exchange rate, IMF is facing new demands
        on its cash, but they should be able to
        afford it.

689.   Reutlinger, Shlomo, and Marcelo Selowsky.
        MALNUTRITION AND POVERTY; MAGNITUDE AND
        POLICY OPTIONS (World Bank Staff
        Occasional Papers, 23). Baltimore, MD:
        Published for the World Bank by Johns
        Hopkins University Press, 1976. 82 p.
        ISBN 0-8018-1868-0   LCCN 76-17240 *

690.   Rhee, Yung Whee. INSTRUMENTS FOR EXPORT
        POLICY AND ADMINISTRATION: LESSONS FROM
        THE EAST ASIAN EXPERIENCE. Washington,
        D.C.: World Bank, 1985.   *

691.   Rhee, Yung Whee, Bruce Clifford Ross-Larson,
        and Garry Pursell. KOREA'S COMPETITIVE
        EDGE: MANAGING THE ENTRY INTO WORLD
        MARKETS. Baltimore, MD: Published for
        the World Bank by Johns Hopkins
        University Press, 1984.   *

692.   Rice, Gerald, James Corr, and Susan Fennell.
"Maintaining Financing for Adjustment
and Development." FINANCE AND
DEVELOPMENT, vol. 20 (December 1983):
44-47.

     Reports on main themes at 1983
Board of Governors meeting. The Bank
and Fund were challenged with these
themes: growth, diversification of world
economy, and increased interdependence
of constituent parts.

693.   Riemer, Blanca. "Foreign Debt: Only the
Little Guys are Marching to Baker's
Music." BUSINESS WEEK (January 20,
1986): 39.

     When Baker announced his plan, it
was assumed that Argentina, Mexico, and
Brazil were in mind. It appears that
Colombia, Ecuador, Uruguay, Morocco, and
Ivory Coast may be the first to fall in
line. Mexico, Argentina, and Brazil are
not sure they want the funds on the
terms of Baker's plan.

694.   Riemer, Blanca, John Templeman, et al.
"Good Luck, Mr. Conable -- You'll Need
It." BUSINESS WEEK (July 7, 1986): 74.

     World Bank needs more capital,
economic restructuring, and better
relations with IMF. Everyone expects
Conable to solve the debt crisis, get
more funds from Congress, and shake up
the Bank's bureaucratic organization.

695.   Rimmer, P.J.   "The World Bank's Urban
         Transport Policy: Authorized Version,
         Revised Version, and the Apocrypha
         (Research Policy and Review 20)."
         ENVIRONMENT & PLANNING, vol. 19
         (December 12, 1987): 1569-1577.

              Examines the characteristics of the
         Bank's initial policy paper on urban
         transport. Summarizes the new policy
         statement, and outlines the criticisms
         of the revision. Privatization and
         buses are the cornerstones of the Bank's
         new policy.

696.   Ringen, Stein.   "Fruits of the United
         Nations: the Distribution of Development
         Aid." JOURNAL OF PEACE RESEARCH,
         vol. 11, no. 1 (1974): 51-6.

              Describes conflict of interest
         between developing and developed
         nations. Examines justice (UN
         principle) and economic interests.
         Points out difference in principles
         between World Bank and other UN
         affiliates. Perhaps due to World Bank
         being more linked with capitalism (as an
         economic activity), while others (UNDP
         and WHO) are more in accord with UN
         ideals.

697.   "Rites of Autumn." BANKER, vol. 137, no. 741
         (November 1987): 128.

              Discusses the 1987 Board of
         Governors meeting, and how the effect of
         Reaganomics on the US economy impacts on
         the Bank. Describes how US indebtedness
         threatens international financial
         markets.

698.   Roeet, Riordan.   "Brazil's Debt Crisis and
        U.S. Policy." ADJUSTMENT CRISIS IN THE
        THIRD WORLD, ed. by R. Feinberg and V.
        Kallab. New Brunswick, NJ: Transaction
        Books, 1984. p. 139-146.

        Argues that US should increase
        funding to the Bank, IMF, and IADB in
        order to aid Brazil and other heavily
        indebted nations. See also Entry 282.

699.   Roessner, Jill and Morallina George.   "Little
        Romance: Five Bank Couples and How They
        Met." BANK'S WORLD, vol. 7 (February
        1988): 8-10. *

700.   Roosa, Robert V.   "How World Banker Role
        Benefits the U.S." BANKING, vol. 56
        (November 1963): 47-48. *

701.   Rosenberg, Robert.   "World Bank Sets Up World
        Class Net." ELECTRONICS, vol. 58
        (August 5, 1985): 22+,24.

        Describes how World Bank spent
        three years studying its own
        communication needs. Discusses how the
        Bank came up with a plan for largest
        local area network created (Howard
        Conrad, Chief, Network Communications).

702.   Rossi, R.   "World Bank." ECONOMIC REVIEW
        (Helsinki), vol. 1 (1954): 10-18. *

703.   Rotberg, Eugene.   "Eugene Rotberg."
        INSTITUTIONAL INVESTOR, vol. 21 (June
        1987): 60-63. *

        Special issue in honor of
        INSTITUTIONAL INVESTOR's 20th
        anniversary featuring oral history on
        the World Bank from Rotberg's experience
        as World Bank Treasurer.

704.   Rotberg, Eugene H.   "World Bank: A Financial
         Appraisal."   FINANCE AND DEVELOPMENT
         (September 1976): 14-18.

              Examines borrowing programs,
         capital structure, liquidity policies,
         and investors. Describes the balance
         maintained between creditors and member
         country shareholders. See Entry 948.

705.   Rotberg, Eugene H.   WORLD BANK: A FINANCIAL
         APPRAISAL. Washington, D.C.: 1981.
         35 p.   LCCN 81-117396

              Summarizes remarks made at various
         seminars concerning financial operations
         of the World Bank (but not IDA or IFC).

706.   Rowen, Hobart.   "Baker, Conable Ask Raise in
         World Bank Funds."   WASHINGTON POST
         (February 17, 1988): 72.   *

707.   Rowen, Hobart.   "Baker Criticizes House
         Leadership for Rejecting World Bank
         Request."   WASHINGTON POST (May 7,
         1988): D11-D12.   *

708.   Rowen, Hobart.   "Baker Pushes for World Bank
         Funds."   WASHINGTON POST (March 31,
         1988): B3.   *

709.   Rowen, Hobart.   "Jim Baker's Global
         Blueprint."   INSTITUTIONAL INVESTOR,
         vol. 20 (September 1986): 302-304 +.   *

710.   Rowen, Hobart.   "World Bank Sees 'Bad News'
         On Third World Debt."   WASHINGTON POST
         (January 19, 1988): E1,E2.   *

711.   Rowen, Hobart.   "World Finance Leaders Still
         Predict Moderate Economic Growth for
         '88."   WASHINGTON POST (April 16, 1988):
         D1,D18.   *

712.   Rowley, Anthony. "Facing the Need for
        Fundamental Economic Reforms." FAR
        EASTERN ECONOMIC REVIEW, vol. 138, no.
        40 (October 1, 1987): 74-75.

        Indonesia has a long-standing
        relationship with IMF and World Bank.
        It has experienced a balance of payments
        deficit and depleted foreign exchange
        reserves. Indonesia also has the second
        largest foreign debt in Asia.

713.   Rowley, Anthony. "Plans, Plans, But Debt
        Won't Go Away." FAR EASTERN ECONOMIC
        REVIEW, vol. 138, no. 40 (October 1,
        1987): 59-60.

        Describes plans for reducing debt
        and progress (very little) made in past
        few years. Summarizes the Baker Plan,
        the Bradley Plan, and a few others.

714.   Rowley, Anthony. "Rational Collection of
        Functions." FAR EASTERN ECONOMIC REVIEW,
        vol. 138, no. 40 (October 1, 1987):
        56-57.

        Discusses criticism aimed at the
        World Bank (i.e., failure to provide
        leadership in debt crisis) and creation
        of Policy, Planning, and Resources
        Division to fill that mandate.

715.   Rowley, Anthony. "Reforms Remain the Price
        of Access to Money." FAR EASTERN
        ECONOMIC REVIEW, vol. 138, no. 40
        (October 1, 1987): 65.

        Discusses structural adjustment
        lending programs, and the shift to
        sectoral adjustment loans (more limited
        but more productive). Both are linked
        to policy reforms.

716.   Rowley, Anthony. "View from the Top of a New
        Look Bank." FAR EASTERN ECONOMIC REVIEW,
        vol. 138, no. 40 (October 1, 1987):
        51-53.

        Interview with Barber Conable,
        World Bank President, on the
        reorganization of Bank's administration.

717.   Rowley, Anthony. "World Bank Finds Headroom
        a Tight Squeeze." FAR EASTERN ECONOMIC
        REVIEW, vol. 138, no. 40 (October 1,
        1987): 58-59.

        Discusses maneuvering the level of
        outstanding loans relative to capital
        base (headroom) and its 10-year record.

718.   Rowley, Anthony. "World Bank's Big Bang."
        FAR EASTERN ECONOMIC REVIEW, vol. 138,
        no. 40 (October 1, 1987): 47-50.

        Describes new approach as World
        Bank management is reorganized by
        Conable, and events leading up to his
        reorganization (status of Bank
        management, loan operations, etc.).

719.   Ryrie, William. "Bringing Order Out of
        Chaos: Challenges Call for Creativity
        and Invention." BANK'S WORLD, vol. 6
        (November 1987): 12-13.   *

720.   Ryrie, William. "Private Investments in
        Developing Countries: Issues and
        Prospects." ARAB BANKER: JOURNAL OF THE
        ARAB BANKERS ASSOCIATION, vol. 7
        (November/December 1987): 21-23,28-30.*

721.   Sachs, Jeffrey. CONDITIONALITY, DEBT RELIEF
        AND THE DEVELOPING COUNTRY DEBT CRISIS
        (NBER Working Paper, 2644). Cambridge,
        MA: National Bureau for Economic
        Research, 1988.

            Evaluates the role of IMF and World
        Bank lending as part of the plan to stem
        LDCs' debt. Argues that effectiveness
        of conditionality could be improved by
        approving fewer programs and aiming for
        macroeconomic stabilization.

722.   Sagnier, Thierry. "Field Security Moves to
        GSD: Sleep Well, Mr. Theodores." BANK'S
        WORLD, vol. 6 (September 1987): 9-10.   *

723.   Salmen, Lawrence F. LISTENING TO THE
        PEOPLE: PARTICIPANT-OBSERVER ASSESSMENT
        OF WORLD BANK DEVELOPMENT PROJECTS. New
        York: Published by Oxford University
        Press for the World Bank, 1987.

            Argues that people-oriented
        projects often fail to achieve their
        potential, because they do not
        understand the concerns of the people.
        Describes participant-observer
        assessment in planning and evaluating
        World Bank development programs,
        beginning in 1982 in Bolivia and
        Ecuador. See Entry 724.

724.   Salmen, Lawrence F. "Listening to the
        People: Participant-Observer Assessment
        of World Bank Development Projects."
        FINANCE AND DEVELOPMENT, vol. 24 (June
        1987): 36-39.

            Abstracts LISTENING TO THE PEOPLE
        (Entry 723), which argues that socio-
        cultural context is often forgotten or
        ignored in development projects.

725.   Samuelson, Robert J. "Global Finance: Can
         the System Support Us? or Money Makes
         the World Go Round -- But What If It
         Can't Anymore?" NATIONAL JOURNAL, vol.
         12, no. 39 (September 17, 1980):
         1956-1608.

             Describes climate prior to 1980
         Board of Governors meeting. Discusses
         how the world economy has come to depend
         on the flows of money in the form of
         international loans and investments.
         Rising oil prices and political
         instability threaten the credit system.

726.   Sanderson, Warren C., and Jeffrey G.
         Williamson. ADJUSTING TO EXTERNAL
         SHOCKS IN DEVELOPING COUNTRIES: A REVIEW
         OF SOME WORLD BANK MACRO MODELS
         (Institute for Economic Research
         Discussion Paper, 1039). Cambridge, MA:
         Department of Economics, Harvard
         University, 1984. *

             Employs several World Bank
         macroeconomic models to assess
         structural adjustment to external
         shocks.

727.   Sanford, Jonathan. "Development Theory and
         the Multilateral Development Banks: An
         Assessment of the Effectiveness of
         Strategies Used in International
         Finance." AMERICAN JOURNAL OF ECONOMICS
         AND SOCIOLOGY, vol. 34, no. 2 (April
         1975): 175-195.

             Assesses project approach,
         macroeconomic approach, and social
         welfare in the context of multilateral
         development such as the World Bank,
         IADB, and others. Concludes they serve

several functions, and it is appropriate they employ several approaches to development.

728. Sanford, Jonathan, and Margaret Goodman. CONGRESSIONAL OVERSIGHT AND THE MULTILATERAL DEVELOPMENT BANKS. Washington, D.C.: U.S. House of Representatives, 1974. *

Analyses operations of international institutions of which the US is a member, and assesses US policy for Congress.

729. Sanford, Jonathan, and Margaret Goodman. "Congressional Oversight and the Multilateral Development Banks." INTERNATIONAL ORGANIZATION, vol. 29, no. 4 (Autumn 1975): 1055-1064.

Argues that national governments need to oversee operations of international organizations, and there must be sufficient access to information, so government and citizens can regulate these institutions. Describes the NAC, and its relation to multilateral development banks, as well as the status of US policy with multilateral development banks.

730. Sankaran, Sundaram. "World Bank: Act as Role Dictates." MALAYSIAN BUSINESS (September 16, 1988): 43-44. *

731. Sankaran, Sundaram. "World Bank: Making a Bid for Global Contracts." MALAYSIAN BUSINESS (November 16, 1988): 54-55. *

732.   Sarker, Subhash Chandra. "World Development
         Report 1987: Is World Bank's Economic
         Policy Prescription Helpful for India?"
         COMMERCE WEEKLY (INDIA), Vol. 155, no.
         3973 (July 11, 1987): 7-12.

         "Efficient industrialization" as
         presented in WORLD DEVELOPMENT REPORT
         1987 (see Entry 505) is discussed.
         Comments on the IMF-IBRD scandal
         (mismanagement of LDCs' economies) under
         structural adjustment lending. Argues
         US dominates the World Bank and the
         nations being "helped" by the Bank.

733.   Sarker, Subhash Chandra. "World Finance:
         Agencies Abet in Spreading Confusion."
         COMMERCE WEEKLY (INDIA), vol. 155, no.
         3986 (October 10, 1987): 5-13.

         Describes how World Bank, IMF, and
         Asian Development Bank have launched a
         campaign to open developing nations'
         economies to exploitation by developed
         nations. Discusses disruption of
         already developed public sector in LDCs
         under the guise of "liberalization" and
         "privatization."

734.   Schaaf, Robert W. "Information Policies of
         International Organizations."
         GOVERNMENT PUBLICATIONS REVIEW, Vol. 17,
         NO. 1 (1990): 49-61.

         Examines international
         organizations and the types of materials
         used to transfer information to library
         users. Studies UN, UNESCO, FAO, World
         Bank, IMF, WHO, ITU, and GATT.
         Discusses access to IGO information in
         electronic format.

735.   Schaffer, B.B.   "Advising About
           Development: The Example of the World
           Bank Report of Papua and New Guinea."
           JOURNAL OF COMMONWEALTH POLITICAL
           STUDIES, vol. 4, no. 1 (March 1966):
           30-46.

           Critiques IBRD report on
           development of New Guinea and Papua
           (first external investigation). See
           Entry 410. Argues that lack of other
           reports on Papua and New Guinea gives
           this one too much weight. Calls for
           more reliance on Australia for
           development aid.

736.   Schirano, Louis. "Bum Rap for the World
           Bank." INTERNATIONAL ECONOMY, vol. 1
           (October/November 1987): 36-38.*

737.   Schmidt, Wilson E.   "Rethinking the
           Multilateral Development Banks." POLICY
           REVIEW, vol. 10 (Fall 1979): 47-61.

           Reviews issues raised by Congress
           on overall growth rates, coordination
           between multilateral development banks,
           and project audit agency. Since US is
           largest source of funds, it is natural
           for it to examine these banks closely:
           World Bank, IADB, African Development
           Bank, and Asian Development Bank.

738.   Schrenk, Martin, Cyrus Ardalan, and Nawal El
           Tatawy. YUGOSLAVIA: SELF-MANAGEMENT
           SOCIALISM AND THE CHALLENGES OF
           DEVELOPMENT -- REPORT OF A MISSION SENT
           TO YUGOSLAVIA BY THE WORLD BANK (World
           Bank Country Economic Report).
           Baltimore, MD: Published for the World
           Bank by Johns Hopkins University Press,
           1979. 329 p. ISBN 0-8018-2263-7;
           0-8018-2278-5 (paper) LCCN 79-84316

Traces institutional changes of
1970s, and reviews economic goals of
1976-1980. Analyzes issues of economic
development Yugoslavia has faced over
the years: stabilization, resource
allocation and mobilization, regional
development, and balance of payments.

739.   "Schools Brief -- Investing in Growth." THE
         ECONOMIST, vol. 306 (February 13, 1988):
         70-71.

         Describes World Bank through its
         five phases (reconstruction bank,
         conservative bank, development lender,
         poverty concern, and policy reform).
         Describes differences between IDA and
         World Bank lending. Discusses how US
         has traditionally named the World Bank
         President, but Japan is getting a bigger
         role in the future.

740.   Schultheis, Michael J. "World Bank and
         Accelerated Development: the
         Internationalization of Supply-side
         Economics." AFRICAN STUDIES REVIEW,
         vol. 27, no. 4 (December 1984): 9-16.

         Summarizes ACCELERATED DEVELOPMENT
         (Entry 378). Criticizes its basic
         assumptions. Reflects on initial
         hostile responses of its readers, which
         AFRICA: PROGRESS REPORT (Entry 456).

741.   Schuman, C.A.W. "World Bank and
         Infrastructure Development in Developing
         Countries." DEVELOPMENT SOUTHERN
         AFRICA, vol. 3 (February 1986):
         82-105. *

742.   Schwark, Eberhard. "Investment of IMF Assets
        in World Bank Securities -- An
        Alternative to the 'Link'." JOURNAL OF
        WORLD TRADE LAW, vol. 7, no. 6
        (November/December 1973): 607-618.

            Proposes alternatives to "linking"
        IMF's SDR to development finance. One
        alternative is to use the monies accrued
        by IMF for financing development via the
        World Bank (i.e., investing IMF assets
        in World Bank bonds).

743.   Scott, Ian. URBAN AND SPATIAL DEVELOPMENT IN
        MEXICO. Baltimore, MD: Published for
        the World Bank by Johns Hopkins
        University Press, 1982.
        ISBN 0-8018-2499-0; 0-8018-2498-2
        (paper) LCCN 80-8023

            Explains the structure and
        development of the urban system.
        Analyzes demographic and economic
        contrast in the systems. Reviews option
        in formulating urban and spatial
        structures. Based on two unpublished
        World Bank reports.

744.   Selassie, Bereket Habte. "World Bank: Power
        and Responsibility in Historical
        Perspective." AFRICAN STUDIES REVIEW,
        vol. 27, no. 4 (December 1984): 35-46.

            Describes debates between Left and
        Right over various aspects of the Bank,
        as well as historical perspective of the
        current controversy. Examines political
        aspects of capital structure, staff, and
        governance.

745.   Sen, Gita. "Industrialization and Foreign
        Trade: A Critical Review." ECONOMIC AND
        POLITICAL WEEKLY, vol. 23, no. 7
        (February 13, 1988): 304-306.

            Presents results of WORLD
        DEVELOPMENT REPORT 1987 (Entry 505)
        which examined state policy and
        industrial growth. Notes the rate of
        growth is affect by its orientation
        toward international trade. Argues the
        relationship between orientation, state
        policy, and foreign trade is weak.

746.   Sen, Sunanda. "Debt Crisis: Fund-Bank
        Policies in the Dock." ECONOMIC AND
        POLITICAL WEEKLY, vol. 23, no. 40
        (October 1, 1988): 2043-2044.

            Presents results of world monetary
        system tribunal. Argues that reduced
        imports and World Bank-IMF adjustment
        programs jeopardize the livelihood of
        workers. Analyzes global debt problem.

747.   Sender, Henny. "Shearson Lehman Goes It
        Alone." INSTITUTIONAL INVESTOR, vol. 20
        (February 1986): 29. *

748.   Serageldin, Ismail. TOOLS FOR MANPOWER
        PLANNING. Washington, D.C.: 1983.
        ISBN 0-8213-0183-7 *

749.   Shank, Margaret. "World Bank/IMF -- Will
        Rhetoric Be Reality?" WEST AFRICA,
        no. 3662 (October 19, 1987): 2069-2070.

            Reports on 1987 Board of Governors
        meeting and discusses structural
        adjustment facility. Presents US
        Secretary of Treasury James Baker's
        comments. Questions whether Bank will

follow through with its verbal
commitment to Africa.

750.   Shapiro, Paul S.   SCIENCE AND TECHNOLOGY IN
        WORLD BANK OPERATIONS.   Washington,
        D.C.: 1982.   LCCN 82-7071   *

751.   Sharkansky, Ira, and Dennis L. Dresang.
        "International Assistance: Its Variety,
        Coordination, and Impact Among Public
        Corporations in Kenya and the East
        African Community."   INTERNATIONAL
        ORGANIZATION, vol. 18, no. 2 (Spring
        1974): 207-231.

            Based on the experience in East
        Africa, argues that competition and lack
        of candor in donor's reports limit the
        effectiveness in coordination.   Kenya
        was a pioneer in joint cooperative
        efforts.   Describes experience in Kenya
        and East Africa, and the possibility of
        transferring this experience to other
        LDCs.

752.   Shelton, C.J.   "Financial Structure and
        Operations of the IBRD."   BANK OF
        ENGLAND QUARTERLY BULLETIN,   vol. 25
        (March 1985): 47-56.   *

            Addresses the possibility of a
        capital increase for the World Bank.

753.   Shenoy, B.R.   "Aid to India from the World
        Bank Group."   POLITICO, vol. 36, no. 3
        (September 1971): 523-548.   *

754.   Shirley, Mary.   "Promoting the Private
        Sector."   FINANCE AND DEVELOPMENT (March
        1988): 32-36.

            Describes how IDA and World Bank
        are helping to strengthen the private

sectors during the 1980s. IFC is
support stock market development. Both
IFC and World Bank are important sources
of foreign finance for private
enterprise in LDCs.

755.   Silkenat, James R. "Role of International
Development Institutions in
International Financing: IBRD, IFC, and
Co-financing Techniques." INTERNATIONAL
LAWYER, vol. 17, no. 4 (Autumn 1983):
615-624. *

756.   Sinclair, Ward. "Message on the Potato Bag."
WASHINGTON POST (November 20, 1987):
A17. *

757.   Singh, Inderjit, Lyn Squire, and John
Strauss. AGRICULTURAL HOUSEHOLD MODELS:
A SURVEY OF RECENT FINDINGS AND THEIR
POLICY IMPLICATIONS (Discussion Paper,
474). New Haven, CT: Economic Growth
Center, Yale University, 1985. 44 p.

Provides a comparative analysis of
empirical and policy applications of
household models in India, Indonesia,
Korea, Malaysia, Nigeria, Senegal,
Sierra Leone, Taiwan, and Thailand. See
also Entries 758 and 785.

758.   Singh, Inderjit, Lyn Squire, and John Strauss
(eds.). AGRICULTURAL HOUSEHOLD MODELS:
EXTENSIONS, APPLICATIONS, AND POLICY.
Baltimore, MD: Published for the World
Bank by Johns Hopkins University Press,
1986. xi,335 p. ISBN 0-8018-3149-0
LCCN 85-45102

Provides an overview of results,
policy conclusions, and methodology, as
well as recent applications of
agricultural household models. Case

studies are presented (Japan, Korea, Malaysia, Nigeria, Sierra Leone, Taiwan, and Thailand). See also Entry 757.

759.   Singh, Shamser, Jos de Vries, et al. COFFEE, TEA, AND COCOA: MARKET PRODUCTS AND DEVELOPMENT LENDING (World Bank Staff Occasional Paper, 22). Baltimore, MD: Published for the World Bank by Johns Hopkins University Press, 1977. xii,129 p. ISBN 0-8018-1869-9 LCCN 76-17239

Assesses prospects for export earnings (coffee, cocoa, and tea) to support lending for increased production. Examines consumption, imports, and market outlook (coffee is second to oil as a major LDC export).

760.   Smith, Patrick. "Embarrassing Predicament for the IMF and the World Bank." WEST AFRICA, no. 3711 (September 26-October 2, 1988): 1803.

States World Bank and IMF have been received more from the Third World than they paid out, as a result of membership subscriptions. Advises commercial banks to resist pressure from the Bank and IMF to lend more money to the Third World, and to consider the trouble caused by not being able to reschedule loans.

761.   Smithies, Arthur. "International Bank for Reconstruction and Development." AMERICAN ECONOMIC REVIEW, vol. 34, no. 4 (December 1944): 785-897.

Describes the need for IBRD, its structure, its contribution to international investment, financial soundness of the Bank, relation to private lending, effect on balance of payments, and relationship to the Export-Import Bank. Concludes foreign investment will be more extensive and constructive as a result of IBRD.

762. Sommers, Davidson. "Institution Emerges." FINANCE AND DEVELOPMENT (June 1984): 4-6.

World Bank's General Counsel (1949-1956) and Vice President (1956-1959), D. Sommers recounts the earlier struggles of the World Bank, and the evolution of the World Bank's Executive Board and management.

763. "Special Report of the National Advisory Council: Text of the Second Special Report of the National Advisory Council on the Operations and Policies of the International Monetary Fund and International Bank for Reconstruction and Development." FEDERAL RESERVE BULLETIN, vol. 36, no. 6 (June 1950): 661-677.

Text of report transmitted to Congress by the US President, May 1950. Covers IBRD and IMF operations and policies, as well as recommendations on whether to decrease or increase funding.

764. Spier, Gerald L.E. "Going for World Bank Business?" CIVIL ENGINEERING (London), (September 1985): 26-7. *

765.   Squire, Lyn, and H.G. van der Tak. ECONOMIC
        ANALYSIS OF PROJECTS (World Bank
        Research Publication). Baltimore, MD:
        Published for the World Bank by Johns
        Hopkins University Press, 1975. 153 p.
        ISBN 0-8018-1818-4; 0-8018-1817-6
        (paper) LCCN 75-40228 *

766.   Srodes, James. "Bid to Cut Out Indochina."
        FAR EASTERN ECONOMIC REVIEW, vol. 96,
        no. 24 (June 17, 1977): 106,111.

            Debate in Congress over US support
        of World Bank, in light of aid to
        Vietnam (a controversial issue), led to
        a Congressional amendment to prevent
        assistance to Thailand and Cambodia.
        The amendment would require US
        representatives in the Bank to veto aid
        to these countries.

767.   Srodes, James. "Carter Sends Out Signals."
        FAR EASTERN ECONOMIC REVIEW, vol. 96,
        no. 18 (May 6, 1977): 55.

            Despite growing opposition to
        McNamara and thoughts that he would not
        finish his term, he was reappointed as
        World Bank President for the third time.
        This signals the Carter administration's
        determination to continue foreign aid
        and development assistance.

768.   Srodes, James. "Congress Stalls on World
        Bank Funds." FAR EASTERN ECONOMIC
        REVIEW, vol. 97, no. 39 (September 30,
        1977): 38-39.

            US unlikely to fulfil its pledge of
        money to IMF and the World Bank.
        Describes problems and loss of overall
        impact in providing aid. Argues the
        need for the Carter administration to

fight growing resentment against foreign aid in Congress.

769.   Srodes, James. "Congress New Guard Keeps Asia Waiting." FAR EASTERN ECONOMIC REVIEW, vol. 100, no. 14 (April 7, 1978): 104-105.

Describes worsening relations between international financial assistance agencies (such as the World Bank) and US Congress. Secretary of Treasury Michael Blumenthal calls for more cuts, especially to the salaries of US nationals at the Bank.

770.   Srodes, James. "Early Exit for McNamara." FAR EASTERN ECONOMIC REVIEW, vol. 108 (June 13, 1980): 118+. *

771.   Srodes, James. "Empty Bag for McNamara." FAR EASTERN ECONOMIC REVIEW, vol. 106 (December 28, 1979): 40. *

772.   Srodes, James. "Enigma at the World Bank." FAR EASTERN ECONOMIC REVIEW, vol. 106 (November 16, 1979): 82. *

773.   Srodes, James. "McNamara and Co. Under Fire." FAR EASTERN ECONOMIC REVIEW, vol. 94, no. 50 (December 10, 1976): 45-46.

Describes the breach of solidarity in the World Bank (citing T. Hori's speech leaked to the press), and the impact of R. McNamara and US politics on the Bank's operations and policy.

774.   Srodes, James. "Putting the Bite on the Rich." FAR EASTERN ECONOMIC REVIEW, vol. 102, no. 40 (October 6, 1978): 74-77. *

775.   Srodes, James. "Vacant Seat for China." FAR
        EASTERN ECONOMIC REVIEW, vol. 103, no. 2
        (January 12, 1979): 70-71.

            Taiwan currently has recognition in
            the World Bank and IMF. China is also
            applying for membership which should be
            granted, but questions remain regarding
            the funds borrowed by Taiwan, and
            whether both could have their own
            "seats."

776.   Srodes, James. "Working Harder, but Little
        Progress." FAR EASTERN ECONOMIC REVIEW,
        vol. 92, no. 17 (April 23, 1976):
        74-75,77.

            Describes the Bank's less-than-
            optimistic environment following
            McNamara's presidency. Discusses the
            "secret" study on petroleum resources in
            LDCs, especially in Bangladesh, India,
            and Pakistan. Updates the status of
            foodgrains in Latin America and Asia.

777.   Srodes, James. "World Bank: A Cause for
        Concern." FAR EASTERN ECONOMIC REVIEW,
        vol. 95 (January 7, 1977): 41-42.

            Describes the opposition to R.
            McNamara in developing countries. World
            Bank Executive Director Charles Cooper's
            remarks supports T. Hori's views.
            Argues McNamara's policy of setting
            annual lending quotas for specific
            countries could lead to problems.

778.   "Staff Association Plans Agenda: A
        Conversation with the Chairman." BANK'S
        WORLD, vol. 7 (February 1988): 16-18.   *

779.   Staple, Gregory C.   "U.S. Law May Boost
        Telecom Development in the Third World."
        TELEPHONY,   vol. 210 (April 28, 1986):
        42-43. *

            Comments on World Bank loans for
        telecommunications facilities.

780.   "Statement from the World Bank." BUSINESS
        AMERICA, vol. 9, no. 3 (February 3,
        1986): 8.

            Brief statement of origins,
        purpose, governance, and current lending
        emphasis in this special issue on
        multilateral development banks.

781.   Stauffer, Robert B. MANILA-WASHINGTON
        CONNECTION: CONTINUITIES IN THE
        TRANSNATIONAL POLITICAL ECONOMY OF
        PHILIPPINE DEVELOPMENT (University of
        Sydney, Transnational Corporations
        Research Program, Research Monograph,
        17). Sydney, Australia: 1983.   40 p.
        ISBN 0-908470-31-2   LCCN 85-226921

            Presented at 1983 Association for
        Asian Studies meeting. Argues US, IMF,
        and World Bank pursue development in the
        Philippines, and control the structure
        of the Philippine economic development
        (capitalist development model).

782.   Stephens, Philip. "Private Smiles, Public
        Unease." FINANCIAL TIMES (September 22,
        1987): 26. *

783.   Stern, Ernest. "World Bank General Capital
        Increase." FINANCE AND DEVELOPMENT
        (June 1988): 20-23.

            Discusses how large capital
        increase will permit 10% growth in World

Bank lending program. Also discusses
the history of capital increases.

784.   Stockwin, Harry. "Beefing Up Developing
        Nations." FAR EASTERN ECONOMIC REVIEW,
        vol. 86, no. 43 (November 1, 1974):
        42,43,45.

            Illustrates the recent World Bank
        report on world beef market and the
        World Bank's role in increasing
        production. Describes a project in Asia
        where over 33% of the world's cattle are
        produced but it is the lowest portion of
        world trade (less than 0.1%).

785.   Strauss, John. OVERVIEW OF AGRICULTURAL
        HOUSEHOLD MODELS: THEORY (Center
        Discussion Paper, 450). New Haven, CT:
        Economic Growth Center, Yale University,
        1984.   44 p.

            Compares theoretical models of
        agricultural households, and the link
        between consumer and producer behavior.
        See also Entry 757.

786.   Streeten, Paul, et al. FIRST THINGS FIRST:
        MEETING BASIC HUMAN NEEDS IN THE
        DEVELOPING COUNTRIES. New York:
        Published for the World Bank by the
        Oxford University Press, 1981.
        ISBN 0-19-520368-2;   0-19-520369-0
        LCCN 81-16836

            Emphasizes that meeting basic needs
        of LDCs' population is the only way to
        increase productivity of poor. Argues
        that meeting those basic needs
        (education, health, housing, water
        supply, sanitation, nutrition) must be
        considered in formulation of poverty
        reduction policies.

787.   Stryker, Richard E.   "World Bank and Third
        World Development."   GOVERNMENT
        PUBLICATIONS REVIEW, vol. 6, no. 2
        (1979): 1975-1976.

            Summarizes the role of the World
        Bank in international finance, and its
        contribution to development literature.

788.   Stryker, Richard E.   "World Bank and
        Agricultural Development: Food
        Production and Rural Poverty."   WORLD
        DEVELOPMENT, vol. 7, no. 3 (1979):
        325-336.

            During 1970s, World Bank has become
        the leading international institution
        for development financing, and designing
        development strategies. Following the
        1972-1974 food crisis, the Bank began a
        major shift toward agriculture and rural
        development to increase food production
        and to reduce rural poverty. Their
        efforts have not been as successful as
        they could be.

789.   Syz, John.   INTERNATIONAL DEVELOPMENT BANKS.
        Dobbs Ferry, NY: Oceana Publications,
        1974. xxvii, 296 p. ISBN 0-379-0021-3
        LCCN 73-5040

            Provides a comparative legal
        analysis of international development
        banks (membership, privileges,
        functions, organization, legal standing,
        source of funds, etc.). Covers ten
        development banks: IBRD, IFC, IDA, IADB,
        European Investment Bank, Asian
        Development Bank, African Development,
        East African Development Bank, Caribbean
        Development Bank, and the Central
        American Bank for Economic Integration.

790.   Taft, Robert A.   "International Bank."
        COMMONWEALTH AND FINANCIAL CHRONICLE,
        vol. 162, no. 4404 (July 19, 1945):
        299+.

        US Senator Taft asks for
        postponement in approving World Bank.
        Argues that planning to lend on the
        scale envisioned by the Bank is
        dangerous. Calls it a serious deviation
        from US foreign policy. Argues credit-
        financed foreign trade is inflationary.

791.   "Taking Up the Running: a Survey of the World
        Bank." THE ECONOMIST, vol. 300
        (September 27, 1986): survey 1-56.   *

792.   Taylor, Carl E., and Rashid Faruquee.   CHILD
        AND MATERNAL HEALTH SERVICES IN RURAL
        INDIA: THE NARANGWAL EXPERIMENT.
        Baltimore, MD: Published for the World
        Bank by Johns Hopkins University Press,
        1984.   2 v. (v.1 - xxv,256 p.;   v.2 -
        xxxiii,252 p.)   ISBN 0-8018-3064-8
        LCCN 82-23915

        World Bank recognized the need for
        a longitudinal field study of nutrition
        and primary health care system to help
        in improving nutrition. This study grew
        out of the Narangwal Nutrition Project
        in India (1961).

793.   Tenorio, Vyvyan.   "Manila's Tariff
        Modification." FAR EASTERN ECONOMIC
        REVIEW, vol. 109, no. 33 (August 8,
        1980): 46,51.

        The Philippines gets a World Bank
        loan to assist with balance of payments
        problem (structural adjustment loan), to
        help meet the costs of imports used in
        implementing the industrialization

program and development of export
industries. The Philippines began a
review of the tariff schedule to modify
duties on imported finished goods.

794.   Tenorio, Vyuyan. "Power Push: India, World
Bank Team Up on Major Power Projects."
ENGINEERING NEWS RECORD, vol. 216
(February 20, 1986): 13-14. *

795.   Tetzlaff, Rainer. "World Bank: The Way It
Functions and Its Political Importance
for the Third World." ECONOMICS,
vol. 19 (1979): 118-135.

        Calls the Bank the "most important
and controversial international
organization." Describes its beginnings
at Bretton Woods, the establishment of
IDA, and the continuing problem of
financing IDA (it is dependent on the
goodwill of governments to supply
funds). Concludes describing the
political power under R. McNamara, and
who benefits from World Bank programs.

796.   Thackeray, Fred. "World Bank: Energy
Investment in LDCs." PETROLEUM
ECONOMIST, vol. 53 (July 1986):
261-263. *

797.   "Those Simple Bare Necessities." THE
ECONOMIST, vol. 265 (December 31,
1977): 66-67.

        Comments on R. McNamara's address
to the Board of Governors, calling for
change in using conventional wisdom in
providing basic services to the poor.
Discusses the growth of development aid
business, in contrast to little change
in solving global poverty. Describes
new strategy in which UNICEF is using

the poor to reach the poor, but that
approach has some problems too.

798. Tran, Mark. "Carnage in the Corridors."
SOUTH, no. 83 (September 1987): 10-11.

Describes the reorganization of the
World Bank and its ramifications (China
cancels a visit by a World Bank
delegation; E. Rotberg, World Bank
Treasurer since 1968, leaves for Wall
Street; Benjamin King leaves after 40
years with the Bank, etc.). Criticizes
the shakeup for its clumsiness, and the
setback in the World Bank's vision.

799. "Transformation of International Lending."
MIDLAND BANK REVIEW (August 1955):
5-7,10.

Compares World Bank loans, and
sources of capital for the Bank with the
Export-Import Bank. Also compares the
World Bank with the Commonwealth
Development Finance Company (UK
corporation whose purpose is to provide
financing to develop resources in any
country in the British Commonwealth).

800. "Transport and Urban Form." EKISTICS,
vol. 42, no. 248 (July 1976): 5-10.

Presents World Bank policy on urban
use, its plan for achieving better urban
transport, and the difficulties of
evaluating urban transport. Abstracts
Chapter 5 from World Bank's Urban
Transport Sector Policy Paper (1975).

801. Tun, M.C. "Burma Maps Out Improvements."
FAR EASTERN ECONOMIC REVIEW, vol. 99,
no.2 (January 13, 1978): 58-59.

Burma conducts feasibility studies
with World Bank assistance, and
identifies 5 areas: improving rice,
cotton and groundnut seed distribution;
rubber; urea fertilizer; hydroelectric
plant; and road improvements. Funding
has been made for the seed project.

802.   Turnbull, Laura Sherer. CURRENT ASPECTS OF
UNITED STATES FOREIGN LENDING ON
EXPORT-IMPORT BANK, INTERNATIONAL BANK
FOR RECONSTRUCTION AND DEVELOPMENT, AND
INTERNATIONAL MONETARY FUND: SELECTED
BIBLIOGRAPHY OF TEXTS AND COMMENTS.
Princeton, NJ: Princeton University,
1947. *

803.   Turvey, Ralph, and Dennis Anderson.
ELECTRICITY ECONOMICS: ESSAYS AND CASE
STUDIES. Baltimore, MD: Published for
the World Bank by Johns Hopkins
University Press, 1977. xvii,364 p.
ISBN 0-8018-1866-4; 0-8018-1867-2
(paper) LCCN 76-9031

Investigates pricing and investment
policy in LDCs which furthers economic
development in the electricity sector in
Tunisia, Sudan, Thailand, and Turkey
(1972-1973). Examines economic theory,
and the practice of pricing and
investment in electricity industry.

804.   Tyler, Christian. "Paying Back a Green
Debt." FINANCIAL TIMES (December 13,
1987): Weekend, FT1. *

805.   Ugochukwu, Onyema. "IMF/World Bank: Growth
of Positive Trend." WEST AFRICA,
no. 3713 (October 10-16, 1988): 1888-89.

IMF and World Bank resolve to
intensify efforts to reduce poverty.

Represents a step forward in recognition of the role played by industrialized countries in adjustment process.

806. Ul Haq, Mahbub, and S.J. Burki. MEETING BASIC NEEDS: AN OVERVIEW. Washington, D.C.: IBRD, 1980.

Emphasized basic needs must be balanced against growth. Meeting these needs (housing, nutrition, education, and health) is essential to long-term sustainable growth.

807. UK Chancellor of the Exchequer. PROPOSALS FOR INCREASING THE RESOURCES OF INTERNATIONAL MONETARY FUND AND INTERNATIONAL BANK FOR RECONSTRUCTION AND DEVELOPMENT. London: HMSO, 1959. iii,30 p. *

808. US Citizens Advisory Committee to Study Financial Aspects of Expansion of International Trade. STUDY OF THE FINANCIAL ASPECTS OF INTERNATIONAL TRADE AND OF THE EXPORT-IMPORT BANK AND THE WORLD BANK. Washington, D.C.: GPO, 1954. vi,54 p. *

Report to the US Senate Committee on Banking and Currency.

809. US Congress. ORGANIZATIONAL SURVEY OF THE INTERNATIONAL BANK FOR RECONSTRUCTION AND DEVELOPMENT. Washington, D.C.: GPO, 1953. iv,10 p. *

810. US Congress. House. Committee on Banking and Currency. ANGLO-AMERICAN FINANCIAL AGREEMENT (Hearing, HJ Res 311 and SJ Res 311, May-June 1946). Washington, D.C.: GPO, 1946. 675 p.

Joint resolution to implement
Bretton Woods Agreements Act.
Authorizes the Secretary of the Treasury
to carry out the agreement with UK.

811.   US Congress. House. Committee on Banking
        and Currency. BRETTON WOODS AGREEMENTS
        ACT (Hearing, HR 2211, March and April
        1945). Washington, D.C.: GPO, 1945.
        2 v. 1334 p.

        Bill to provide US participation in
        IMF and IBRD. Hearings, statements, and
        testimony of experts are included
        (HR 2211 superseded later by HR 3314).
        See Entry 812.

812.   US Congress. House. Committee on Banking
        and Currency. BRETTON WOODS AGREEMENTS
        ACT (Hearing, HR 3314, June 1945).
        Washington, D.C.: GPO, 1945. 670 p.

        Bill to provide US participation in
        IMF and IBRD (supercedes HR 2211). See
        Entry 811.

813.   US Congress. House. Committee on Banking
        and Currency. BRETTON WOODS AGREEMENTS
        ACT AMENDMENT (Hearing, HR 10162,
        February 1962). Washington, D.C.: GPO,
        1962. 165 p.

        Amends the Bretton Woods Agreements
        Act to authorize US participation in
        loans to strengthen the money system.

814.   US Congress. House. Committee on Banking
       and Currency. EIGHTH SPECIAL REPORT ON
       THE OPERATIONS AND POLICIES OF THE
       INTERNATIONAL FINANCIAL INSTITUTIONS OF
       WHICH THE US IS A MEMBER, FOR THE 2-YEAR
       PERIOD APRIL 1960-MARCH 1962 (88th
       Congress, 1st Session. House Document,
       175). Washington, D.C.: 1963.
       vi,39 p. *

            Published annually, covers
       operations and policies of the various
       international financial institutions
       (IBRD, IFC, IDA, and IADB) to which the
       US belongs.

815.   US Congress. House. Committee on Banking
       and Currency. EXPANDING OF THE
       RESOURCES OF THE INTERNATIONAL
       DEVELOPMENT ASSOCIATION (Hearing,
       HR 9022, December 1963). Washington,
       D.C.: GPO, 1963. 81 p.

            Amends the IDA Act to authorize the
       US to participate in an increase of the
       resources for IDA.

816.   US Congress. House. Committee on Banking
       and Currency. IBRD AND IFC ARTICLES OF
       AGREEMENT (Hearings, HR 8816 AND S 1742,
       July 1965). Washington, D.C.: GPO,
       1965. 83 p.

            Authorizes the US government to
       agree to the amendments of IFC and IBRD,
       and to allow the US government
       representatives (on the Board of
       Governors) to vote for capital increases
       when it does not involve an increase in
       the US subscription.

817.   US Congress. House. Committee on Banking
        and Currency. INTERNATIONAL BANKS
        (Hearings, HR 7405 and HR 7406, July
        1963). Washington, D.C.: GPO, 1963.
        33 p.

        Amends Bretton Woods Agreements Act
        to authorize the US government to vote
        for an increase in the World Bank's
        authorized capital stock, and increased
        participation in IADB.

818.   U. S. Congress. House. Committee on Banking,
        Finance and Urban Affairs. MANDATE FOR
        DEVELOPMENT: THE FUTURE OF THE WORLD
        BANK; Hearing, September 5, 1985 (99th
        Congress, 1st Session, Serial
        no. 99-40). Washington, D.C.: GPO,
        1986. iii,41 p. *

        Former World Bank president Robert
        McNamara testifying on US support for
        aid to developing countries.

819.   US Congress. House. Committee on Banking,
        Finance and Urban Affairs. US PROPOSALS
        ON INTERNATIONAL DEBT CRISIS; Hearing,
        October 22, 1985 (99th Congress, 1st
        Session, Serial no. 99-39). Washington,
        D.C.: GPO, 1986. iii,65 p. *

        Discusses proposals made at 1985
        Board of Governors meeting in Seoul.

820.   US Congress. House. Committee on Foreign
        Affairs. Subcommittee on Africa.
        AFRICA, THE WORLD BANK, AND THE IMF: AN
        APPRAISAL -- HEARING (98th Congress,
        Second Session, February 23, 1984).
        Washington, D.C.: GPO, 1984.
        iii,103 p. *

821. US Congress. Senate. Committee on Banking
        and Currency. STUDY OF EXPORT-IMPORT
        BANK AND WORLD BANK. Washington, D.C.:
        GPO, 1954. iii,1301 p. *

822. US General Accounting Office. LOW US
        SHARE OF WORLD BANK-FINANCED
        PROCUREMENT. Washington, D.C.: 1974.
        65 p. LCCN 74-602866 *

823. US Library of Congress. UNITED STATES AND
        THE MULTILATERAL DEVELOPMENT BANKS.
        Washington, D.C.: GPO, 1974. xv,230 p.

        Surveys the operations of
        multilateral development banks and US
        policy towards them. Covers IADB, Asian
        Development Bank, and World Bank, the
        largest of the 9 development banks.

824. US National Advisory Council on
        International Monetary and Financial
        Problems. REPORT OF ACTIVITIES COVERING
        ITS ACTIVITIES FROM JANUARY 1-JUNE 30,
        1961, IN ACCORDANCE WITH SECTION 4(b)(5)
        OF BRETTON WOODS AGREEMENTS ACT (87th
        Congress, 2nd Session. House Document,
        402). Washington, D.C.: 1962.
        vii,83 p. *

        Provides information about US
        participation in international financial
        organizations.

825. US National Advisory Council on
        International Monetary and Financial
        Problems. SPECIAL REPORT TO THE
        PRESIDENT AND TO THE CONGRESS ON THE
        SELECTIVE CAPITAL INCREASE. Washington,
        D.C.: 1977. 18 p.

        Recommends an increase of Bank
        capital, so it can continue its work in

LDCs. Comments on basis for US support, and Bank's lending operations and resources. Analyses the proposal for a capital increase.

826. US POLICIES TOWARD THE WORLD BANK AND THE INTERNATIONAL MONETARY FUND. New York: 1982. ISBN 0-934654-40-9 LCCN 82-13569 *

827. "US Wants Increase in International Funds." ENGINEERING-NEWS RECORD, vol. 215 (October 17, 1985): 10. *

828. Van de Laar, Aart J.M. WORLD BANK AND THE POOR (Institute of Social Studies Series on the Development of Societies, 6). Boston, MA: Martinus Nijhoff, 1980. xii,269 p. ISBN 0-89838-042-1 LCCN 80-12011

Discusses adequacy of Bank policies in light of: (1) lack of information on the Bank's internal functioning, or lack of public access to this information; and (2) negative reaction to public criticism, and unwillingness to establish an open dialogue. Examines the Bank's past, and considers trends in Bank policy. Discusses whether the World Bank can change to serve the poorest of the poor.

829. Van de Laar, Aart J.M. "World Bank and the World's Poor." WORLD DEVELOPMENT, vol. 4, no. 10/11 (October-November 1976): 837-851.

Analyzes Bank's policy statements and shows that, while Robert McNamara expressed intentions of doing more for the poor, limited progress was made. Project, sector, and institutional constraints, as well as a deficient World Bank framework limited progress.

830. Van de Laar, Aart J.M. "World Bank: Which Way?" DEVELOPMENT AND CHANGE, vol. 7, no. 1 (January 1976): 67-97.

Reviews the Bank's structural position and growth through 1975. Describes the Bank's accomplishments and the problems being faced.

831. Van de Laar, Aart J.M. "Young Professionals Programme of the World Bank: An Analysis of an Elite Group." DEVELOPMENT AND CHANGE, vol. 6, no. 3 (July 1975): 5-26.

Analyzes the Young Professionals Program, how participants are selected, and how UN personnel policies affect the World Bank. The program's purpose is to recruit talented graduate students to receive training at the Bank, and then retained them as permanent staff.

832. van der Tak, Herman G. ECONOMIC CHOICE BETWEEN HYDROELECTRIC AND THERMAL POWER DEVELOPMENT, WITH A NOTE ON JOINT COSTS IN MULTIPURPOSE PROJECTS (World Bank Staff Occasional Paper, 1). Baltimore, MD: Distributed for the World Bank by Johns Hopkins Press, 1966. x,70 p.

Compares alternative developments of a power system. Analyses problems of choosing smaller investments in thermal power at a future date, or larger investments in hydro power at the present time.

833.   Van Meerhaeghe, M.A.G.   INTERNATIONAL
             ECONOMIC INSTITUTIONS, 4th ed.
             Dordrecht, The Netherlands: Martinus
             Nijhoff, 1985.   ISBN 90-247-2972-6
             LCCN 84-7967

                     Focus on institutions (IMF, IBRD,
             GATT, UNCTAD, OECD, and EEC) which
             influence the national economies of its
             member nations.

834.   Venugopal, Reddy Y.   WORLD BANK, BORROWERS'
             PERSPECTIVES.   New Delhi, India: 1985.
             x,143 p.   ISBN 81-207-0032-5
             LCCN 85-904345 *

835.   Villegas, Edberto M.   REFORMS IN THE
             PHILIPPINE FINANCIAL SYSTEM AND
             CONTRADICTIONS WITHIN US CAPITALISM
             (Third World Studies Paper, 31).
             Diliman, Quezon City, Philippines:
             University of Philippines, College of
             Arts and Sciences, 1982   52 p.
             LCCN 84-179346

                     Illustrates how IMF and World Bank
             backed reforms contributing to the
             recession in the US economy.   Explores
             the major industrial programs in the
             Philippines.   Argues the Philippines
             financial system promotes the expansion
             of US capitalism.

836.   Vogl, Frank.   "Annual Meetings: The Observer
             in Berlin."   BANK'S WORLD, vol. 7
             (November 1988): 6-11.   *

837.   "Volker to Advise World Bank."   WASHINGTON
             POST (September 30, 1987): F1.   *

838.   Vu, My T.   SHORT-TERM POPULATION PROJECTIONS,
        1980-2020 AND LONG-TERM PROJECTIONS 2000
        TO STATIONARY STAGE BY AGE AND SEX FOR
        ALL THE COUNTRIES OF THE WORLD.
        Washington, D.C.: IBRD, 1983.   385 p.

        Detailed projections at 5-year
        intervals with implied fertility and
        mortality rates.   Summarizes the WORLD
        DEVELOPMENT REPORT 1983 (Entry 501).

839.   Wall, Roger.   "Development, Instability and
        the World Bank."   INST. RESEARCH PEACE
        VIOLENCE, vol. 7, no. 2 (1977): 83-98.   *

840.   Wallich, H.C.   "Financing the International
        Bank."   HARVARD BUSINESS REVIEW, vol. 24
        (Winter 1946): 164-182.   *

        Comprehensive discussion on large-
        scale export of capital and sale of
        bonds.   Summarizes different viewpoints
        to guarantee loans and floating bonds.

841.   Walsh, John.   "World Bank Pressed on
        Environmental Reforms."   SCIENCE,
        vol. 234 (November 14, 1986): 813-815.

        Critics of the World Bank view the
        nomination of Barber Conable as on way
        the World Bank is being receptive to
        ecological reform.   While encouraged by
        Conable's stance, environmentalists will
        not decrease their pressure on the Bank.

842.   Walsh, John.   "World Bank Puts Priority on
        Africa Program."   SCIENCE, no. 226
        (October 12, 1984): 148-149,152.

        Describes the problems of injecting
        science and technology into the Sub-
        Saharan Africa development program.
        Emphasizes the World Bank's new focus on

utilizing science and technology,
especially low cost technology.

843.   Walstedt, Bertil. STATE MANUFACTURING
        ENTERPRISE IN A MIXED ECONOMY: THE
        TURKISH CASE (World Bank Research
        Publication). Baltimore, MD: Published
        for the World Bank by Johns Hopkins
        University Press, 1980. xxii,354 p.
        ISBN 0-8018-2226-2; 0-8018-2227-0
        (paper) LCCN 78-21398

        Discusses the role of state
        enterprise in the development of
        Turkey's manufacturing sector. Turkey
        is one of the few democratic LDCs.

844.   Walters, Alan Arthur. ECONOMICS OF ROAD USER
        CHARGES. Baltimore, MD: Published for
        the World Bank by Johns Hopkins Press,
        1968. 243 p. LCCN 68-8702 *

845.   Webberman, Ben. "Smart Answers to Dumb
        Questions." FORBES, vol. 137 (May 19,
        1986): 110,113.

        Interviews Eugene Rotberg (World
        Bank Treasurer) about the Bank's
        portfolio, interest rates, and financial
        analysis. The Bank handles $5 trillion
        transactions per year.

846.   Weinwurm, Ernest H. "Worldwide Investment
        Expected for World Bank Bonds."
        COMMONWEALTH AND FINANCIAL CHRONICLE,
        vol. 163, no. 4486 (May 2, 1946):
        2354,2375.

        Points out that a global market
        will be created when the World Bank
        floats its bonds. It will act as
        international reserves, and have the

broadest market in all countries. See
also Entries 687, and 840.

847.   Weiss, Charles. "World Bank's Support for
        Science and Technology." SCIENCE,
        no. 227 (January 18, 1985): 261-5.

        Describes the Bank's role as an
        unsung hero in the development of
        science and technology in LDCs. It
        provides education and training in
        technology, development policy, research
        in sanitation, renewable energy
        resources, agriculture, health, etc.
        Now it is examining its approach, as
        available funds decrease.

848.   Westlake, Melvyn. "Shape Up or Ship Out."
        SOUTH, no. 95 (September 1988): 17.

        Describes the proposed US
        contributions vs. Japan's contributions,
        and voting shares. Notes that Japan is
        second biggest shareholder. The fight
        in Congress over the capital increase
        could change this, especially since
        James Baker is no longer there to fight
        for the increase (the Bank's ally in
        Congress).

849.   Wheatley, Alan. "World Bank Looks at
        Mortgage Debt." WASHINGTON TIMES (March
        22, 1988): C4. *

850.   White, John. REGIONAL DEVELOPMENT BANKS: THE
        ASIAN, AFRICAN AND INTER-AMERICAN
        DEVELOPMENT BANKS (Praeger Special
        Studies in International Economics and
        Development). New York: Published for
        ODI by Praeger, 1972. vii,204 p.
        LCCN 74-184033

Presents these alternatives to the World Bank Group as international development financing sources, by studying their structure and prospects.

851.   Whitman, Marina von Neumann. GOVERNMENT RISK-SHARING IN FOREIGN INVESTMENT. Princeton, NJ: Princeton University Press, 1965. 358 p. LCCN 65-14314

Discusses six agencies engaged in risk-sharing activities with US funds between 1945 and 1963, including Export-Import Bank, IBRD, and IADB. Examines the contributions of US capital on foreign economic development.

852.   Weiss, Charles, and Nicolas Jequier (eds.). TECHNOLOGY, FINANCE AND DEVELOPMENT: AN ANALYSIS OF THE WORLD BANK AS A TECHNOLOGICAL INSTITUTION. Lexington, MA: Lexington Books, 1984. vi,342 p. ISBN 0-669-07762-3 LCCN 83-49213

Surveys the World Bank's impact on the diffusion of technology as a result of its mission to acts as a development agency. Suggests conclusions for policy makers, and examines technology at the sector level. Discusses the approach of appropriate technology, and problems of technology transfer. Concludes with efforts to build global research networks.

853.   Williamson, J. "World Bank Stands at the Crossroads." TELEPHONY, vol. 213 (September 28, 1987): 149-151. *

854.   Wilson, Geoffrey M. "Operations of the World Bank." WORLD TODAY, vol. 20, no. 2 (February 1964): 84-92.

Describes allocation of voting power, financial resources, loan commitments, and IDA. Discusses how World Bank is widening its horizons in terms of loan rates and repayment, and technical assistance. It still will continue to be cautious and pragmatic, but more sympathetic.

855.   Wilson, Stanley. "Can Barber Conable Get the World Bank Moving Again? The New World Bank Chief Has a Talent for Compromise and Political Contacts Aplenty -- But is That Enough?" INSTITUTIONAL INVESTOR, Vol. 20 (May 1986): 304-306+. *

Examines former Congressman Conable's career, and projects the possible outcome as he becomes the new World Bank president.

856.   Wirth, David A. "World Bank and the Environment." ENVIRONMENT, vol. 28 (December 1986): 33-4. *

857.   W'obanda, Chango B. Machyo. "World Bank, IMF and Deepening Misery in Uganda (the Mbale Experience)." MAWAZO: A JOURNAL OF THE FACULTIES OF ARTS AND SOCIAL SCIENCES, MAKERERE UNIVERSITY (UGANDA), vol. 6 (June 1985): 27-49. *

858.   Wohlmuth, Karl. "IMF and World Bank Structural Adjustment Policies: Cooperation or Conflict?" INTERECONOMICS, vol. 19, no. 5 (October 1984): 226-234.

Discusses relationship between IMF and World Bank, as well as areas of cooperation, alternatives for structural adjustment and conditionality. Argues members should give political support in process of structural adjustment.

859.   "World Bank: Accounting for the Environment." THE ECONOMIST, vol. 299 (June 21, 1986): 70,72.

        World Bank will double its spending on forestry in Africa. It will examine environmental damage caused by previous development projects like those in Indonesia, India, and Brazil, and will work to correct them.

860.   "World Bank: A Friend or Foe?" BUSINESS IN ECOWAS, vol. 1, no. 5 (October 5, 1987): 17-31.

        Explores the paradox in which West Africa tends to view the World Bank as maintaining poverty, instead of alleviating it. Expresses viewpoints by officials in Ghana, Nigeria, etc.

861.   "World Bank: After Clausen." THE ECONOMIST, vol. 298 (February 1, 1986): 78.

        Describes how US generally picks the World Bank President, while the IMF President is usually European, but various factors come into play. Examines possible candidates for World Bank presidency: William Brock, John Petty, Jack Hemingway, etc.

862.   "World Bank Assesses Effects of Oil Price Plunge." OIL & GAS JOURNAL, vol. 84 (August 11, 1986): 30.   *

863.   "World Bank Attaches Strings to LDC Loans." JOURNAL OF COMMERCE (April 15, 1988): 11A.   *

864.   "World Bank Branches Out." THE ECONOMIST,
            vol. 274 (March 22, 1980): International
            Banking Survey 21-22.

            Describes how the World Bank is
            trying to change its operations to
            "program lending," because the project
            financing cycle takes about ten years
            from identifying to completing a
            project. This change is controversial,
            because it sets conditions on the loan.
            But project financing is not being
            completely abandoned.

865.   World Bank: EMGF Kicks Off." BANKER,
            vol. 136 (April 1986): 60. *

            Describes the Emerging Markets
            Growth Fund program.

866.   "World Bank Gets Capital Increase." AFRICA
            ECONOMIC DIGEST, vol. 9 (May 6-12,
            1988): 2. *

867.   "World Bank: Global Financing of
            Impoverishment and Famine." ECOLOGIST,
            vol. 15, no. 1-2 (1985): 4-81. *

            Presents remarks by Anders Wijkman,
            Lloyd Timberlake, and N.D. Jayal.

868.   "World Bank/IMF Await Their Fate." WEST
            AFRICA, no. 3708 (September 5-11, 1988):
            1639-40.

            Both are seeking capital increase
            from the US, and must wait for the 1988
            Board of Governors meeting to see what
            Congress will do. If the US fails to
            come through with the funding, Japan
            could decide to buy up the shares the US
            turns down and thereby, increase its

share. Congress has been in the habit of blocking increases in recent years.

869. "World Bank/IMF: Beyond Debt Swaps."
FINANCIAL MAIL (SOUTH AFRICA), vol. 106
(October 2, 1987): 53-54. *

870. "World Bank Leads the Way." BANKER,
vol. 105, no. 357 (October 1955):
230-234. *

871. "World Bank: Much Bigger Game, Same Rules."
MASS TRANSIT, vol. 13 (April 1986):
16+.*

872. "World Bank Needs a Little Self-Help." THE
ECONOMIST, vol. 298 (March 22, 1986):
71.

Awaiting confirmation as new World
Bank President, Barber Conable faces
obstacles of getting more money to lend
(increasing capital base), and changes
in terms of loans (conditions).

873. "World Bank Outlines Opportunities."
TELEPHONY, vol. 212 (January 5, 1987):
24. *

874. "World Bank Raising Cash." ENGINEERING NEWS
RECORD, vol. 220 (March 3, 1988): 15. *

Describes the shift in policy from
construction projects to economic
stability projects.

875. "World Bank Reorganization." FINANCE AND
DEVELOPMENT, vol. 24 (September 1987):
46-47.

Organization chart after
reorganization in May 1987 by Barber
Conable who stated the purpose of the

reorganization was to make the Bank more responsive and efficient. Created four areas: Administration; Finance; Operations; and Policy, Planning, and Research. Each of the four areas are headed by a senior Vice President.

876. "World Bank -- Running in Place." FINANCIAL MAIL (SOUTH AFRICA), vol. 107 (February 26, 1988): 66. *

877. World Bank Scramble -- Editorial." JOURNAL OF COMMERCE (April 14, 1988): 8A. *

878. "World Bank Sees Slower Global Economic Recovery, Says Open Trade Policies are Best for Growth." BUSINESS AMERICA, vol. 10, no. 15 (July 20, 1987): 14-15. Based on WORLD DEVELOPMENT REPORT 1987 (Entry 505). Presents the highlights, focusing on trade and industrialization. Examines protectionism, trade policy, industrialization and the Uruguay Round.

879. "World Bank Supporting Hydro." ALTERNATIVE SOURCES OF ENERGY, no. 75 (September/October 1985): 58.

Describes hydroelectric power projects in Nepal, Yugoslavia, India, and China.

880. "World Bank to Assist Yugoslav Gas Projects." OIL & GAS JOURNAL, vol. 83 (July 22, 1985): 58+ *

Studies the role of AID, Export-Import Bank, IBRD, IFC, IADB, and Investment Guaranty Program in capital movements.

881. "World Bank to Stress Environment
      Protection." CHEMICAL & ENGINEERING
      NEWS, vol. 65 (May 11, 1987): 5-6. *

          Calculates the environmental costs
      of Bank programs.

882. "World Bank's Development Primer." THE
      ECONOMIST, vol. 296 (September 14,
      1985): 73.

          Abstracts INVESTING IN DEVELOPMENT
      (see Entry 141). Describes IDA and
      World Bank loans approved by sector
      (agriculture and rural development,
      water, energy, transport, education,
      population and health, etc.).

883. "World Bank's Natural Gas Program." FINANCE
      AND DEVELOPMENT, vol. 23 (June 1986):
      12-13.

          Describes Thailand, Argentina, and
      Tanzania as examples of exploiting
      natural gas, gas utilization, and fuel
      substitutions, respectively. World Bank
      is trying to assist LDCs to implement
      energy policies. Currently 25% of Bank
      lending goes to energy sector.

884. "World Bank's Plan for $75 Billion Rise in
      Capital Backed By Baker, Greenspan."
      WALL STREET JOURNAL (February 17, 1988):
      42. *

885. "World Bank's Prescription: Electronics."
      ECONOMIC AND POLITICAL WEEKLY, vol. 22,
      no. 39 (September 26, 1987): 1625.

          Comments on World Bank's
      recommendation to India on completing
      the process of delicensing electronics
      industry. The Bank advises the

fostering of electronics monopolies.
reduction of import duties, and adoption
of economies of scale -- all of which
were already being pursued by India.

886.   Wright, L.C. "Fund, the Bank, and I.F.C."
        SCOTTISH BANKERS MAGAZINE, vol. 48, no.
        191 (November 1956): 145-152.

        Claims that after 10 years, IMF is
        inept while the Bank is ingenious.
        Describes the objectives, failures, and
        accomplishments. World Bank was
        established as type of international
        investment institution, and it has been
        successful in its financial policy. IFC
        was intended to underwrite projects
        outside the scope of the World Bank.

887.   Yagci, Fahrettin, Steve Kamin, and Vicki
        Rosenbaum. STRUCTURAL ADJUSTMENT
        LENDING: AN EVALUATION OF PROGRAM DESIGN
        (World Bank Staff Working Paper, 735).
        Washington, D.C.: World Bank, 1985.
        137 p. ISBN 0-8213-0545-X
        LCCN 85-9521*

888.   Yokota, Yozo. "Non-political Character of
        the World Bank." JAPANESE ANNUAL OF
        INTERNATIONAL LAW, vol. 20 (1976):
        39-64. *

889.   Young, Kevin, Willem C. F. Bussink, and
        Parvez Hasan (eds.). MALAYSIA: GROWTH
        AND EQUITY IN A MULTIRACIAL SOCIETY
        (World Bank Country Economic Report).
        Baltimore, MD: Published for the World
        Bank by Johns Hopkins Press, 1980.
        xix,345 p. ISBN 0-8018-2384-6;
        0-8018-2385-4 (paper) LCCN 79-3677

Reviews Malaysian economy since 1960. Discusses current issues, and addresses future prospects.

890.   Yudelman, Montague. WORLD BANK AND AGRICULTURAL DEVELOPMENT: AN INSIDER'S VIEW (World Resources Institute Papers, 1). World Resources Institute, 1985. 37 p. ISBN 0-915825-11-2 *

891.   Zakiriya, Hasan S. "Petroleum Lending Programme of the World Bank." JOURNAL OF WORLD TRADE LAW, vol. 17, no. 6 (November/December 1983): 471-495. *

892.   Zymelman, Manuel. ECONOMIC EVALUATION OF VOCATIONAL TRAINING PROGRAMS, with the assistance of Alan Woodruff. Baltimore, MD: Published for the World Bank by Johns Hopkins Press, 1976. 122 p. ISBN 0-8018-1855-9 LCCN 76-4868

INTERNATIONAL CENTRE FOR SETTLEMENT OF INVESTMENT DISPUTES

893.   Baker, James C. "ICSID: An International Method for Handling Foreign Investment Disputes in LDCs." FOREIGN TRADE REVIEW, vol. 21 (January/March 1987): 411-421. *

894.   Balekjian, W.H. "Convention of the International Bank on the Settlement of Investment Disputes Between States and Nationals of Other States." ANNUAIRE DES AUDITEURS ET ANCIENS AUDITEURS DE L'ACADEMIE ET DROIT INTERNATIONAL DE LA HAYE, vol. 37-38 (1967/68): 108-120. *

895. Coll, Richard J. "United States Enforcement
      of Arbitral Awards Against Sovereign
      States: Implications of the ICSID
      Convention." HARVARD INTERNATIONAL LAW
      JOURNAL, vol. 17, no. 2 (Spring 1976). *

896. International Centre for the Settlement of
      Investment Disputes. ANNUAL REPORT,
      1966/67-. Washington, D.C.: 1967- *

897. International Centre for Settlement of
      Investment Disputes. CONTRACTING STATES
      AND ACTIONS TAKEN BY THEM PURSUANT TO
      THE CONVENTION (ICSID/8/Rev.4).
      Washington, D.C.: n.d. *

898. International Centre for Settlement of
      Investment Disputes. CONVENTION ON THE
      SETTLEMENT OF INVESTMENT DISPUTES
      BETWEEN STATES AND NATIONALS OF OTHER
      STATES, AND ACCOMPANYING REPORT OF THE
      EXECUTIVE DIRECTORS OF THE INTERNATIONAL
      BANK FOR RECONSTRUCTION AND DEVELOPMENT
      (ICSID/2). Washington, D.C.: n.d. *

899. International Centre for Settlement of
      Investment Disputes. ICSID TENTH ANNUAL
      REPORT, 1975/1976. Washington, D.C.:
      1976. 34 p.

          Reviews activities, and presents
      the financial statement. Lists members,
      provisions, and publications.

900. International Centre for Settlement of
      Investment Disputes. LIST OF
      CONTRACTING STATES AND OTHER SIGNATORIES
      OF THE CONVENTION (ICSID/3).
      Washington, D.C.: n.d. *

901.   International Centre for Settlement of
            Investment Disputes. LIST OF MEMBERS OF
            THE PANELS OF CONCILIATORS AND
            ARBITRATORS (ICSID/10). Washington,
            D.C.: n.d. *

902.   International Centre for Settlement of
            Investment Disputes. MODEL CLAUSES
            RECORDING CONSENT TO THE JURISDICTION OF
            THE INTERNATIONAL CENTRE FOR SETTLEMENT
            OF INVESTMENT DISPUTES (ICSID/5).
            Washington, D.C.: n.d. *

903.   International Centre for Settlement of
            Investment Disputes. MODEL CLAUSES
            RELATING TO THE CONVENTION ON SETTLEMENT
            OF INVESTMENT DISPUTES DESIGNED FOR
            BILATERAL INVESTMENT TREATIES (ICSID/6).
            Washington, D.C.: n.d. *

904.   International Centre for Settlement of
            Investment Disputes. PROVISIONAL
            REGULATIONS AND RULES (ICSID/1).
            Washington, D.C.: n.d. *

                    Superseded by Entry 907.

905.   International Centre for Settlement of
            Investment Disputes. PROVISIONS
            RELATING TO ICSID IN INTERNATIONAL
            AGREEMENTS AND NATIONAL INVESTMENT LAWS
            (ICSID/9/Rev. 2). Washington, D.C.:
            n.d. *

906.   International Centre for Settlement of
            Investment Disputes. PUBLICATIONS OF
            ICSID (ICSID/7). Washington, D.C.:
            n.d.*

907.   International Centre for Settlement of
            Investment Disputes. REGULATIONS AND
            RULES (ICSID/4/Rev.1). Washington,
            D.C.: n.d. *

See also Entry 904.

908.   Ryans, John K., Jr., and James C. Baker.
        "International Centre for the Settlement
        of Investment Disputes (ICSID)."
        JOURNAL OF WORLD TRADE LAW
        (January/February 1976): 65-79.

        ICSID provides a structure to
        resolve contractual disputes between
        host country and corporate donor. Most
        African nations belong. Calls for Latin
        American nations to join, and to settle
        current cases being considered by ICSID.
        Since these countries are high risk, not
        having them as members is one of ICSID's
        shortcomings.

909.   Schmidt, John T. "Arbitration Under the
        Auspices of the International Centre for
        Settlement of Investment Disputes
        (ICSID): Implications of the Decision on
        Jurisdiction in Alcoa Minerals of
        Jamaica, Inc. v. Government of Jamaica."
        HARVARD INTERNATIONAL LAW JOURNAL,
        vol. 17 (1976): 90-109. *

910.   West, Luther C. "Award Enforcement
        Provisions of the World Bank
        Convention." ARBITRATION JOURNAL,
        vol. 23, no. 1 (1968): 38-53.

        Points out how ICSID allows World
        Bank to make arbitration agreements
        binding. Describes paper autonomy and
        its relation to IMF, expropriation, and
        treaty violation. Concludes that while
        it is worthwhile, ICSID is not perfect,
        because it encourages member countries
        to agree to arbitration.

INTERNATIONAL DEVELOPMENT ASSOCIATION

911.   "Agreement Reached on a Sixth Replenishment
         of IDA." FINANCE AND DEVELOPMENT,
         vol. 17 (March 1980): 3.

              Representatives agree to increase
         IDA's resources (1980-1983).

912.   "Aid: Mean, Meaner, Meanest." THE ECONOMIST,
         vol. 290 (January 21, 1984): 62-63.

              Describes outcome of cuts to IDA
         funding ($9 down from $16 million),
         leading to more bilateral aid. This is
         tied to manufacturers' contracts in
         donor countries, instead of the free-
         market advice which accompanies
         multilateral assistance.

913.   "Aiding IDA." THE ECONOMIST, vol. 289
         (December 3, 1983): 18.

914.   Baldwin, David A. "International Development
         Association: Theory and Practice."
         ECONOMIC DEVELOPMENT AND CULTURAL
         CHANGE, vol. 10 (October 1961): 86-96.

              Studies IDA in terms of political
         dimensions. Defines "soft loans"
         (backbone of IDA lending). Presents
         disadvantages and advantages of soft
         lending, and how countries view IDA.

915.   Bleiberg, R.M. "Look Before You Leap: Red
         China's Credit Has Suffered Another
         Blow." BARRONS, vol. 62 (November 8,
         1982): 11. *

916.   Blitzer, Charles. "Financing the World
        Bank." BETWEEN TWO WORLDS: THE WORLD
        BANK'S NEXT DECADE, by R. Feinberg, et
        al. New Brunswick, NJ: Transaction
        Books, 1986. p. 135-160.

        Recommends a large capital increase
        to give the Bank more flexibility in
        increasing disbursements. See also
        Entry 283.

917.   Bowring, Philip. "No Credit Where It Is
        Due." FAR EASTERN ECONOMIC REVIEW,
        vol. 83 (February 11, 1974): 34.

        US Congress turned down a request
        to replenish IDA, even though the US was
        committed to it (another signal of US
        withdrawal from foreign aid). LDCs will
        suffer. Argues the cause is poor
        nations' general opposition to US
        policy, especially in Middle East.

918.   "China Receives IDA Credit for Drainage and
        Irrigation Project." BUSINESS AMERICA,
        vol. 5, no. 14 (July 12, 1982): 35.

        Agriculture accounts for more than
        30% of China's GDP, but only 10% of the
        land is arable. Discusses the first
        attempt to control soil salinity and
        waterlogging in China. Largest Bank
        member in terms of population, this is
        its second IDA credit project.

919.   Dupuy, R.J. RIGHT TO DEVELOPMENT AT THE
        INTERNATIONAL LEVEL. Published for
        Kluwer Academic by Sijthoff and
        Noordhoff, 1981. 458 p.
        ISBN 90-286-0990-3 *

920.   "Ebenezer Reagan." THE ECONOMIST, vol. 289
        (December 17, 1983): 62. *

921.   "Filling the Coffers." THE ECONOMIST,
            vol. 284 (September 4, 1982): 14+.   *

922.   Fleming, Stewart. "Equipping the Fund and
            Bank for the Long Haul: the Long-Term
            Nature of the Debtor Nations' Problems
            is Raising Basic Questions About the
            Purpose of IMF Credits, the Role of the
            World Bank, and Ways in Which the Two
            Institutions Might Seek to Work
            Together." BANKER, vol. 135 (September
            1985): 58-59.   *

            Examines role of IDA, IMF credits,
            and the capital needs of the World Bank.

923.   Fleming, Alexander, and Mary Oakes Smith.
            "Raising Resources for IDA: The Eighth
            Replenishment." FINANCE AND
            DEVELOPMENT, vol. 24 (September 1987):
            23-26.

            Discusses how $12.4 billion was
            raised for IDA, and key policy issues
            were resolved (i.e. burden sharing, IDA-
            8 size, allocation of IDA-8 resources
            and changes in IDA-8 terms).

924.   Grant, J. "Strings Attached: Will Congress
            Finally Hobble the World Bank?"
            BARRONS, vol. 57 (July 18, 1977): 3+.   *

925.   Heywood, P. "US Seeks Harder Terms for
            Bank's Softest Loans." ENGINEERING NEWS
            RECORD (February 6, 1986): 13.*

926.   Hornstein, R.A. "Cofinancing of Bank and
            IDA Projects." FINANCE AND DEVELOPMENT,
            vol. 14 (June 1977): 40-43.   *

927.   International Bank for Reconstruction and
        Development. MULTILATERAL REGIONAL
        FINANCING INSTITUTIONS (joint IBRD and
        IDA publication). Washington, D.C.:
        IBRD and IDA, 1968. ii,102 p.

        Describes cofinancing (World Bank
        funds and funds from external sources).
        Analyzes what it means to the Bank, as
        well as to member countries.

928.   "IDA Assists Sudan's Second Highway Project."
        FINANCE AND DEVELOPMENT, vol. 16 (June
        1979): 6.

        Describes the approval of $41
        million IDA credit for a highway
        project, especially maintenance and
        detailed engineering studies for
        analyzing future needs in Sudan.

929.   "IDA Credit to Mechanize Maldivian Fishing
        Industry." FINANCE AND DEVELOPMENT,
        vol. 16 (September 1979): 3.

        Describes the IDA $3.2 million
        credit for establishment of repair
        centers, mechanization of fishing craft,
        and installation of navigation aids to
        increase water safety in the Maldives.
        Ultimately the project will increase
        fishing productivity, and provide
        training for fishermen.

930.   "IDA Crosses $10 Billion Mark in Aid Funds."
        FINANCE AND DEVELOPMENT, vol. 13
        (September 1976): 4.

Announces milestone in IDA lending
($10 billion), and 90% are credits to
countries with less than $200 per capita
income. Describes the main sources of
IDA contributions, and IDA credits
disbursed in 1976.

931.   "IDA Difference: Quiet Help for the Poorest."
         THE ECONOMIST, vol. 299 (April 5, 1986):
         16.

Contrasts funds raised by Band Aid
and Bob Geldof (the highly publicized
$100 million) with the unpublished funds
raised and distributed by IDA (almost
100 times as much).

932.   "IDA's Golden Opportunity." THE ECONOMIST,
         no. 251 (June 29, 1974): 51.

Describes gold amendment attached
to IDA funding by US Congress (allowing
US citizens to buy and hold gold for the
first time in 40 years). Discusses how
it was attached to IDA legislation which
was initially turned down by the Senate,
and Congress is being asked to vote in
support of IDA due to gold amendment.

933.   International Bank for Reconstruction and
         Development. BY-LAWS. Washington,
         D.C.: 1962. 10 p.

Presents World Bank by-laws,
especially those covering terms of
service for Board of Governors.

934.   International Development Association.
         ANNUAL REPORT, 1960/61- . Washington,
         D.C.: 1961-

Published with the WORLD BANK
ANNUAL REPORT (see Entry 380).

935.   International Development Association. IDA:
        INTERNATIONAL DEVELOPMENT ASSOCIATION.
        Washington, D.C.: IBRD, 1977. 48 p.

        Describes IDA's purpose, and
        disbursement of funds.

936.   International Development Association. IDA
        IN RETROSPECT: THE FIRST TWO DECADES OF
        THE INTERNATIONAL DEVELOPMENT
        ASSOCIATION. New York: Published for
        IDA and IBRD by Oxford University Press,
        1982. 142 p.

        Describes origins, evolution, and
        activities. Assesses IDA's place in
        economic assistance to LDCs.

937.   Jackson, Robert G.A. CASE FOR AN
        INTERNATIONAL DEVELOPMENT AUTHORITY.
        Syracuse, NY: Syracuse University Press,
        1959. 70 p. LCCN 59-9104

        Lectures by Jackson on the value of
        IDA, its role in economic progress,
        IDA's operations, and its purpose.
        Presents essay by Harland Cleveland on
        the history behind the proposal for IDA.

938.   Libby, Ronald T. "International Development
        Association: a Legal Fiction Designed to
        Secure an LDC Constituency."
        INTERNATIONAL ORGANIZATION, vol. 29,
        no. 4 (Autumn 1975): 1065-1072.

        Argues IDA is a pseudo-division
        which allows the Bank to increase
        lending to LDCs via IDA loan terms,
        without jeopardizing World Bank's long-
        term investments. Argues that without
        IDA, the Bank would be prevented from
        working in 25 of its poorest member
        countries. Contends IDA is important

precisely, because of difficulties with repayment of conventional term loans.

939.   Mehra, S. "Fifth Replenishment of IDA Completed." FINANCE AND DEVELOPMENT, vol. 14 (June 1977): 6-7.

Negotiations were completed March 1977, but awaiting approval from member countries' legislatures. IDA will allocate funds based on poverty level, lack of creditworthiness, adequate economic performance, and availability of program suitability for IDA lending.

940.   "Mr. Simon Says No." THE ECONOMIST, no. 261 (October 9, 1976): 111.

William Simon, US Secretary of Treasury, turns down the IDA replenishment. Discusses Henry Kissinger's idea of a World Bank-managed Resources Bank for providing funds to produce minerals in the Third World.

941-946. Omitted.

947.   Nations, Richard. "New Right Attacks." FAR EASTERN ECONOMIC REVIEW, vol. 111, no. 9 (February 20, 1981): 70-71.

Describes effects of US budget cuts on IDA, World Bank, and other international agencies, as a result of cuts in foreign aid. Cuts under the Reagan administration will seriously affect the Bank (especially IDA), which enjoyed political support from the Carter administration.

948.   "Poor IDA." THE ECONOMIST, no. 250 (February 2, 1974): 44.

Describes how Congress barely passed the aid bill, and IDA contributions request is stuck in the US House. The outcome could be disastrous to IDA's programs. Describes political climate in US where bilateral foreign aid is currently unpopular.

949. Prosterman, Roy. "World's 2 Billion Poor People Head Into Their Darkest Times." WAR/PEACE REPORT, vol. 13, no. 1 (1974): 26-29.

While improvements were made in foreign assistance, these efforts were defeated with increasing oil prices and other events. Congress approved new foreign aid bill, and vetoed IDA replenishment. Calls for maintaining oil conservation, concentrating on alternative energy sources, and willingness to share with the world's poor through food exports.

950. Rotberg, Eugene H. "World Bank -- A Financial Appraisal, II: The Role of IDA." FINANCE AND DEVELOPMENT, vol. 13 (December 1976): 36-39.

Focuses on the role of IDA, creditworthiness of borrowers, project appraisal, and Bank lending policies (see Entry 705). IDA facilitates development while providing sound investment for creditors.

951. Sanford, Jonathan E. "Feasibility of a World Bank Interest Subsidy Account to Supplement the Existing IDA Program." WORLD DEVELOPMENT, vol. 16, no. 7 (July 1988): 787-796.

Demonstrates how World Bank could
increase the amount of monies available
in low rate loan subsidies. Costs and
risks, as well as disadvantages and
advantages, are discussed. It would
allow for more innovation in using
resources, without increasing budget
commitments from member countries.

952.   Schwartz, Pushpa Nand. "Improving Education
in Tanzania Sixth IDA Project in Sector
Approved." FINANCE AND DEVELOPMENT,
vol. 16 (March 1979): 2-4.

Describes IDA-funded education
programs in Tanzania. The objectives of
these programs were to increase the
number of middle managers, to develop
the training for skills needed, to
strengthen vocational management
training, and to provide women with
greater access to technical education
and accounting skills.

953.   "Time for IDA: How to Agree on More Money for
the Poorest Countries." THE ECONOMIST,
vol. 300 (August 30, 1986): 14.

Describes raising funds for IDA, US
and Japan relations, and voting power.

954.   US National Advisory Council on
International Monetary and Financial
Problems. SPECIAL REPORT TO THE
PRESIDENT AND TO THE CONGRESS ON THE
PROPOSED REPLENISHMENT OF THE RESOURCES
OF THE INTERNATIONAL DEVELOPMENT
ASSOCIATION. Washington, D.C.: 1977.
15 p.

Recommends US approval of the 5th
replenishment of IDA ($7.6 billion).

955.   Van de Laar, Aart J.M. INTERNATIONAL
        DEVELOPMENT ASSOCIATION. The Hague:
        1976. 32 p. LCCN 77-352650   *

956.   Vibert, Frank. "Process of Replenishing IDA
        Finances." FINANCE AND DEVELOPMENT
        (September 1977). 25-77+.

            Examines negative process that led
        to Fifth Replenishment being approved by
        donor countries. Offers improvements in
        procedures.

957.   Weaver, James H. INTERNATIONAL DEVELOPMENT
        ASSOCIATION: A NEW APPROACH TO FOREIGN
        AID (Praeger Special Studies in
        International Economics and
        Development). New York: Praeger, 1965.
        ix,268 p. LCCN 65-19792

            Presents origin of IDA, and its
        role in foreign assistance in developing
        countries.

958.   "World Bank and IDA Approve Loans to Seven
        Countries." BUSINESS AMERICA, vol. 5,
        no. 14 (July 12, 1982): 34.

            Describes IDA projects: India
        (irrigation, and power plants), Malawi
        (improved water supply and sanitation),
        Sri Lanka (building power station), Togo
        and Yemen (technical assistance), and
        Zaire (fisheries investment and
        technical assistance).

959.   "World Bank and IDA Approve Loans Totalling
        $778 Million to 11 Countries." BUSINESS
        AMERICA, vol. 5, no. 12 (June 14, 1982):
        35.

            Describes IDA-approved projects in
        Burma (construction industry), Kenya

(telecommunications facility), Mexico
(pollution control), Uganda (economic
recovery), Tunisia (agricultural
production), Philippines (fish handling
and marketing facility), Brazil
(agricultural development), Cameroon
(oil palm and rubber plantation
productivity), Jordan (power plant
construction), Turkey (structural
adjustment and economic recovery, and
pollution control), and Yugoslavia
(farmland drainage).

960.   "World Bank and IDA Approve Loans Totalling
        $800 Million to 11 Countries." BUSINESS
        AMERICA, vol. 5, no. 11 (May 31, 1982):
        35.

            Describes IDA-approved projects in
        Brazil (electric power distribution),
        Pakistan (irrigation and agricultural
        productivity), Paraguay (highway
        maintenance), Peru (water supply and
        sewerage), Turkey (highway
        rehabilitation), Benin (primary and
        secondary education), Zaire (technical
        assistance), Burma (transmission
        facilities), Korea (small-scale
        industries), Mexico (capital goods
        manufacturing industry), and Thailand
        (telecommunications).

961.   "World Bank and IDA Approve $93.4 Million to
        Seven Countries." BUSINESS AMERICA,
        vol. 5, no. 11 (October 18, 1982): 34.

            Describes IDA-approved projects in
        Indonesia, Mauritania, and Tunisia
        (technical assistance), Thailand
        (economic and social infrastructure to
        Agricultural Land Reform Office), Upper
        Volta (agricultural technology),

Zimbabwe (farmers' credits), and the
Philippines (vocational training).

962.   "World Bank and IDA Lend for Urban Impact
         Projects." FINANCE AND DEVELOPMENT,
         vol. 14 (March 1977): 4-5+.

         Describes IDA and World Bank loans
         for projects: Greece (sewage and
         industrial wastes), India (transport
         development), Afghanistan (agricultural
         education), Ivory Coast (urban
         development), and Paraguay (rural
         education).

INTERNATIONAL FINANCE CORPORATION

963.   Baker, James C. INTERNATIONAL FINANCE
         CORPORATION: ORIGIN, OPERATIONS, AND
         EVALUATION (Praeger Special Studies in
         International Economics and
         Development). New York: Praeger, 1968.
         xxi,271 p. LCCN 68-54999

         Analyses IFC's first 10 years, and
         provides historical information.

964.   Bell, Carl. "Promoting Private Investment:
         the Role of the International Finance
         Corporation." FINANCE AND DEVELOPMENT,
         vol. 18 (September 1981): 16-19.

         Reviews IFC expenditures, and the
         impact on development of business
         opportunities in member countries.
         Describes how its financial sector
         studies work to break down barriers
         between private and public sectors.

965.   "Catalytic Role of IFC is Growing in
         Importance." FINANCE AND DEVELOPMENT,
         vol. 14 (September 1977): 2.

During 1956-1977, IFC invested in
more than 300 programs, generating
investment funds from local and foreign
sources, and assisting domestic
enterprises needing finance. IFC is
expected to continue support in natural
resource development (forestry,
agriculture, and fisheries) in the
coming years.

966.   Chowdhury, Amitabha. "Rich Bargains From
        Poor Countries." ASIAN FINANCE (HONG
        KONG), vol. 13 (September 15, 1987):
        86-89. *

967.   Cunningham, N.J. "Public Funds for Private
        Enterprise: the International Finance
        Corporation." JOURNAL OF DEVELOPMENT
        STUDIES, vol. 2, no. 3 (April 1966):
        268-296.

        Defines the problems encountered by
        channeling aid into the private sector,
        and suggests some future developments.
        Surveys nature of IFC's work and its
        limitations. Discusses "economic
        priority" as investment criteria used by
        IFC, and presents operating constraints
        that will impact future work.

968.   "Debt Doubts." THE ECONOMIST, no. 260
        (September 18, 1976): 113.

        Discusses the indexation vs. debt
        between North and South as stated in a
        recent IFC report.

969.   Donlan, T.G. "Troubled Portfolio: IFC
        Investments Go Sour." BARRONS, vol. 65
        (May 13, 1985): 16+. *

970.   Dumaine, Brian.   "Frontier Investing."
        FORTUNE, vol. 110 (November 12, 1984):
        143-144.

            Describes how IFC is major
        underwriter of Korea Fund, along with
        Lehman Brothers and First Boston, giving
        US investors the opportunity to purchase
        Korean stocks without much bureaucratic
        red tape.   IFC's Capital Markets
        Department is studying other likely
        candidates (i.e., Brazil and India).
        IFC is able to both help the LDCs'
        economy and make money for IFC and its
        investors.

971.   "Expanded Role for International Finance
        Corporation with Major Capital
        Increase."   FINANCE AND DEVELOPMENT,
        vol. 15 (June 1978): 2-3,40.

            Describes increase from $100
        million to $650 million (first increase
        since IFC's inception in 1960).   Total
        resources have steadily increased
        through other investors.   One IFC dollar
        yields four dollars by investors.

972.   Finn, Edwin A., Jr.   "Shot in the Foot."
        FORBES, vol. 138 (July 14, 1986): 80.

            Discusses the conflicts with
        private funds in international
        investing.   Describes John Templeton's
        mutual fund program for IFC, and how IFC
        botched it.   States how the Emerging
        Markets Growth Fund sounded like a good
        idea, but IFC is killing it.

973.   Friedland, J.   "Will Anyone Bet on Third
        World Stocks?"   INSTITUTIONAL INVESTOR,
        vol. 19 (July 1985): 155-156+.   *

974.   Gill, David, and Peter Tropper. "Emerging
         Stock Markets in Developing Countries."
         FINANCE AND DEVELOPMENT (December 1988):
         28-31.

              Describes the IFC's role in
         encouraging foreign portfolio investment
         using EMGF. Illustrates strong equity
         markets can accommodate foreign
         investment.

975.   Grenier, D. "International Finance
         Corporation." MOORGATE AND WALL STREET
         (1967): 42-54.   *

976.   Hornbostel, P.A. "New Emphasis for IFC:
         Development as a Risk Business."
         COLUMBIA JOURNAL OF WORLD BUSINESS
         (November/December 1969).   *

977.   Huehne, Luther H. "International Finance
         Corporation -- Creation, Record and
         Outlook." PUBLIC FINANCE, vol. 19,
         no. 2 (1964): 142-155.

              Describes creation of IFC (its
         advocates and adversaries), IFC's
         origins (legally separate from World
         Bank), and financial operations. IFC
         cannot lend or borrow from World Bank
         but must raise its own capital from
         member countries. The outlook for IFC
         is good. It acts as an advisor for
         fiscal policies.

978.   "IFC At A Glance." FINANCE AND DEVELOPMENT,
         vol. 25 (December 1988): 39-40.

              IFC was created to "promote
         development by supporting private
         enterprise." Describes number of
         projects, portfolio by sector, and
         evolution of lending from 1961 to 1988.

979.   "IFC is Keen on India." BUSINESS INDIA,
           no. 250 (October 5, 1987): 31. *

980.   International Bank for Reconstruction and
           Development. INTERNATIONAL FINANCE
           CORPORATION -- ARTICLES OF AGREEMENT AND
           EXPLANATORY MEMORANDUM AS APPROVED BY
           THE EXECUTIVE DIRECTORS OF INTERNATIONAL
           BANK FOR RECONSTRUCTION AND DEVELOPMENT
           ON 11 APRIL, 1955. London, UK: HMSO,
           1955. 25 p. *

981.   "International Finance Corporation: Ryrie
           Wastes No Time." BANKER, vol. 135
           (March 1985): 66-67. *

           Discusses actions taken by William
       Ryrie, IFC's new Executive Vice
       President.

982.   International Finance Corporation. ANNUAL
           REPORT, 1956- . Washington, D.C.:
           1956- .

           Covers activities, and financial
       record for past year.

983.   International Finance Corporation. IFC:
           BY-LAWS. Washington, D.C.: 1956. 7 p.

           Presents by-laws as of October
       1956.

984.   International Finance Corporation. IFC:
           GENERAL POLICIES. Washington, D.C.:
           1976. 7 p.

           Summarizes objectives, capital
       resources, basic operations, limits,
       terms, and relations with other
       institutions.

985.   International Finance Corporation.   IFC IN
         AFRICA.   Washington, D.C.: 1971.   44 p.

              Covers operations and origins of
         IFC, as well as private investment in
         Africa (arranged by investment industry:
         development financial institutions,
         mining, and textiles).

986.   International Finance Corporation.   IFC IN
         LATIN AMERICA.   Washington, D.C.: 1971.
         98 p.

              Covers operations and origins of
         IFC, as well as private investment in
         Latin America (arranged by investment
         industry: cement, chemical production,
         and mining).

987.   International Finance Corporation.   IFC: WHAT
         IT IS, WHAT IT DOES, HOW IT DOES IT.
         Washington, D.C.: 1971.   16 p.   *

988.   International Finance Corporation.
         INAUGURAL REPORT, JULY 24, 1956-
         SEPTEMBER 15, 1956.   Washington, D.C.:
         1956.   12 p.

              Presents IFC's Articles of
         Agreements (effective July 1956) and
         two-months report (update on membership,
         director, etc.) at the 1956 Board of
         Governors meeting.   See also Entry 980.

989.   International Finance Corporation.
         INTERNATIONAL FINANCE CORPORATION.
         Washington, D.C.: 1956.   15 p.

              Describes IFC's role in increasing
         production and trade.

990.   International Finance Corporation. PRIVATE
         DEVELOPMENT FINANCE COMPANIES.
         Washington, D.C.: 1964, 15 p.

         Examines ownership, capital
         structure, relationship of the Bank and
         IFC, and limitations of development
         finance companies.

991.   "LDCs Eye Private Funds." ENGINEERING NEWS
         RECORD, vol. 211 (September 29, 1983):
         49. *

992.   Lowe, John W. "IFC and the Agribusiness
         Sector." FINANCE AND DEVELOPMENT (March
         1977): 25-28.

         Discusses IFC experience in
         agribusiness ventures, and government
         involvement in appropriate technology.
         In 1976, IFC committed funds for coconut
         oil processing in the Philippines,
         vegetable growing in Senegal, tea
         growing in Rwanda, and sugar production
         in Ecuador and Nicaragua.

993.   Matecki, Bronislaw. E. "Establishment of the
         International Finance Corporation: a
         Case Study." INTERNATIONAL
         ORGANIZATION, vol. 10, no. 2 (May 1956):
         261-275.

         Summarizes Entry 992 discussing the
         origins of IFC. Analyzes the origins of
         the idea behind proposing the creation
         of IFC. Evaluates the impact of
         international organizations on US for
         economic policy.

994.   Matecki, Bronislaw E.   ESTABLISHMENT OF THE
        INTERNATIONAL FINANCE CORPORATION AND
        UNITED STATES POLICY: A CASE STUDY IN
        INTERNATIONAL ORGANIZATION.   New York:
        Praeger, 1957.   194 p.   LCCN 57-7075

            Studies the origins of IFC (not its
        operations).   Examines the influence of
        IFC on US foreign economic policy,
        especially what caused US to support
        IFC.

995.   McWilliams, Bruce W.   "IFC Results, FY87: Net
        Income More Than Doubles."   BANK'S
        WORLD, vol. 6 (September 1987): 5-6.   *

996.   "New Instruments: IFC Comes to Grips."
        BANKER, vol. 136 (October 1986): 44.   *

            Describes the Guaranteed Recovery
        of Investment Principal program at IFC.

997.   Pfeffermann, Guy P., and Andrea Madarassy.
        TRENDS IN PRIVATE INVESTMENT IN 30
        DEVELOPING COUNTRIES (International
        Finance Discussion Paper, 6).
        Washington, D.C.: IFC, 1989.

            Presents annual private investment
        data (1970-1988) in 30 developing
        countries.   Shows how private sector
        plays a role in domestic investment.
        Indicates that private investment is on
        the rise.

998.   Purcell, John F.H., and Michelle B. Miller.
        "World Bank and Private Capital."
        BETWEEN TWO WORLDS: THE WORLD BANK'S
        NEXT DECADE, by R. Feinberg, et al.   New
        Brunswick, NJ: Transaction Books, 1986.
        p. 111-134.

Describes difference between IFC and MIGA, and private capital's role in development. See also Entry 283.

999. Riemer, Bianca. "Pioneering a Brave Third World of Mutual Funds." BUSINESS WEEK (February 17, 1986): 66-67.

Describes the models for IFC fund: Korea Fund, and Nomura Pacific Basin Fund. Discusses Third World mutual fund (Emerging Markets Growth Fund) to be launched in March 1986.

1000. Rosen, Martin M. "IFC Recruits Capital for Development." COLUMBIA JOURNAL OF WORLD BUSINESS, vol. 3, no. 6 (November/December 1968): 1-10.

Describes IFC's mission. Presents information on diversification, local participation, criteria, and agribusiness opportunities.

1001. Rowley, Anthony. "Debt Crisis and Reaganomics Give IFC a New Lease on Life." FAR EASTERN ECONOMIC REVIEW, vol. 141 (September 29, 1988): 107-109.

Describes how pro-privatization stance of Reagan administration and Third World debt crisis is bringing IFC into higher profile. IFC concentrates on providing equity for projects, which reduces the debt ratios in LDCs.

1002. Ryrie, William. "IFC: An Investment Bank for Development." BANK'S WORLD, vol. 7 (November 1988): 18. *

1003.   Ryrie, William. "IFC: Growth and
         Diversification." FINANCE AND
         DEVELOPMENT, vol. 25 (December 1988):
         22-24.

              Interviews William Ryrie (IFC
         Executive Vice President) on the global
         environment, profitability vs.
         development, MIGA and IFC, poverty and
         Sub-Saharan African, equity investments,
         and IFC's relationship to the World
         Bank.

1004.   "Ryrie's Catalyst." BANKER, vol. 135
         (September 1985): 63. *

1005.   Sethnewss, Charles O. "Capital Market
         Development." FINANCE AND DEVELOPMENT
         (December 1988): 32-33.

              Discusses technical assistance,
         investment, and loans to IFC member
         countries through Capital Markets
         Program.

1006.   Sharan, Vyuptakesh. "International Finance
         Corporation and the Less Developed
         Countries: An Appraisal." COMMERCE
         WEEKLY, vol. 155, no. 3973 (July 11,
         1987): 20-26,30.

              Describes technical and financial
         assistance by IFC, financial resources
         (where IFC funds come from), and funding
         operations during the first 30 years.
         Examines whether IFC has provided enough
         funds to others.

1007.   Shreeve, Gavin. "Profile: IFC's David Gill:
         A True Believer." BANKER, vol. 137
         (September 1987): 24-25. *

1008.   Silkenat, James R.   "GRIP: Guaranteed
         Recovery of Investment Principal."
         INTERNATIONAL FINANCIAL LAW REVIEW,
         vol.7 (March 1988): 39-40.   *

1009.   Snaveley, William P.   "International Finance
         Corporation: a New International
         Investment Agency."   AMERICAN JOURNAL OF
         ECONOMICS AND SOCIOLOGY, vol. 17, no. 4
         (July 1958): 341-52.

             Describes establishment of World
         Bank and IMF, and later IFC.   Discusses
         operating procedures, accomplishments,
         and future prospects.   Concludes there
         is a urgent need for additional capital
         in LDCs in coming years.

1010.   UN Conference on Trade and Development.
         FINANCING FOR AN EXPANSION OF
         INTERNATIONAL TRADE: PRIVATE DEVELOPMENT
         FINANCE COMPANIES, prepared by the IFC
         (UN Document E/CONF.46/23).   New York:
         1964.   11 p.   *

             Describes capital structure,
         organization, and management of private
         development companies, as well as World
         Bank and IFC assistance.

1011.   US Congress. House.   Committee on Banking
         and Currency.   INTERNATIONAL FINANCE
         CORPORATION (Hearing, HR 6228, July
         1955).   Washington, D.C.: GPO, 1955.
         107 p.

             Superseded by S1894 (bill to
         provide for US participation in IFC).

1012.   US Congress. House.   Committee on Banking
         and Currency.   INTERNATIONAL FINANCE
         CORPORATION (Hearing, HR 6765, May
         1961).   Washington, D.C.: GPO, 1961.
         33 p.

         Authorizes the acceptance of the
         amendment to the IFC's Articles of
         Agreement, permitting investment in
         capital stock.

1013.   US National Advisory Council on
         International Monetary and Financial
         Problems.   SPECIAL REPORT TO THE
         PRESIDENT AND TO THE CONGRESS ON THE
         CAPITAL EXPANSION OF THE INTERNATIONAL
         FINANCE CORPORATION.   Washington, D.C.:
         1976.   22 p.

         Recommends US approval of proposed
         increase of $540 million.   IFC has not
         requested a capital replenishment since
         1956.   The increase would allow $480
         million for projects.   See Entry 1014.

1014.   US National Advisory Council on
         International Monetary and Financial
         Problems.   SPECIAL REPORT TO THE
         PRESIDENT AND TO THE CONGRESS ON THE
         CAPITAL EXPANSION OF THE INTERNATIONAL
         FINANCE CORPORATION.   Washington, D.C.:
         1977.   26 p.

         Same proposal recommended for
         approval (not approved in 1976).   See
         Entry 1013.

MULTILATERAL INVESTMENT GUARANTEE AGENCY

1015.   Brostoff, Steven. "World Bank OKs Political
        Risk Unit." NATIONAL UNDERWRITER
        (PROPERTY AND CASUALTY/EMPLOYEE BENEFITS
        ED.), vol. 91 (April 13, 1987): 6+. *

1016.   "Global Insurance Addressed." ENGINEERING
        NEWS RECORD, vol. 218 (June 11, 1987):
        15-16. *

1017.   Green, Paula L. "World Bank Unit Plans
        Political Risk Cover." JOURNAL OF
        COMMERCE (February 16, 1988): 9A. *

1018.   Harris, Anthony. "World Bank Unveils
        Investment Risk Plan." FINANCIAL TIMES
        (April 13, 1988): 4. *

1019.   Lawrence, Richard. "World Bank Guarantee
        Agency May Begin Operating in Spring."
        JOURNAL OF COMMERCE (December 24, 1987):
        7A. *

1020.   Lota, G.-P. "Multinational Investment
        Guarantee Agency: Benefits." CREDIT AND
        FINANCIAL MANAGEMENT, vol. 88 (January
        1986): 38. *

1021.   Lota, G.-P. "Multinational Investment
        Guarantee Agency: History." CREDIT AND
        FINANCIAL MANAGEMENT, vol. 87 (December
        1985): 46. *

1022.   "Multinational Investment Guarantee Agency
        Launched." FINANCE AND DEVELOPMENT,
        (June 1988): 14.

        MIGA became effective on April 12,
        1988, although it was actually approved
        a few years earlier.

1023.   "Multinational Investment Guarantee Agency:
          an Update." FINANCE AND DEVELOPMENT,
          vol. 22 (December 1985): 54.

              MIGA was approved at 1985 Board of
          Governors meeting, but it did not become
          effective until almost three years
          later.

1024.   Shihata, I. "Bringing MIGA to Birth."
          EUROMONEY (November 1985): 14-15.   *

1025.   Shihata, Ibrahim. "MIGA: A Fresh Instrument
          for Cooperation." EFTA BULLETIN
          (European Free Trade Association,
          Geneva), Vol. 26 (October-December
          1985): 6-7.   *

1026.   Shihata, Ibrahim F.I. MIGA AND FOREIGN
          INVESTMENT. Boston, MA: Martinus
          Nijhoff, 1987. xvi,540 p.   *

              Explains origins, function, and
          policy issues resulting from MIGA's
          creation.

1027.   Viehe, Karl William. "Multilateral
          Investment Guarantee Agency."
          INTERNATIONAL FINANCIAL LAW REVIEW,
          vol. 6 (October 1987): 37-38.   *

1028.   Voss, Jurgen. "MIGA and the Code of
          Conduct." CTC REPORTER: UNITED NATIONS
          CENTRE ON TRANSNATIONAL CORPORATIONS,
          No. 22 (Autumn 1986): 51-55.   *

1029.   "World Bank's MIGA Gets Under Way." AFRICAN
          BUSINESS, no. 118 (June 1988): 76-77.   *

WORLD BANK

See:
INTERNATIONAL BANK FOR RECONSTRUCTION
AND DEVELOPMENT

UN MONETARY CONFERENCE

See:
BRETTON WOODS

APPENDICES

APPENDIX A.

HISTORICAL HIGHLIGHTS

HISTORICAL HIGHLIGHTS

1944 United Nations Monetary & Financial
Conference (Bretton Woods, New Hampshire).
Proposals for the World Bank and
International Fund are reviewed.

1945 Articles of Agreement are signed.

1946 Inaugural Meeting of the Board of Governors
held. Eugene Meyer is appointed first
President (June-December 1946).
First Annual Meeting of the Board of
Governors held.

1947 John McCloy appointed President (March
1947-June 1949). Mission to Poland (First
mission).

1949 Eugene Black appointed President (July
1949-December 1962). Technical assistance
program starts.

1955 Economic Development Institute (EDI)
established.

1956 International Finance Corporation (IFC)
established. Robert Garner is appointed
President of IFC (July 1956-October 1961).

1960 International Development Association (IDA)
established.

1961 Eugene Black appointed President of IFC
(October 1961-December 1962).

1963 George Wood appointed President of the Bank,
IFC, & IDA (January 1963-March 1968).

1966 International Centre for Settlement of
Investment Disputes (ICSID) established.

1968 Robert McNamara appointed President of the
Bank, IFC, & IDA (April 1968-June 1981).

1971 Consultative Group on International
      Agricultural Research (CGIAR) established
      (co-sponsored by World Bank and UN).

1974 Joint Ministerial Committee of the Board of
      Governors of the World Bank and the
      International Monetary Fund on the Transfer
      of Real Resources to Developing Countries
      (Development Committee) established.

1981 A.W. Clausen appointed President of the Bank,
      IFC, & IDA (July 1981-June 1986).

1985 Special Facility for Sub-Saharan Africa began
      operations.

1986 Barber Conable appointed President of the
      Bank, IFC, & IDA (July 1986-September 1991).
      Bank membership up to 151 countries.

1987 Bank reorganized into four complexes:
      Finance; Operations; Administration; and
      Policy, Planning and Research.

1988 Multilateral Investment Guarantee Agency
      (MIGA) established.

1991 Lewis T. Preston under consideration as
      President of the Bank, IFC, & IDA (to replace
      Barber Conable in September).

APPENDIX B.

WORLD BANK INFORMATION PRODUCTS

WORLD BANK INFORMATION PRODUCTS

Access to bibliographic information is available through the World Bank's INDEX TO PUBLICATIONS IN PRINT, the Library of Congress bibliographic system, and National Technical Information Service (NTIS).

SALES LITERATURE

CATALOG OF EDUCATIONAL MATERIALS (annual)
Teaching guides aimed at high school courses in history, economics, and current affairs.
CATALOG OF STAFF WORKING PAPERS, 1967-1986
Series discontinued. Useful for subject access and retrospective verification.
INDEX OF WORLD BANK PUBLICATIONS IN PRINT (annual)
Author, title, country, and subject access to publications in print as of January 1.
NEW PUBLICATIONS CATALOG (2x/yr)
Author, title, and series access to titles published in last six months.
PUBLICATIONS UPDATE (irregular; about 6x/yr)
Announces newest publications in last few months. No index, but arranged by broad subjects.

MAJOR SERIES
(Arranged by Publication Frequency)

ANNUAL
ABSTRACTS OF CURRENT STUDIES - WORLD BANK RESEARCH PROGRAM
Title varies. Abstracts of current research programs.
COMMODITY TRADE AND PRICE TRENDS
Handbook on developing countries' trade statistics.
CURRICULA OF COURSES
Reading lists and assignments of EDI classes.
DEVELOPING COUNTRY DEBT
Abridged version of WORLD DEBT TABLES.
EMERGING STOCK MARKETS FACTBOOK
New reference work, 1988. 1980-1988 data on developed stock market and leading securities in developing countries. Will be updated annually.

ICSID ANNUAL REPORT
    Reviews ICSID activities.
IFC ANNUAL REPORT
    Reviews IFC activities.
SUMMARY PROCEEDINGS OF THE BOARD OF GOVERNORS
    Covers Board of Governors meetings for IBRD, IDA,
    and IFC.
WORLD BANK ANNUAL REPORT
    Reviews IBRD and IDA activities.
WORLD BANK ATLAS
    Population data for member countries. Published
    in English, French and Spanish.
WORLD DEBT TABLES
    Statistics on external debt of developing
    countries. Issued annually with 3 supplements.
WORLD DEVELOPMENT REPORT
    Focus on development problems of low and middle
    income countries. Published in English, French,
    Spanish, Arabic, Chinese, Portuguese, German, and
    Japanese.
WORLD TABLES
    New frequency with 1987 edition. Will be
    published annually (see description below).

REGULAR

MONTHLY OPERATIONAL SUMMARY (monthly)
    Information on potential loans.
TECHNICAL DATA SHEETS (weekly)
    Current information on World Bank-financed
    projects and IDA credits.
PRICE PROSPECTS FOR MAJOR PRIMARY
COMMODITIES, 1988-2000 (quarterly)
    New series, 1989. Up-to-date data on market
    performance of 44 commodities.
QUARTERLY REVIEW OF COMMODITY MARKETS (quarterly)
    Price prospects and forecasts for 44 commodities.
STATEMENT OF LOANS-STATEMENT OF
DEVELOPMENT CREDITS (quarterly)
    Cumulative history of financial transactions.
URBAN EDGE (10x/yr)
    Practical approaches to urban problems in
    developing countries. Published in English,
    Spanish and French.
WORLD BANK ECONOMIC REVIEW (3x/yr)
    Refereed professional journal. Intended for
    specialists. Emphasis on policy relevance and
    operations aspects of economics.

WORLD BANK RESEARCH OBSERVER   (2x/yr)
     Intended for generalists with some knowledge of
     economics.   Summarizes recent development
     research.
WORLD BANK RESEARCH NEWS   (quarterly)
     Description of current research and publications.
WORLD BANK TELEPHONE DIRECTORY   (quarterly)
     IBRD, IDA, and IFC staff and phone numbers.

IRREGULAR
CGIAR STUDY PAPERS
     Focus on collaboration of CGIAR and individual
     countries (i.e., CHILE AND THE CGIAR CENTERS).
DEVELOPMENT DATA BOOK AND TEACHING GUIDE
     Presents statistical concepts useful for studying
     the development process.
EDI DEVELOPMENT POLICY CASE SERIES
     New series, 1988.   Case studies for teaching
     economic and political decision making.
EDI POLICY SEMINAR REPORTS
     New series, 1988.   Summaries of EDI policy
     seminars, focusing on public affairs.
HIGHWAY DESIGN AND MAINTENANCE STANDARDS
STUDY SERIES
     Focus on physical and economic relationship of
     road design in developing countries.
IFC DISCUSSION PAPERS
     Informal reports focusing on the private sector in
     developing countries.
INTERNATIONAL BUSINESS OPPORTUNITIES SERVICE
(IBOS)
     Description of procurement opportunities on
     upcoming Bank-financed projects.
LIVING STANDARDS MEASUREMENT STUDY
WORKING PAPERS SERIES
     Intermediate findings on economic well-being and
     the distribution of welfare.
MANAGING AGRICULTURAL DEVELOPMENT IN AFRICA
(MADIA) SERIES
     Informal discussion papers series on agricultural
     in Cameroon, Kenya, Malawi, Nigeria, Senegal, and
     Tanzania.
SOCIAL DIMENSIONS OF ADJUSTMENT IN SUB-SAHARAN
AFRICA SERIES
     New series, 1990.   Informal documents to assist
     Sub-Sahara African governments in becoming
     integrated in structural adjustment programs.

POLICIES AND OPERATIONS: WORLD BANK, IDA AND IFC
    Title varies. Covers origin, relationships, and
    other factors relating operations and policies.
WORLD BANK COUNTRY STUDIES
    "Formal" economic reports based on earlier works.
WORLD BANK COMMODITY WORKING PAPERS
    Focus on developments in a particular commodity.
WORLD BANK COMPARATIVE STUDIES
    New series, 1988. Focus on sectoral and economy-
    wide data.
WORLD BANK DEVELOPMENT RESEARCH CENTER PAPERS
    Informal reports circulated for comments. Ceased
    publication in 1988.
WORLD BANK DISCUSSION PAPERS
    New series, 1986. Preliminary results of projects
    circulated for comments.
WORLD BANK POLICY, PLANNING AND RESEARCH
WORKING PAPERS
    New series, 1988. Informal report of findings.
WORLD BANK OCCASIONAL PAPERS
    New series, 1987. Informal reports.
WORLD BANK OPERATIONS EVALUATIONS STUDIES
    Review of World Bank projects and programs.
WORLD BANK POLICY STUDIES
    Focus on current situation and existing policy in
    a particular area.
WORLD BANK SECTOR POLICY PAPERS
    Reviews a specific field, i.e. Fisheries.
WORLD BANK STAFF WORKING PAPERS
    1967-1976. Research results from early stages of
    World Bank projects. Ceased publication in 1976.
WORLD BANK SYMPOSIUM SERIES
    Collected essays by World Bank staff and external
    consultants on a particular topic.
WORLD BANK TECHNICAL PAPERS
    Informal papers on technical aspects of research
WORLD TABLES
    Published annually effective 1987 edition.
    Economic and social time-series data.

NONPRINT FORMATS
EDUCATION FINANCE SIMULATION MODEL (EDFISIMO)
    User's manual and MS-DOS disk for use with Lotus
    1-2-3; useful in education sector decision making.
HIGHWAY DESIGN AND MAINTENANCE STANDARDS MODEL
(HDM-III)
    User's manual, sourcebook, and MS-DOS disks.

POSTER KITS
#1-Life Expectancy at Birth; #2-Population Growth
Rate. Teaching guide, 6 posters, and map.
SOFTWARE FOR INDUSTRIAL, TRADE AND INCENTIVES ANALYSIS
(SINTIA-T): TARIFF AND NOMINAL PROTECTION ANALYSIS
User's manual and MS-DOS disk. Useful in analysis
of trade incentives.
TOWARD A BETTER WORLD
Multimedia learning kits. Five kits with
filmstrips, teaching guide, and student books.
VIDEOCASSETES
VHS format. Teaching guide. Focus on daily life
in a developing country: Brazil, Bangladesh,
India, Kenya, Mexico, West Africa.
WORLD DEBT TABLES
Magnetic tape. Continuous historical series and
projections. Basis for WORLD DEBT TABLES.
WORLD DEVELOPMENT INDICATORS
User's manual and MS-DOS disks (.WKS or .PRN
format). Useful for regression analysis,
comparing country data. Basis for WORLD
DEVELOPMENT REPORT.
WORLD TABLES
Magnetic tape. Economic, demographic and social
data; basis for WORLD TABLES.

For further information, contact:

World Bank Publications Department
1818 H St., N.W.
Washington, D.C. 20433

All World Bank print publications are
available in microfiche or photocopy from NTIS
when they are out-of-print at the World Bank.

JOINT IMF-IBRD PUBLICATIONS

QUARTERLY
FINANCE AND DEVELOPMENT
Articles on IBRD and IMF activities, as well as
general topics in international economics.

<u>MONTHLY</u>
JOINT IMF-IBRD LIBRARY LIST OF PERIODICAL ARTICLES
Indexes working papers, newspaper articles and
periodical articles as received by the Joint
Library. Arranged by subject and geographic
region.
JOINT IMF-IBRD LIBRARY LIST OF RECENT ADDITIONS
Items added to the Joint Library. Arranged by
reference works, general works, and geographic
regions, then by LC classification.

For additional information on these publications,
contact:

International Monetary Fund
Washington, D.C. 20431

APPENDIX C.

ELECTRONIC SOURCES

ELECTRONIC SOURCES

Printed indexes were used for locating World Bank citations for this work. However, a number of the sources are also available in electronic format. It is helpful to be aware of these, especially in keeping up-to-date on materials about the World Bank.

A quick survey of electronic sources, using "World Bank" as the only search term, yielded the results shown below. These results should be used only for comparison purposes. A thorough search would have used additional terms, as was done when conducting the citation research for this work.

CD-ROM PRODUCTS
Infotrac (1985-88)	498 citations
Social Science Index (1983-88)	216 citations
Reader's Guide (1983-88)	172 citations
ERIC (1983-88)	95 citations

WILSONLINE DATABASES
LC MARC Books (1977-87)	888 citations
Cumulative Book Index (1982-87)	229 citations
Social Science Index (1983-87)	203 citations
Business Periodical Index (1982-87)	192 citations

DIALOG DATABASES
NTIS (1964-89)	923 citations
CIS (1971-1988)	450 citations
PAIS (1976-88)	388 citations
ASI (1974-88)	275 citations
Dissertations Abstracts (1861-1988)	106 citations
Economic Literature (1969-88)	93 citations

Since all World Bank publications (but not their documents) are catalogued through the Library of Congress, and made available through NTIS when they are no longer in print, it is no surprise that these databases have the largest number of citations. A few other databases (U.S. Political Science Documents, and Legal Resource Index), as well as other CD-ROM products (Library Literature, Psych Literature) were also surveyed; less than fifty citations were retrieved.

The electronic sources listed represent the ones most likely to yield a significant number of citations, to keep abreast of new World Bank citations.

APPENDIX D.

RELATED WORKS AND SOURCES CONSULTED

SOURCES CONSULTED

The sources used for locating World Bank citations were major U.S. national and trade bibliographies, as well as various indexing and abstracting services. Most of the citations came from the following sources: Business Periodical Index, Cumulative Book Index, International Bibliography of Economics, International Bibliography of Political Science, Public Affairs Information Service Bulletin, Reader's Guide to Periodical Literature, Social Science/Humanities Index, and Vertical File Index.

These sources were searched using several terms. In addition to the "WORLD BANK" and "INTERNATIONAL BANK FOR RECONSTRUCTION AND DEVELOPMENT," the following were used as search terms: EDI, IDA, IFC, ISCID, MIGA, CGIAR, UN MONETARY CONFERENCE, and BRETTON WOODS.

RELATED WORKS

The following is a list of related works. They were examined to determine whether this work would duplicate another effort, or whether it would be similar to other works.

Atherton, Alexine L. INTERNATIONAL ORGANIZATIONS: A GUIDE TO INFORMATION SOURCES. Detroit: Gale, 1976.
Baer, George, ed. INTERNATIONAL ORGANIZATIONS 1918-1945. Wilmington, DE: Scholarly Resources, 1981.
Collester, J. Bryan. EUROPEAN COMMUNITY: A GUIDE TO THE INFORMATION SOURCES. Detroit: Gale, 1979.
Haas, Michael. INTERNATIONAL ORGANIZATIONS: AN INTERDISCIPLINARY BIBLIOGRAPHY. Stanford, CA: Hoover Institution Press, 1971.
Hajnal, Peter I. GUIDE TO UNITED NATIONS ORGANIZATION, DOCUMENTATION AND PUBLISHING. Dobbs Ferry, NY: Oceana, 1962.
Hajnal, Peter I. INTERNATIONAL INFORMATION: DOCUMENTS, PUBLICATIONS AND INFORMATION SYSTEMS OF INTERGOVERNMENTAL ORGANIZATIONS. Englewood, CO: Libraries Unlimited, 1988.
"International Monetary Fund, 1984: a selected bibliography," IMF STAFF PAPER 32, December 1985.

Jeffries, John. A GUIDE TO THE OFFICIAL PUBLICATIONS
      OF THE EUROPEAN COMMUNITY, 2nd ed. London:
      Mansell, 1981.
Marulli, Luciana. DOCUMENTATION OF THE UNITED NATIONS
      SYSTEM. Metuchen, NJ: Scarecrow, 1979.
Meerhaeghe, M.A.G. van. INTERNATIONAL ECONOMIC
      INSTITUTIONS. Dordrecht, The Netherlands:
      Martinus Nijhoff, 1985.
Palmer, Doris, ed. SOURCES OF INFORMATION ON THE
      EUROPEAN COMMUNITY. London: Mansell, 1979.
Richard, J. H. INTERNATIONAL ECONOMIC INSTITUTIONS.
      London: Holt, Rinehart, & Winston, 1970.
Winton, Harry N. PUBLICATIONS OF THE UNITED NATIONS
      SYSTEM; A REFERENCE GUIDE. New York: Bowker,
      1972.

APPENDIX E.

ORGANIZATIONAL CHART

ORGANIZATIONAL CHART

In 1987, the World Bank implemented its first major reorganization since 1972. It was described as a way of strengthening the Bank's organizational responsiveness in providing development assistance.

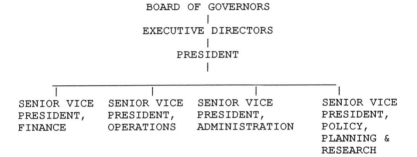

```
                    BOARD OF GOVERNORS
                             |
                    EXECUTIVE DIRECTORS
                             |
                         PRESIDENT
                             |
     _____
    |               |               |               |
SENIOR VICE     SENIOR VICE     SENIOR VICE     SENIOR VICE
PRESIDENT,      PRESIDENT,      PRESIDENT,      PRESIDENT,
FINANCE         OPERATIONS      ADMINISTRATION  POLICY,
                                                PLANNING &
                                                RESEARCH
```

In addition to the Senior Vice Presidents, the General Counsel and Secretary also reported directed to the President.

Under each of the Senior Vice Presidents were the following departments:

SENIOR VICE PRESIDENT - FINANCE
  VP FINANCIAL POLICY & RISK MANAGEMENT
  VP PENSION FUND
  VP TREASURER
  VP CONTROLLER

SENIOR VICE PRESIDENT - OPERATIONS
  VP AFRICA
  VP ASIA
  VP EMENA
  VP LAC
  VP FINANCIAL INTERMEDIATION SERVICES
  VP COFINANCING

SENIOR VICE PRESIDENT - POLICY, PLANNING & RESEARCH
    VP DEVELOPMENT ECONOMICS AND CHIEF ECONOMIST
    VP SECTOR POLICY AND RESEARCH

SENIOR VICE PRESIDENT - ADMINISTRATION
    VP PERSONNEL
    VP EXTERNAL AFFAIRS

INDEX

INDEX

Indexes authors, editors, chief of missions, titles, countries, and subjects, using entry numbers.

305